GOSPEL TRUTH?

To Roger, Michael
and Nicola

GOSPEL TRUTH?

New Light on Jesus and the Gospels

Graham Stanton

TRINITY PRESS
INTERNATIONAL
Valley Forge, Pennsylvania

First U.S. edition published in 1995 by
Trinity Press International,
P.O. Box 851, Valley Forge, PA 19482

First published in Great Britain in 1995 by
HarperCollins Publishers

Library of Congress Cataloging-in-Publication Data

Stanton, Graham,
    Gospel truth?: new light on Jesus and the Gospels / Graham
Stanton.
        p.   cm.
    Includes bibliographical references and index.
    ISBN 1-56338-137-0 (alk. paper)
    1. Bible. N.T. Gospels–Criticism, interpretation, etc.
2. Jesus Christ–Historicity. 3. Bible. N.T. Gospels–Criticism,
interpretation, etc.–History–20th century. 4. Christian
antiquities–Palestine. 5. Palestine–Antiquities. 6. Excavations
(Archaeology)–Palestine. 7. Jesus Christ–Person and offices.
I. Title.
BS2555.2.S667   1995
226'.06–dc20   95-37709
                                                          CIP

Printed and bound in Great Britain

95 96 97 98 99   10 9 8 7 6 5 4 3 2 1

Contents

Preface   vii

I   Searching for Gospel Truth   1

II   First-century Fragments of Matthew's Gospel?   11

III   Mark's Gospel among the Dead Sea Scrolls?   20

IV   How Reliable are the Manuscripts of the Gospels?   33

V   Between Jesus and the Gospels   49

VI   Q: A Lost 'Gospel'?   63

VII   Other Gospels: Peter, Egerton, Thomas and 'Secret Mark'   77

VIII   One Gospel and Four Gospellers   96

IX   Jesus: the Archaeological Evidence   111

X   Jesus Traditions Outside the Gospels   122

XI   Jesus Traditions Inside the Gospels   135

XII   Jesus: the Aftermath   145

XIII   Jesus: a Magician and a False Prophet   156

XIV   Jesus: Disciple of John   164

XV   Jesus: King of the Jews   173

XVI   Gospel Truth about Jesus   188

Notes   194

For Further Reading   207

General Index   213

List of Illustrations

Plate 1 Magdalen College Oxford fragments (reproduced by kind permission of Magdalen College, Oxford)

Plates 2 & 3 The earliest fragment of the New Testament from c. AD 125, featuring part of John's Gospel (reproduced by courtesy of the Director and University Librarian, the John Rylands University Library of Manchester)

Plate 4 Codex Sinaiticus (reproduced by kind permission of the British Library)

Plate 5 Cave no. 7 at Qumran (© ASAP/Garo Nalbandian)

Plate 6 An enlarged photograph of 7Q5 (© ASAP/David Rubinger)

Plate 7 A diagrammatic representation of 7Q5 (S.R. Pickering)

Plate 8 A diagrammatic representation of two letters from 7Q5 (Geoffrey Jenkins)

Plate 9 Papyrus Egerton 2 (reproduced by kind permission of the British Library)

Plate 10 A close-up of the octagonal church at Capernaum (© ASAP/Garo Nalbandian)

Plate 11 A close-up of the synagogue at Capernaum (© ASAP/Israel Talby)

Plate 12 Capernaum – aerial view (© ASAP/Garo Nalbandian)

Plate 13 A *mikveh* from the Palatial Mansion in Jerusalem (© ASAP/Garo Nalbandian)

Plate 14 The Celsus Library at Ephesus (© Lennox Manton)

Plate 15 Latin inscription found at Caesarea (© ASAP/Garo Nalbandian)

Plate 16 The Wailing Wall, Jerusalem (© Sonia Halliday Photographs)

PREFACE

The recent wave of media interest in Jesus of Nazareth and in the origin of the Gospels has not surprised me. For many years now I have found that Christians and non-Christians alike are keen to inquire into the evidence for the life of Jesus and to consider the claims of the evangelists. Early versions of many parts of this book have been given as talks or lectures in settings as varied as modest village halls and splendid Cathedrals. Adults, students and sixth formers have plied me with questions which have often prompted me to consider issues or points of view I might otherwise have by-passed.

Over the past three or four years the reading public has not been well served by books published on Jesus and the Gospels. Too many have been written by sensation seekers who have twisted evidence to fit fancy theories. Although their books have been so inept that most scholars have not bothered to take them seriously, they have caught the eye of readers who have sorely needed a winnowing fork to sift the wheat from the chaff. Other books on Jesus and the Gospels have been written by journalists, some of whom have done little more than feed rather irresponsibly off the work of scholars.

For these reasons I accepted the request to write this book. The support and encouragement of my scholarly friends and colleagues are deeply appreciated. I am particularly grateful to those who have responded to my requests for advice, several of whom have generously sent me drafts or proofs of unpublished articles. I wish to acknowledge the help of the following scholars who are not in any way responsible for my conclusions: Prof. Dr Barbara Aland (Münster); Dr George Brooke (Manchester); Prof. James

Charlesworth (Princeton); Prof. J. A. Fitzmyer (Washington); Prof. Dr K. Haacker (Wuppertal); Canon C. J. A. Hickling (Arksey); Dr G. Jenkins (Melbourne); Prof. Alan Millard (Liverpool); Prof. Peter Parsons (Oxford); Dr Stuart Pickering (Sydney); Mr T. C. Skeat (London); Prof. Christopher Tuckett (Manchester); Dr Klaus Wachtel (Münster).

I am most grateful to Mr Giles Semper of HarperCollins for initiating the project and for his exemplary support. Barbara Chapman, Rosamund Webber and their colleagues at HarperCollins have been thoroughly professional and efficient throughout.

As always, my wife has helped in numerous ways. This book is dedicated to our three children to whom we owe so much.

Graham Stanton
2 July 1995

CHAPTER I

SEARCHING FOR
GOSPEL TRUTH

THIS BOOK BEGAN life at the breakfast table on Christmas Eve 1994. My 18-year-old daughter, knowing that study of Matthew's Gospel had taken up several years of my life, passed a copy of *The Times* to me and said, 'You'll be interested in this.' A front-page story was entitled, 'Oxford papyrus is "eyewitness record of the life of Christ".' The article reported the claim by the German scholar, Dr Carsten Thiede, that three papyrus fragments of Matthew's Gospel held in Magdalen College Oxford library since 1901 date from the mid-first century, within twenty years or so of the life of Jesus.

'Not since the discovery of the Dead Sea Scrolls in 1947', the story continued, 'has there been such a potentially important breakthrough in biblical scholarship.' *The Times* devoted nearly two full pages to Carsten Thiede's claims, including an editorial which likened the alleged new discovery not only to the finding of the Dead Sea Scrolls, but also to Howard Carter's discovery of Tutankhamun's treasures in 1922, and to Schliemann's location of Troy. On 26 December *The Times* carried an extended interview with Dr Thiede, thereby giving still more oxygen to his claims about three tiny papyrus fragments of Matthew's Gospel.

Abraham Lincoln once said that *The Times* (founded in 1785) was one of the greatest powers in the world. While few would make that claim today, *The Times* is still an influential voice in the English-speaking world. What it says today is echoed in other countries tomorrow. Until recently *The Times* has rarely indulged in sensationalist reporting, so many readers have assumed that genuinely new evidence has been found for the early dating, eye-witness character and reliability of the Gospels.

I was surprised to learn that Matthew's Gospel had made the front page of *The Times*. I was equally surprised to find that my daughter, not known for her interest in the finer points of biblical scholarship, had already read avidly every word of the lengthy articles. Thiede's claims were reported in the BBC radio national news bulletins that same day, and were then picked up quickly in many parts of the world in television and radio programmes, and in newspapers and magazines.

In its 23 January 1995 issue the international edition of *Time* magazine devoted a full page to the story, with the provocative headline, *A Step Closer to Jesus?* In its cover story on Miracles on 10 April 1995, just before Easter, *Time* magazine drew attention once again to the importance of the alleged discovery.

As media people say, the story 'has legs'. Not since March 1963, when the Sunday newspaper, *The Observer*, published extracts from John Robinson's forthcoming book, *Honest to God,* has there been so much interest in the media in a story about the Bible or Christian Theology.

This wide interest is not unexpected. New discoveries which have a bearing on the life and teaching of Jesus of Nazareth will always catch the eye. Many Christians who hanker after 'proof' for their faith tend to snatch at such claims – and if in the process the noses of 'sceptical' scholars are put out of joint, so much the better. Many non-Christians who are fascinated by Jesus of Nazareth have a keen interest in new manuscript and archaeological discoveries.

Even allowing for possible exaggeration by a journalist from *The Times*, I was so astonished by the bold claims that even in the midst of preparations for a family Christmas, I faxed a letter to the Editor. I noted that since the initial publication of the papyrus fragments of Matthew in 1953, several leading palaeographers and New Testament scholars have dated the Oxford Matthew fragments to the end of the second century, or even early in the third century. I also suggested (mistakenly, as it has turned out) that Carsten Thiede's claims concerning the very early date and alleged eyewitness character of Matthew's Gospel would not merit serious discussion by specialists. Thiede's theory has attracted so much interest that, like it or not, specialists have been forced to discuss it.

In my letter to *The Times* I also drew attention to Carsten Thiede's equally controversial views about another papyrus fragment. I recalled an earlier front-page story *The Times* had run concerning a 'discovery' of a Biblical manuscript. On 16 March 1972 *The Times* reported the claim by the Spanish papyrologist José O'Callaghan that a papyrus fragment in Greek from Cave 7 at Qumran (7Q5) was part of Mark 6: 52-3. I recall vividly the moment when I read this story while travelling on a crowded commuter train from my home to King's College in central London, where I teach. That very day a colleague and I spent every spare moment following up the story in our library. We were amazed to discover that a photograph of the fragment had been under our noses in our own College library for ten years!

According to *The Times*, part of Mark's Gospel had allegedly turned up in the most surprising place of all: not in Rome, where most scholars thought it was written, but in a cave very close to the sectarian Jewish community at Qumran, near the Dead Sea. And since the scroll was hidden before the Roman Tenth Legion marched through the area in AD 68, Mark's Gospel must have been written earlier than most scholars had supposed. Many widely held views about earliest Christianity would have to be reconsidered.

O'Callaghan has continued to champion this theory; in 1984 Carsten Thiede joined the cause. For many years their views attracted little attention. Until recently, few specialists on Mark's Gospel took seriously the possibility that a fragment of Mark had been discovered in a cave near Qumran. Interest has now been fuelled by the publication in 1992 of Thiede's book, *The Earliest Gospel Manuscript? The Qumran Fragment 7Q5 and its Significance for New Testament Studies* which has made his views more widely known in the English-speaking world.[1] 1992 also saw the publication of an important set of scholarly papers by Thiede and others which were given at a symposium on the theory and its implications held in Eichstätt in Germany. The significance of these papers is only now being appreciated.[2]

This is also a story which will run and run in the months and years ahead. Has a fragment of a very early *Christian* writing been found in the library of a conservative *Jewish* community? I predict that very shortly the public will hear a great deal about the claim that a fragment of Mark's Gospel has turned up among the Dead Sea Scrolls. This fascinating theory has already featured in several German television programmes.

There is plenty of precedent for keen interest in a story about the Scrolls. Ever since their discovery in 1948, they have featured regularly in the media and in mass market books. Long delays in the publication of the fragments have led to allegations of a Vatican conspiracy to hide evidence in the Scrolls said to be damaging to traditional Christianity. Several authors and publishers have recently cashed in unscrupulously on public interest in the Scrolls with bizarre claims about their importance for early Christianity.

So two intriguing stories about the origin of the Gospels are running in tandem. Papyrus fragments of parts of Matthew 26 and a papyrus fragment from a Dead Sea Scroll alleged to contain part of Mark 6 are both said to date from the first century, and thus underpin the reliability of the Gospels. Until now, the earliest surviving fragment of a New Testament writing is generally held to be a piece of papyrus from c. AD 125 with a few lines of John 18 on it (see Plates 2 and 3). If either of the new claims turns out to be correct, parts of the history of earliest Christianity will have to be rewritten from top to tail. This book includes the first full appraisal of both claims.

❧

The Gospels are the foundation documents of Christianity. For Christians there is a great deal at stake when the Gospels are put under the scholar's microscope. Do they contain 'Gospel truth'? In the light of modern scholarship, what do we know about the life and teaching of Jesus of Nazareth?

On the further reaches of the right wing of contemporary Christianity (both Roman Catholic and Protestant), 'the truth of the Gospel' hangs on the historical reliability of every single word of all four Gospels. Interest in the new claims about the fragments of Matthew and Mark has been keenest in this wing of the church. On the radical left, some scholars insist that recent research has undermined the 'truth' of the Gospels: as products of the early church, they tell us next to nothing about Jesus of Nazareth. The earliest Christians, we are told, held such widely diverging views about the significance of Jesus that we have to talk about a set of 'Christianities' – and modern Christians can pick and choose according to their tastes. I shall argue that at both ends of the spectrum justice is not being done to the historical evidence.

Since the Gospels are woven into many strands of our culture, they are also of perennial interest to non-Christians. On almost any definition, the Gospels are 'classic texts'. For nearly two thousand years they have had an impressive 'after-life', so they deserve to be taken very seriously indeed. Readers of this book, whether Christians or not, will expect me to set out the evidence fairly, and to take fully into account non-Christian as well as Christian sources. I am a Christian. My research and teaching are carried out in a School of Humanities proud of its international reputation. So my methods as a scholar have to pass muster with colleagues in departments of Classics, History and English.

Following the discussion in *Chapters II* and *III* of the papyrus fragments of Matthew and the alleged fragment of Mark, I turn in *Chapter IV* to the manuscript evidence for the text of the Gospels. How many early manuscripts do we have, and how reliable are they? I include a discussion of passages from the Gospels where there are important variations in the manuscripts.

In *Chapter V* I take up a baffling question: What happened to traditions about the life and teaching of Jesus between his crucifixion and the writing of the earliest Gospel, Mark? Even on a conservative dating of Mark's Gospel, there is a gap of about 35 years. Did eyewitnesses ensure that the Jesus traditions were transmitted with little or no distortion? Or did the beliefs and practices of the post-Easter Christian communities all but smother the original thrust of the teaching of Jesus?

Many scholars hold that Matthew and Luke both incorporated an earlier large collection of sayings of Jesus. This source, known as Q, has recently been referred to as a 'lost Gospel'. Is Q our most reliable source for the teaching of Jesus? Should this 230-verse source be referred to as a 'Gospel'? These questions are discussed in *Chapter VI*.

In the second century AD, a number of writings known as 'Gospels' failed to find their way into the New Testament. Since they are 'unofficial', even esoteric, they are of interest to many today. Several writers have recently proposed that four of these 'Gospels' contain invaluable evidence for the serious student of the life of Jesus. These claims are discussed in *Chapter VII*. The chapter which follows examines how and why the early church eventually settled on *four* Gospels, no more, no less.

In the second half of this book, the focus changes from the Gospels to Jesus. *Chapter IX* discusses some recent archaeological discoveries which are relevant for the quest for the historical Jesus. In *Chapter X*, literary evidence from outside the Gospels is assessed – evidence in pagan, Jewish and Christian writings. *Chapter XI* examines the literary genre of the Gospels, and the criteria which may be used to uncover authentic Jesus traditions from them.

For many readers *Chapters XII, XIII , XIV* and *XV* will be of particular interest. I discuss questions which are easy to pose but difficult to answer: Who was Jesus of Nazareth? What do we know about his life and teaching?

These questions will be considered from unconventional angles. In *Chapter XII* I start with the 'aftermath' of the Jesus movement in the post-Easter period. I argue that the smoke which swirls around in the early years after the crucifixion of Jesus helps us to locate 'the fire' which caused it.

Historians like to look at the records left not only by history's 'winners', but also history's 'losers', the opponents of a prominent individual or movement. Searching for the voices of the opponents of Jesus of Nazareth is rarely attempted, for his followers were not keen to give the opposition a platform. The reader is invited to join the hunt in *Chapter XIII* for the limited number of clues we do have.

In *Chapters XIV* and *XV* I emphasize the importance of evidence which was *embarrassing* to the first followers of Jesus, but which they retained none the less. Not many readers will be aware of the striking similarities between Jesus and John the Baptist. Traditions which put John on a par with Jesus were an embarrassment in the early church. Since they are unlikely to have been invented, they deserve close attention.

In *Chapter XV* I start with the embarrassment of the crucifixion of Jesus and ask why Jesus the prophet from Nazareth was put to death in this most horrendous of all methods of execution.

The final chapter takes up the broader issues which lurk behind many earlier parts of this book. The relationship between historical inquiry and the evangelists' claims about the significance of Jesus is considered. Could the historian's results conceivably either undermine or prove Christian claims about Jesus?

✺

The title of this book, *Gospel Truth?*, is intended to provoke reflection on a set of questions. In the light of recent discoveries and modern scholarship, how much 'truth' do the Gospels contain? Are the evangelists concerned with 'Gospel truth' understood as the *factual reliability* of their stories? Or is their primary interest 'Gospel truth' understood in a very different sense: the *significance* of Jesus as the one who stood in a unique relationship to God as the Messiah-Christ, the Son of God?

The phrase 'Gospel truth', which is used in English today in both senses, has an interesting history. In many contexts today it is used to affirm the truthfulness of a fact or statement. This usage seems to go back no further than the early nineteenth century when the reliability of the written Gospels was contested fiercely. In the seventeenth and eighteenth centuries the phrase referred to the truthfulness of the *content* of the Christian message about Jesus. No doubt this usage was influenced strongly by the use of the phrase 'the truth of the Gospel' in the Authorized Version translation (1611) of Galatians 2:5, 14. In this fiery letter Paul uses this phrase twice to refer to the proclaimed message of good news about the death and resurrection of Christ. In both verses in Galatians the phrase 'the truth of the Gospel' is still found in the New Revised Standard Version (1989) and in the Revised English Bible (1989).

The second half of this book is concerned with the question 'What can the historian say about the life and teaching of Jesus of Nazareth?' Questions of this kind have been asked only since the eighteenth-century Enlightenment. The father of modern historical inquiry into the Gospels is H.S. Reimarus. He recognized that by pressing rigorously historical questions he would be perceived to be undermining traditional Christianity's 'Gospel truth', so he decided not to allow his writings to be published in his lifetime. Six years after his death in 1768, the philosopher-theologian Lessing began to publish extracts from Reimarus's writings anonymously under the title *Wolfenbüttel Fragments*. In 1788 Lessing published his own book about the origin of Matthew and its relationship to Mark and Luke. And so began intensive study of the Gospels which continues to this day.

This was not the first time some of the issues discussed in this book were considered. Martin Luther was well aware of the mistakes and inconsistencies in Scripture. For example, he recognized that Matthew 27:9 mistakenly cited Jeremiah for Zechariah. He knew that there was a serious discrepancy between Matthew and John over the date of the cleansing of the temple: Matthew placed it at end of the ministry of Jesus, John at the beginning. Luther commented as follows:

> These are questions that I am not going to try to settle. Some people are so hairsplitting and meticulous that they want to have everything absolutely precise. But if we have the right understanding of Scripture and hold to the true article of our faith that Jesus Christ, God's Son, died and suffered for us, it won't matter much if we cannot answer all the questions put to us.

In other words, Luther concluded that 'Gospel truth' was not undermined by discrepancies. Not all Luther's colleagues took the same line. Andreas Osiander was convinced that proven contradictions would undermine 'Gospel truth', so with great ingenuity he tried to harmonize the apparent discrepancies. This led him to conclude that Jesus must have been crowned with thorns twice, and that Peter must have warmed himself four times in the high priest's courtyard.[3]

Similar issues were discussed over a thousand years earlier by Origen. This immensely learned and influential third-century church father has a strong claim to be considered the father of serious inquiry into Biblical manuscripts, an inquiry we shall pursue in *Chapters II, III* and *IV*.

Origen reflected on the reliability and purpose of the Gospels in the face of a stern challenge from the first important pagan opponent of Christianity, Celsus, who wrote between AD 177 and 180. Celsus drew on several strands of Greek philosophical and religious thought in defending what he called 'an ancient doctrine which has existed from the beginning', a tradition which 'newly arrived' Christians had corrupted.

Sixty years later Celsus's attack on Christianity was still making such strong waves that Origen decided that he had no option but to respond to it vigorously. Although Celsus's work, *The True Doctrine*, has not survived, Origen quoted from it at length, and replied to it point by point.

One of the exchanges between Celsus and Origen takes us to the heart of my concerns in this book. In the opening round of his attack, Celsus utilizes the distinctive views of a Jewish opponent of Jesus and his followers. Celsus's Jew says to Jesus:

> When you were bathing near John (at the time of your baptism) you say that you saw what appeared to be a bird fly towards you out of the air. What trustworthy witness saw this apparition, or who heard a voice from heaven adopting you as son of God? There is no proof except for your word and the evidence which you may produce of one of the men who were punished with you.
> (*Contra Celsum* I:41)

Celsus is unimpressed by the eyewitness testimony of a disciple, and asks for *independent* reliable witnesses.

Origen knows that this challenge must be taken seriously. He acknowledges immediately that 'an attempt to substantiate almost any story as historical fact, even if it is true, and to produce complete certainty about it, is one of the most difficult tasks and in some cases is impossible.' He then cites episodes from Greek history, and Greek myths and legends, in order to show how difficult it is to discover historical truth and how difficult it is to decide which traditions may be discerned to have a deeper, allegorical meaning. He then writes as follows:

> We have said this by way of introduction to the whole question of the narrative about Jesus in the Gospels, not in order to invite people with intelligence to mere irrational faith, but with a desire to show that readers need an open mind and considerable study, and, if I may say so, need to enter

into the mind of the writers to find out with what spiritual meaning each event was recorded. (*Contra Celsum* I:42)[4]

These issues are still with us today. Origen's perceptive comments set out an agenda for our own quest. He refuses to allow his readers to shield their personal faith from difficult questions concerning the eyewitness character and reliability of the Gospels. On the other hand, Origen knows that narratives about Jesus in the Gospels were not recorded as mere historical records, but for the sake of the 'Gospel truth' they contain.

CHAPTER II

FIRST-CENTURY FRAGMENTS
OF MATTHEW'S GOSPEL?

NO ONE DISPUTES that, with only one possible exception, the Magdalen College Oxford fragments are the earliest evidence we have for the Greek text of Matthew's Gospel.[1] For this reason they will always be of special interest. It is to Carsten Thiede's credit that he has redirected attention to these fascinating three small scraps of papyrus with writing on both sides, known to New Testament scholars as P64 *(see Plate 1)*.

The first fragment contains parts of Matthew 26:7-8 on one side and parts of Matthew 26:31 on the other; the second fragment contains parts of v. 10 and of vv. 32-3; fragment 3 contains parts of vv. 14-15 and of 22-23. Because there is writing on both sides of the fragments, they come from a codex (the predecessor of the modern book) and not a roll. The fragments were acquired at Luxor in Egypt in 1901 by the Rev. Charles B. Huleatt, a former scholar of Magdalen College; he gave them to his College in the same year.

For fifty years they attracted little attention. They were first published (with photographs) in 1953 by the distinguished papyrologist C. H. Roberts. He noted that the codex had two columns to the page, a rather unusual arrangement. He also concluded that since the entire Gospel of Matthew must have run to about 150 pages, in all probability it contained nothing else. We shall see later in this chapter that this is the only one of Roberts' major observations which must now be revised.

On the basis of a comparison with five papyri, Roberts concluded that P64 is an early predecessor of the well-attested 'Biblical Uncial' hand, 'whose peculiar style began to form towards the end of the second century'.[2] Roberts reported that

on showing a photograph of the papyrus to three scholars, Sir
Harold Bell, Mr T. C. Skeat and Professor Turner, 'they independently and without hesitation pronounced in favor of a date
in the later second century; their verdict can, I think, be accepted with confidence.' Since the three scholars mentioned, plus
Colin Roberts himself, were leading specialists of the day, their
opinions carried considerable weight and were not challenged
until Thiede's views were published in *The Times* on Christmas
Eve 1994. Later in this chapter I shall refer to the important
current research of T. C. Skeat, who, over 40 years later, has
returned to close study of the fragments.

In 1962 Colin Roberts recognized that two Barcelona frag-
ments of parts of Matthew 3:9, 15 and 5:20-2, 25-8 (known as
P67) came from the same codex, a view which has won univer-
sal agreement.[3] This was a major step forward as the two
Barcelona fragments contain rather more words than the three
Oxford fragments.

Carsten Thiede's Theory

It will be helpful at this point to sketch briefly the main grounds
on which palaeographers date manuscripts. At the end of manuscripts from the early Middle Ages (and later) the scribe sometimes added the date on which the copy was completed; unfortunately none of the early papyri is dated in this way.
Archaeology helps in some cases: if a manuscript was found at a
place known to have been destroyed, it predates the destruction.
The content sometimes gives important clues; for example, a
fragment which refers to Jesus cannot have been written before
his lifetime. The material used (papyrus or parchment), the size
and shape of the manuscript (roll or codex), the lay-out and
punctuation of the text, are all important. As yet, carbon 14 dating has not been used, as very large samples would be needed for
accurate analysis. Recent advances in this field allow the use of
very tiny samples, but as far as I know, this has not yet been
attempted on manuscripts of the Gospels. If carbon 14 analysis is
used, it will only give a date for the writing material; it will not
tell us when the papyrus or parchment was actually used.

In most cases the most important guide to dating is the style of the handwriting. Several styles of handwriting were used simultaneously in different parts of the Roman Empire. After close analysis manuscripts can often be placed in groups and ranked chronologically. Attention is given to the forms of individual letters, but specialists have often noted that on its own this feature is too arbitrary to be trustworthy. The script as a whole must also be considered. Is the overall style formal or informal? How are letters grouped together? How skilful and consistent was the scribe? Is there a contrast in thickness between vertical, horizontal and diagonal strokes in the formation of individual letters (known as shading)? How much distance is there between lines? Are there any ornamentations (e.g. serifs)? Even after considering these points (and others) palaeographers are normally most cautious about assigning dates to manuscripts.[4] They often appeal to the independent judgement of experienced colleagues when proposing a date.

When were the Magdalen College Oxford fragments written? On the basis of C. H. Roberts' article, the standard reference works all state, 'about AD 200'. So Carsten Thiede's claim in *The Times* that the fragments may date from the mid-first century came as a bolt from the blue. If accepted, this date would revolutionize our understanding of the origin of the Gospels and just about every other aspect of earliest Christianity. No wonder such keen interest is being taken in three tiny fragments of papyrus.

The articles in *The Times* referred to Thiede's forthcoming scholarly discussion of the Magdalen College fragments in the January 1995 issue of the journal, *Zeitschrift für Papyrologie und Epigraphik*, early copies of which were searched for by scholars as if they were gold nuggets. The article turned out to be something of a damp squib. As is appropriate in an academic journal, it set out a number of proposals on technical points concerning the fragments, some of which are certainly correct. Most crucially of all, Dr Thiede concluded his article as follows: 'it may be argued that it (the Matthew papyrus) could be redated from the late second to the late first century, some time after the destruction of the Temple in Jerusalem (in AD 70).'[5]

I am mystified by the discrepancy between the extravagant claims made in *The Times* (and echoed in the media worldwide), and the 'caution' of the academic journal article which did not even mention that on the 'new' dating Matthew's Gospel offers eyewitness testimony to the life and teaching of Jesus. There is a world of difference between dating the fragments of Matthew to the mid-first century and to the late first century! The later date would not change any of the most widely held views about the origins of the Gospels; the earlier dating would change everything.

Is a date in the late first century possible? From time to time it is important in all branches of knowledge to reconsider received opinion. Many new papyri have been discovered since Roberts first published the fragments 40 years ago. In recent years new dates have sometimes been assigned to papyri; in some cases earlier dates, in some cases, later. So Carsten Thiede's proposals deserve careful consideration.

However there are a number of reasons why they cannot be accepted. Scholars who seek to challenge an established view normally take pains to set out the reasons why it can no longer be accepted; only then do they offer evidence and arguments in support of a rival view. I do not allow my Ph.D. students to come up with a fancy new theory unless they can show that there are serious weaknesses with received opinion. So on reading Thiede's journal article I naturally looked immediately for the reasons why he was no longer satisfied by the arguments advanced by Roberts in favour of a late second century date and a clear link with the 'Biblical Uncial' or 'Biblical Majuscule' style of handwriting.[6] No challenge to Roberts' views is mounted; his book *Greek Literary Hands*, still a classic in the field, is not cited.[7]

Although recent work has been done on the 'Biblical Uncial' style, partly in the light of recent discoveries, Thiede does not discuss it. He does not refer either to G. Cavallo's magisterial 1967 study, or to the splendid 1987 book by G. Cavallo and H. Maehler, *Greek Bookhands of the Early Byzantine Period, A.D. 300 – 800*.[8] Both books note that the formal script known as 'Biblical Uncial' (which is not confined to Biblical manuscripts) goes back to the end of the second century; it reaches its definitive form by the third century, and the height of its perfection in the fourth century, the period which produced the famous Biblical manuscripts, Codex Vaticanus and Codex Sinaiticus.[9] Both books list a number of characteristics of both the formation and shape of letters in this script in its 'phase of greatest formal perfection'. Many of these characteristics are found in the fragments of P64. Several leading specialists are as baffled as I am by Thiede's failure to offer reasons for abandoning the consensus view that P64 is an early example of the 'Biblical Uncial' style.[10]

Equally puzzling is his failure to discuss the two rather more substantial Barcelona fragments of Matthew from the same codex (P67). If one is making a comparison of handwriting styles, it is obviously important to use as large a sample as possible.

Thiede rests his case on a comparison of P64 with five recently discovered examples of handwriting from outside Egypt, the origin of P64 and P67. At first sight the examples seem to be well chosen, for the latest dates of these texts can be established on archaeological grounds even before appeal is made to handwriting styles. The three texts from Cave 4 at Qumran must be earlier than the Roman advance in AD 68; the texts from Cave 7 are probably no later than AD 135; and the Greek Minor Prophets Scroll from Nahal Hever is no later than AD 135. Appeal to papyri discovered at Herculaneum (near Pompeii) is also superficially attractive, for they must have been written before they were buried in the eruption of Mt Vesuvius in AD 79.[11]

Of course there is no reason why the style(s) of handwriting found in these first and early second-century texts should not have continued to be used for a very long time. Thiede recognizes this, and accepts that his proposed redating depends on his ability to establish that the form of handwriting found in P64 is also used in the five manuscripts he offers for comparison.

However, there are serious problems with his case. Papyrologists insist that in dating manuscripts both the methods used in the formation of individual letters and their shape should be considered carefully.[12] Thiede very largely ignores the former, and does not offer a full comparison of the latter. While there are similarities between the shape of some of the letters in P64 and their counterparts in the first-century examples appealed to, there are also dissimilar letters which are not discussed.[13]

Even if Thiede had been able to show that P64, the Qumran, Nahal Hever and Herculaneum texts all used the same style of script, he would not necessarily have made out his case for a first-century dating. For as the distinguished Oxford palaeographer Peter J. Parsons noted in 1990, 'there is no special reason to suppose that the same styles of script existed at the same time, and developed at the same pace, in all parts of the Mediterranean world'.[14] In other words, P64 and P67 should be compared first of all with papyri from Egypt, as Roberts did 40 years ago.

There is no reason to abandon the view of Colin Roberts that P64 and P67 date from the end of the second century: there are no persuasive arguments in favour of a first-century dating.[15]

Oxford, Barcelona and Paris

I believe that the Magdalen College Oxford fragments of Matthew are very significant indeed, but for quite different reasons from those which have received so much attention in the media recently. From time to time it has been suggested that P64 (Oxford) and P67 (Barcelona) come from the same codex as P4 (Paris).[16] The latter contains quite extensive parts of Luke 1-6, as well as a fragment which preserves the title of Matthew's Gospel. In his journal article and in a public discussion with me in the Greek Orthodox Cathedral in London in January 1995, Carsten Thiede brushed aside a possible link. But it is now clear that the four Paris fragments (three of which are substantial) hold the key to a major new development of considerable importance for the student of Christian origins.

The Paris fragments were purchased in 1891 in Luxor in Egypt, the same city where the Magdalen College Matthew fragments were purchased 10 years later. They were not published in full until 1938, and they were not studied intensively until 1994-5.[17]

The story of the original discovery, which was made in 1889 in Coptos in Upper Egypt, is quite extraordinary. Colin Roberts tells it as follows:

> While a Graeco-Roman house was being uncovered, it was noticed that one of the walls gave a hollow ring when tapped; it was opened up and in a carefully prepared niche was found a papyrus codex. It had clearly not been touched since it was first placed there; it was complete and still had

attached to it its rather primitive binding. The contents were identified as two treatises of the Graeco-Jewish scholar Philo . . . Stuck in the inside binding of the codex were found some torn scraps of papyrus; they had been glued together to form papier mâché as padding for the leather binding (an obvious and common practice). These when cleaned and edited, turned out to contain fragments of the Third Gospel written in a singularly handsome hand, with two columns to the page . . .[18]

The codex of Philo was dated by A. S. Hunt, one of the most distinguished specialists of the day, to the third century. The Gospel fragments must be earlier, since they were used in its binding. One must also allow some time for a top grade codex to have deteriorated to such an extent that it was torn up and used as padding in the binding of the Philo codex. This suggests that the Gospel codex cannot have been written much, if at all, after AD 200.[19]

In May 1995 Philip Comfort reconsidered the relationship of P4 to P64 and P67 and concluded that while they were all written by the same scribe, they did not come from the same codex. Comfort noted some differences between the fragments and suggested that the scribe wrote P4 at a later date.[20]

In the same month T. C. Skeat generously shared with me some of the results of research he began long before the Magdalen College fragments unexpectedly attracted enormous interest. T. C. Skeat is highly respected for his work on the origins of the codex, to which we shall come in a moment.

T. C. Skeat has convinced me that the script, the lay-out of the text, and the page size are the same in the Oxford, Barcelona and Paris fragments. On the basis of a set of brilliant calculations he is able to show that in all probability the fragments all come from the same codex. The earlier judgement of C. H. Roberts and others (about which some doubts had been expressed) has been vindicated.[21] Skeat, however, has taken a further important step forward by showing that the codex almost certainly contained all four gospels: it may well be the oldest manuscript of a codex of the four.

In an article published in 1994, T. C. Skeat developed consid-

erably some of his own earlier work on the origin of the
Christian codex. He noted that some 42 papyrus fragments of
the Gospels have now come to light, and every one is from a
codex. 'This is an astonishing statistic, if we reflect that among
non-Christian papyri the roll form predominated for centuries,
and it was not until about AD 300 that the codex achieved par-
ity of representation with the scroll, and another two or three
centuries passed before the roll disappeared altogether as a vehi-
cle for literature.'[22]

Why did Christians have such an extraordinary predilection
for the codex form of book as opposed to the roll? Skeat's
answer, which I find convincing, is that Christians adopted the
codex because it could contain the texts of all four Gospels. No
roll could do this. Christians borrowed the codex from the
Romans. They invented it, but began to use it only very slowly;
the familiar roll retained its popularity for book production for a
long time to come.

When did Christians first bring together four Gospels into a
single codex? Until now most scholars have accepted that the
Chester Beatty papyrus codex (P45) from the middle of the third
century is the earliest example of a four-Gospel codex. Skeat has
calculated that the important Bodmer codex of Luke and John
(P75), usually dated to early in the third century, was probably
a four-Gospel codex.

The codex which contained the Oxford, Barcelona and Paris
fragments is somewhat earlier. This codex was originally a most
handsome literary production; the formal handwriting style and
the meticulously planned lay-out of each page suggest that it will
have had ancestors. As we have seen, the dating of papyri is not
an exact science, but if Roberts' judgement is accepted, the
codex was written near the end of the second century. This
strongly suggests that well before the end of the second century
(much earlier than most scholars have supposed) the church
accepted as authoritative four Gospels, no more, no less.

I believe that this conclusion is consistent with other evidence.
I shall take up this important topic again in *Chapter VIII*, where
I shall explain more fully why the decision of the early church to
accept four Gospels was as important as any other decision taken
in the early centuries.

So at last we have uncovered the real significance of the Magdalen College fragments of Matthew's Gospel. They are certainly not from the first century. They may well be part of the earliest surviving copy of the four Gospels brought together in one codex: our earliest witness to a momentous development within early Christianity.

CHAPTER III

MARK'S GOSPEL AMONG THE DEAD SEA SCROLLS?

BETWEEN 1947 AND 1956 an enormous number of Jewish writings were found in eleven caves near Qumran, close to the Dead Sea[1]. For students of the Bible and of early Judaism, this discovery has turned out to be the archaeological find of the century. Shortly before the arrival of the Romans in AD 68, the writings were hidden in eleven nearby caves by the members of the 'Essene' sectarian community whose ruined buildings have been excavated at Qumran. The Qumran community may well have originated as a rift within the Essene movement in the middle of the second century BC. Analysis of the handwriting styles of the manuscripts suggests that most of them were written in the two centuries BC, results which were confirmed in 1991 by carbon 14 analysis of tiny samples of manuscripts undertaken with new techniques.

About 800 manuscripts have been recovered; 225 are copies of Biblical books, the remainder are religious writings. The finds in Cave 4 are mind-boggling: about 15,000 fragments from about 550 different manuscripts. Some of the scrolls are remarkably complete, but there are thousands of tiny fragments. Painstaking study will continue for a long time to come. Some of this work can be likened to assembling a giant jigsaw puzzle with many pieces missing – and to complicate matters it is sometimes not clear how many jigsaw puzzles are on the table!

No other archaeological discovery relating to the Bible has caught the public imagination in quite the same way. In the early years the story of the early discoveries, complete with tales of political intrigue, was often repeated. In 1948 came the dramatic announcement that a complete copy of the Hebrew text of Isaiah

had been discovered: a scroll one thousand years older than any
other complete manuscript of this writing which Jews and
Christians have always valued so highly.

In the 1950s a few scholars claimed that the Scrolls were a
medieval forgery, a view long since abandoned. In that decade
bizarre claims about the relationship of these writings to earliest
Christianity began to emerge – mainly from journalists seeking
to boost their bank balances. This phenomenon continues to the
present day: let the buyer of books about the Dead Sea Scrolls
beware.

In recent years the number of television and radio programmes, as well as books and magazine articles, has increased.
Attention has frequently focused on the failure of some scholars
to publish texts which they had been assigned. This led to quite
unwarranted allegations of a Vatican conspiracy to hide evidence
which would undermine Christianity. The truth is more pro-
saic: in several cases the delays were exacerbated by personal
tragedies; in other cases scholarly reluctance to publish editions
which were less than perfect led to procrastination. This storm
has now blown over, for since 1993 all the material has been
readily available for scholarly study in photographs on no fewer
than 134 microfiches.

In 1991, just in time for the Christmas market, the journalists
Michael Baigent and Richard Leigh published *The Dead Sea
Scrolls Deception,* a book which tries to use some of the Scrolls to
turn the history of earliest Christianity inside out. In Germany
alone over 400, 000 copies were sold in just over a year, largely
as the result of an unprecedented advertising campaign which
played on gullibility and anti-Christian sentiments.[2]

I do not propose to waste another sentence on this absurd
book. Nor shall I discuss the theories of the Australian writer
Barbara Thiering, who allows her vivid imagination to find
polemical references to Jesus as the 'wicked priest' in two of the
most important Scrolls, and who claims that in AD 30 Jesus married Mary Magdalene.[3] Her book was described in a review as
'silly' by the Jewish scholar Herschel Shanks, and merits no further attention.

The Dead Sea Scrolls do not refer or allude to Jesus, John the
Baptist, James, Mary Magdalene, or any early Christians. Nearly

all of them were written during the two centuries *before* Jesus was born. With the exception of only a very few maverick scholars (notably Barbara Thiering and Robert Eisenman), all Qumran specialists in different parts of the world accept these conclusions, whatever their personal religious convictions. Attempts (mainly by journalists) to overturn this consensus all play fast and loose with the evidence of both the Scrolls and the Gospels. The theories of Barbara Thiering and Robert Eisenman are being steadily falsified by rigorous new carbon 14 analysis. None of the writings tested so far has been dated to the first century AD, necessary if they are to contain references to Jesus or his followers.

In this chapter I shall concentrate on one possible direct link between the Dead Sea Scrolls and earliest Christianity: the claim that a fragment of Mark's Gospel known as 7Q5 has been found among the Dead Sea Scrolls. There is a curious irony in the fact that so far this fragment has not featured in any of the mass market books which claim that some of the Dead Sea Scrolls refer to Jesus or to earliest Christianity. Although the theory has been discussed by scholars for some time now, wider interest in 7Q5 has so far been confined largely to conservative Christian circles (both Roman Catholic and Protestant) where it has been seen as offering 'proof' for the early date and reliability of Mark's Gospel.

Given the enormous appetite of the general public for 'new' information about the significance of the Scrolls, I suspect that it may be only a matter of time before media attention is focused on 7Q5. This tiny fragment has already featured in several television programmes in Germany.

Cave 7 at Qumran

In 1955 18 papyrus fragments in Greek (7Q1–18) were discovered in Cave 7 at Qumran (*see Plate 5*). In addition, a set of imprints on the ground (7Q19) was discovered, probably from several texts. Apart from some pottery remains, nothing else was found in the cave. Whereas very nearly all the manuscripts in the other 10 caves were written in Hebrew or Aramaic, the fragments found in Cave 7 are all in Greek. Why were scrolls in

Greek put in a cave on their own? A satisfactory answer to this question cannot at present be given.

The Cave 7 fragments were published in 1962.[4] Only two fragments were identified: 7Q1 as Exodus 28:4-7, and 7Q2 as Baruch 6:43-4 (Epistle of Jeremiah), both of which are close to the text of the Septuagint, the Greek translation of the Old Testament. On the advice of the respected Oxford palaeographer C. H. Roberts, 7Q1-3 were dated at about 100 BC, and 7Q4-18 between 50 BC and AD 50.[5] Some pottery remains were dated to the two centuries BC and prior to AD 68.

There matters rested until 1972. There were plenty of other more promising Qumran writings to occupy the attention of scholars. In 1972 the Spanish scholar José O'Callaghan claimed that 7Q5 contained parts of Mark 6:52-3. He later identified 7Q4 as I Timothy 3:16 – 4:1,3. With much less confidence, he suggested that seven further Cave 7 fragments were parts of New Testament writings: three more of Mark, one each of Acts, Romans, James and II Peter. M. Baillet, the editor of the original publication of the Cave 7 scrolls, rejected O'Callaghan's identifications, as did several other respected scholars.[6]

O'Callaghan's identification of 7Q5 is now being vigorously and tirelessly championed by Carsten Thiede. All participants in the debate agree that unless 7Q5 is accepted as part of Mark 6:52-3, the other proposed links with New Testament writings are no more than interesting speculations. So I shall concentrate on 7Q5.

What if?

Historians do not like playing the game, 'What would have been the outcome *if* x had (or had not) happened?' So I am reluctant to explain the implications of the O'Callaghan/Thiede theory before we have considered the evidence closely. However, the reader may wish to know just what is at stake before we look at the current intense debate over one damaged letter in one tiny fragment among the thousands found in the Qumran caves.

Most scholars believe that Mark's Gospel was written between AD 65 and 75. If Mark's Gospel was written by, say, AD 60, we might have a little more confidence in its historical reliability, but it would not shorten appreciably the gap between the crucifixion of Jesus and the composition of Mark, our earliest Gospel. This gap will be considered in *Chapter V.*

On the basis of analysis of the style of handwriting carried out long before O'Callaghan first advanced his theory, C. H. Roberts suggested that 7Q5 was written between 50 BC and AD 50. So if 7Q5 is from Mark, was this Gospel written no later than AD 50? Of course not. Roberts, like other palaeographers, frequently emphasized that styles of handwriting cannot be dated with any precision.

According to a tradition which goes back to the end of the second century, Mark was written in Rome. This is certainly possible, but an equally good case can be made out in favour of Antioch in Syria, or even Galilee. Cave 7 was not far from main trade routes, so a copy could have been brought south from Antioch or Galilee within a few days. And a copy could have reached Qumran from Rome, via Jerusalem, in weeks rather than months.

O'Callaghan did not stop to consider such questions. Carsten Thiede, however, has not shirked the challenge. He notes that a damaged jar bearing the Hebrew inscription *rwm'* (vocalized *Roma* or *Ruma*) twice on its neck has been found in Cave 7. He then builds on a cautious suggestion made by J. A. Fitzmyer that the inscription might be an attempt at writing *Rome* in Hebrew letters. 'Thus it would indicate the original ownership of the scrolls: they belonged to and came from the Christian community in Rome which supplied the "home communities" in Palestine with material collected and copied in Rome or at any rate of Roman origin (such as the Gospel according to Mark?).'[7] Thiede then sketches out three possible scenarios to explain how Christian scrolls in Greek may have found their way from Rome to Qumran.

Although strong objections can be raised to all three proposals, in the light of the many gaps in our knowledge of first-century Judaism and earliest Christianity, it is not possible to rule them out completely – and it is not at all difficult to envisage still further possible scenarios. This is so, even if one considers (as I do) that the inscription on the jar is more likely to be a proper name than a reference to the origin of the scrolls in Rome.

If 7Q5 is part of Mark, it would undoubtedly be the earliest surviving fragment of any part of the New Testament. At present that honour belongs to a fragment of John 18, usually dated to c. AD 125 (*see Plates 2 and 3*). The Magdalen College Oxford Matthew fragments are not now in contention!

As we saw in the preceding chapter, some 42 papyrus fragments of the Gospels have now come to light, and every single one is from a codex. 7Q5, like the other Qumran writings, is written on only one side, so it is from a roll. An early fragment of Mark from a roll would be an unexpected surprise, but it is not impossible. So far all the earliest papyri of the Gospels have come from Egypt, but discovery in a Qumran cave cannot be ruled out.

Who would have placed a copy of Mark's Gospel in a cave near Qumran? Most scholars assume that the Greek fragments discovered in Cave 7 were placed there by the Qumran community before the Romans advanced through the area in AD 68. Is it conceivable that a member of the Qumran community put a copy of Mark, along with some other texts in Greek, in a cave in isolation from texts in Hebrew and Aramaic?

For two reasons, this is most unlikely. First, the Qumran community had very little interest either in writings in Greek or in religious writings with which they were totally out of sympathy. Apart from the fragments in Cave 7, only a few more fragments in Greek have been found – among the 15,000 in Cave 4.[8] The Greek scrolls were almost certainly brought to Qumran from elsewhere.

And secondly, Mark's Gospel would not have been of any interest at all to members of the Qumran community. Mark and Qumran were at opposite ends of the first-century religious spectrum. Mark is more radical on the question of observance of the Jewish law than Matthew or Luke; only Mark states that Jesus declared all foods clean (7:20). On the other hand, the Qumran community sought to observe the Jewish law more meticulously than many other Jews.

There is a huge gap between the religious worlds of Mark and the Qumran community. So if 7Q5 is part of Mark, perhaps someone other than a member of the Qumran community placed the Greek scrolls in Cave 7. This is not impossible: the Copper Scroll from Cave 3 probably had nothing to do with the rest of the Qumran writings. J. A. Fitzmyer has noted that 'it resembles the rest of the Qumran writings neither in palaeography nor in language (being an early form of Mishnaic Hebrew).'[9]

Was this also the case with the scrolls in Greek in Cave 7? In AD 68 the sounds and smells of war were not far away. In that setting it is just possible that someone without any link with the Qumran community hid some Greek scrolls in Cave 7 in desperation. After all, Cave 7 was not far from north-south, and east-west lines of communication.

If someone other than a member of the Qumran community placed scrolls in Cave 7, when might this have happened? It is natural to assume that the Greek Scrolls (along with all the other scrolls) were hidden shortly before the Romans arrived in AD 68. On the other hand, it is important to note that while there is no archaeological evidence which indicates that Cave 7 was used after AD 68, there is no evidence which rules out that possibility. So if 7Q5 is part of Mark, it is just possible that the scroll was placed in the cave *after* AD 68. Part of Cave 7 has now collapsed: it is most unlikely that it ever will give up any more of its secrets.

Acceptance of the theory that 7Q5 is part of Mark 6 would clearly involve revision of a number of generally held views concerning earliest Christianity. Sometimes scholars do have to consider almost impossible things before breakfast, so we must turn to the evidence. But before we do, it is important to note that acceptance of the theory would neither undermine nor underpin the reliability of Mark's Gospel: *Gospel truth is not at stake.*

Does 7Q5 = Mark 6:52-3?

Do the five lines of 7Q5 contain parts of Mark 6:52-3? In order to assist readers who do not know any Greek, in the five lines of English text below the letters in bold type correspond very approximately to the Greek letters:

> 52 for they did not understand **a**bout the loaves,
> but th**eir** hearts were hard-
> ened.53 **And** when they had crossed over,
> they came (to land) at Ge**nes**saret and
> m**oo**red the boat. 54 When they got out . . .

7Q5 contains only ten Greek letters on four lines which can be read with certainty (*see Plate 6*). I used to tell my students that after only one Greek lesson they could already read an important Greek fragment from Qumran, for it contains only one full word, *kai* (and). However, as Thiede himself has shown, the tiny size of the fragment and the small number of certain letters do not rule out the possibility of identification, for papyrus fragments of comparable size have been identified successfully.[10]

If 7Q5 = Mark 6:52-3, then this text did not contain the Greek phrase *epi tēn gēn* (to land), otherwise line 4 would be nine letters too long. The phrase is found in all Greek manuscripts of Mark and all the early translations into other languages.[11] This is an embarrassment for the theory, but it is not fatal: individual New Testament manuscripts occasionally contain readings not attested in any other manuscript.

In the Greek transcriptions below, a dot beneath a space indicates that the letter above cannot be read with any confidence; a dot beneath a letter indicates a possible or probable reading. The transcription on the left is proposed by the Australian papyrologists S.R. Pickering and R.R.E. Cook.[12] The fuller transcription on the right is Thiede's; O'Callaghan's is similar.[13]

	]ͅ[		]ε[
2	]ͅτωι α ͅ[	2	]υτωνη[
	]η και τ ͅ[		]η καιτι[
4	] ννη ͅ[	4	]ννησͅ[
	] θη ͅͅ[		]ϑησᾳ[
	S.R. Pickering and R.R.E. Cook		C.P. Thiede

[συνῆκαν] ἐ[πὶ τοῖϲ ἄρτοιϲ,]
[ἀλλ᾽ ἦν α]ὐτῶν ἡ [καρδία πεπωρω-]
[μέν]ἡ καὶ τι[απεράσαντεϲ]
[ἦλθον εἰϲ Γε]ννησͅ[αρὲτ καὶ]
[προσωρμίσ]θησᾳ[ν. καὶ ἐξελ-]

Readings and reconstruction
needed to produce Mark 6:52-3

Two letters are clear in line two, *tau* and *omega*. For some time now the next letter has been central to the debate. If 7Q5 is a fragment of Mark, this damaged letter *must* be a *nu*, otherwise the theory collapses (*see Plate* 7). Thiede claims that the difference between what he takes to be a partial *nu* in line 2 and the clear *nu* in line 4 is not significant, for the scribe of 7Q5 did vary his letters slightly. He cites as an example the difference between the *eta* in line four, and the *eta* in line 5.

But a simple test shows that this claim is fallacious. By using tracing paper on an enlarged clear photograph of 7Q5 one can compare the two *etas*: the difference is insignificant (*see Plate 6*). If one then traces the clear *nu* in line 4 and tries to place it over the disputed damaged letter in line 2, it is immediately obvious that a *nu* simply will not fit there.

Very properly, Thiede insists that careful examination of the original is always preferable to photographs, even if they are infrared, or enlargements. He concludes that the *nu* in line 2 is 'highly possible'.[14] Other experienced scholars have looked at the original recently and have concluded that a *nu* is *impossible*. One such scholar is R. G. Jenkins of the University of Melbourne. He has carried out a much more sophisticated version of my tracing paper test. The results are shown in the diagram in Plate 8 of this book.

At this point in the debate, Carsten Thiede will want to produce his trump card, the result of an investigation carried out on 12 April 1992 by the Division of Identification and Forensic Science of the Israel National Police. With German television cameras rolling, a stereo-microscope was used to look closely at the disputed letter in line 2. A photograph is included in the published version of papers given at a symposium held in Eichstätt, Germany in 1991.[15] In the photograph there are faint traces of what Thiede thinks is the top of the diagonal of a *nu* (the Greek letter is shaped like the English letter N). These traces are not visible to the naked eye.

In May 1995 I showed the new enlarged photograph to T. C. Skeat, a very experienced papyrologist. He was certain that there simply wasn't room for a *nu* in this line. He also confirmed the judgement of S. R. Pickering and·R. R. E. Cook that the next damaged letter looks very much like a damaged *alpha* – a further nail in the coffin of the theory that 7Q5 is part of Mark. R. G.

Jenkins, who has been working on all the fragments from Cave 7 for some time, has looked carefully at the original and the new photograph. He has reached the same conclusion: he thinks the faint traces which the stereo-microscope has found may be no more than a shadow.

Several other experienced specialists have concluded that *nu* in line 2 is either very unlikely or quite impossible.[16] Pickering and Cook read an *iota* at this point; they stress the similarity of this damaged letter to the certain *iota* in line 3. This seems to me to be the most likely reading.

One last argument used to support the O'Callaghan/Thiede theory needs to be examined. Computer searches have been mentioned several times in the debate. In particular, appeal has been made to a search at Tyndale House, Cambridge, using the Thesaurus Linguae Graecae (TLG) CD-ROM, a massive database of almost all the Greek writings of antiquity. This search failed to yield any text other than Mark 6:52-3 for the letters of 7Q5 identified by O'Callaghan. This seems to provide impressive support for the O'Callaghan theory until one learns that the Cambridge search did not take account of all the possible ways of reading the damaged letters in 7Q5.[17]

There is an even more serious limitation with computer searches. Although computers can search rapidly databases which incorporate selected editions of texts, not even the TLG CD-ROM is complete. It does not include all possible readings of damaged letters, let alone textual variations in manuscripts. Above all, neither the TLG CD-ROM nor any other database can possibly include lost writings or missing sections of texts! Many Jewish writings in Greek have survived either only in part, or in translations into other languages, or not at all.[18] 7Q5 is almost certainly a fragment of one such writing.

The Dead Sea Scrolls, Jesus and the Gospels

Although it is most unlikely that an early copy of Mark's Gospel found its way to Cave 7, this is not completely impossible. The theory that 7Q5 is part of Mark's Gospel does not collapse for this reason, but simply because the crucial damaged letter in line 2 of 7Q5 *cannot be read as a nu.*

Although Mark's Gospel has not been found among the Dead Sea Scrolls, the discovery of this huge collection of writings sheds a great deal of light on Jesus and the Gospels. There is an important example in *Chapter XV pp. 186–7*). The Dead Sea Scrolls do not refer to Jesus or to any of his followers. How could they, when it is now clear beyond all reasonable doubt that nearly all of them were written before Jesus was born? Their importance lies elsewhere: the Scrolls have revolutionized our knowledge of early Judaism. We now have a much clearer picture of the religious world in which Jesus and his first followers lived and taught. Before the discovery of the Scrolls hardly any other Jewish writings in Hebrew or Aramaic were known from this period. The rabbinic writings are all from later centuries and can be used only with difficulty in reconstruction of Jewish thought and practices at the time of Jesus.

There are, however, two reasons why the Qumran writings cannot be used without further ado as evidence for Judaism at the time of Jesus. They were nearly all written in the two centuries BC; the community's ideas developed considerably during that period. Even more problematic is their origin from an 'Essene' sectarian community, probably a break-away group which parted with the parent Essenes. In the first century, Jewish thought was very diverse, so we must not assume that the Qumran 'sectarian' writings give us direct access to the views of most Jews either in the streets of Jerusalem or in the villages of Galilee.

Even when we keep in mind these two provisos, the Qumran writings confirm and clarify the Jewish roots of the teaching of Jesus, and also the thought patterns and organizational structures developed by the first Christians. Again and again there are clear parallels. For example, in 1QM 14:7 (the War Scroll), but in no other ancient text, there is a parallel to the phrase 'the poor in spirit' in the first beatitude in the Sermon on the Mount (Matthew 5:3).

Perhaps even more striking is the parallel between the way both Mark and 1QS 8:12-16 quote and use Isaiah 40:3. Mark notes that this passage was fulfilled with the appearance of John the Baptist in the desert crying out, 'Prepare the way of the Lord . . .' In 1QS 8:12ff. (the Community Rule) we read:

When the community members exist in Israel in accordance with these rules, they shall separate themselves from the settlement of the men of injustice and shall go into the wilderness to prepare there for the way of him (God), as it is written, 'In the wilderness prepare the way of (God), make level in the desert a highway for our God.' This (way) is the study of the law which he commanded through Moses.[19]

In this passage Isaiah 40:3 is applied to the founding of the Qumran community: its members were to withdraw into the desert in order to prepare there for God's coming. For the Qumran community study and observance of the law are the 'way', whereas for Mark, the way of the Lord is the way of Jesus which he sets out in his Gospel.

Soon after the publication of the first Scrolls to be discovered, several scholars drew attention to parallels between Jesus and the Teacher of Righteousness, the founder and leader of the Qumran community. However, when all the material about the Teacher is assembled, one cannot but be struck by the paucity of it. Although the community was deeply influenced by its respected Teacher, it seems to have survived on a minimum of tradition about him. In contrast, the Gospels give us much fuller portraits of Jesus.

This conclusion has to be modified slightly in the light of the most recently published (1993) major Qumran writing, 4Q394–99, usually known as 4QMMT from the opening Hebrew words. Six incomplete copies of a Cave 4 manuscript seem to be from a letter written by the Teacher of Righteousness to the opponents of the Qumran group. The letter indicates that the Qumran community observed the law much more strictly than its opponents, perhaps Pharisees, or the 'parent' Essenes. 4QMMT alludes to a possible plot against the Teacher of Righteousness. Another Cave 4 writing, 4Q171:3–10, implies that there were plans to kill him. But there is no evidence that this threat was carried out.

The Qumran community, like other Jews of the time, held a variety of expectations concerning an expected Messiah, or Messiahs. The first followers of Jesus undoubtedly drew on some of those expectations as they spelt out their own convictions concerning Jesus, the Messiah-Christ. But there are differences. Although Robert Eisenman's view that 4Q285 refers to a 'slain Messiah' was reported widely in the media in November 1991, it is now agreed that this is a misreading of the text.[20] The Qumran writings do not refer to the death and/or resurrection of a Messiah.

I have referred to several parallels between the Qumran writings and the Gospels. Many more could be added. The parallels do not force us to conclude that either Jesus himself, or the evangelists, drew directly on Qumran writings. The similarities are the result of independent use and reinterpretation of the same Scriptures and other Jewish traditions.

The Scrolls help us to appreciate much more keenly both the teaching of Jesus and the distinctive theological emphases of the evangelists, but they do not anticipate directly 'Gospel truth' about Jesus of Nazareth.

CHAPTER IV

HOW RELIABLE ARE
THE MANUSCRIPTS OF
THE GOSPELS?

IN LATER CHAPTERS of this book we shall see that nearly all our evidence for the life and teaching of Jesus is in the four New Testament Gospels. Do we know exactly what the four evangelists wrote? How reliable are the manuscripts of the Gospels? Questions about manuscripts arise as soon as we start to study any ancient writing. Even with more modern printed texts there are often major variations in different editions of the text: later editors who try to correct errors in earlier editions often introduce more errors. For example, Shakespeare's *The Tempest* contains plenty of problems for textual critics. The text which was printed for the first time in the 'First Folio' 1623 edition contained a large number of errors, probably because it was printed from a prompt's copy. Some scholars have argued that the play as we have it is an abridged version of the original text.

Modern translations of the Gospels include one or two footnote references per page to 'other ancient authorities' (NRSV) or 'some witnesses' (REB). This is a step forward from older translations, including the Authorized (i.e. King James) Version of 1611, which did not alert readers to variations in the manuscripts. The footnotes in modern translations are intended to indicate that translators have genuine doubts about the original words of the evangelists. However the footnotes often have the opposite effect: many readers conclude that since there are so few such notes, variations in the manuscripts are few and far between. Nothing could be further from the truth.

I have taken one page of my copy of the NRSV translation (1989) at random. On the page which sets out the translation of Mark 10:40–11:17, there is no reference to 'other ancient

authorities'. For this same passage, however, the most widely
used edition of the Greek text (the 27th edition of the Nestle-
Aland text, 1993) lists no fewer than 48 places where the manuscripts differ. In those 48 places there are sometimes only two
possibilities; often there are three or more; and in one case (in
Mark 11:3), there are six. Sometimes a variant reading will be
supported by only one or two manuscripts; in other cases, by
hundreds of manuscripts. Other pages from the NRSV would
produce similar figures.

How did so many variations creep into the manuscripts? How
many manuscripts do we have? Which ones are reliable? How do
we reconstruct the most probable wording of the text? What
advances have been made in recent years? These questions will
be discussed in the first part of this chapter. I shall then set out
and assess some of the most interesting and important places
where there are major variations in the manuscripts of the
Gospels, before turning to the most pressing question of all: how
confident can we be that a modern translation is firmly based on
the original words of the evangelists?

Variant Readings

Many of the variations in the manuscripts are minor. At Mark
10:48, for example, the NRSV records that Bartimaeus, the
blind beggar, said to Jesus: 'Son of David, have mercy on me!' In
one manuscript Bartimaeus says to Jesus, 'Lord, Son of David'; in
a few manuscripts, 'Jesus, Son of David'; in a few others, 'the Son
of David'; and in a few more there is a variation in the Greek
which does not affect the translation. Three of these four variations have arisen as a result of conscious or unconscious attempts
to bring the text of Mark into line with the wording of the parallel passage in Matthew 20:31 which the scribe may well have
known by heart.

In a handful of manuscripts, however, the whole of verse 48 is
omitted. Did later scribes expand an original shorter text? In this
case, this is not likely. In most manuscripts in vv. 47b and in 48b
Bartimaeus calls out to Jesus twice over with almost identical
words. So a scribe's eye may well have jumped from one phrase
to the other in adjacent lines, and led him to omit all the words

in between. Since Mark's story about Bartimaeus still made good sense without v. 48, several scribes then repeated the shorter text. Try copying out page after page from a book, and you will see that it is easy to make an error of this kind.

In many cases later scribes thought they were correcting spelling or grammatical slips, whereas in fact they were introducing fresh errors. Occasionally scribes seem to have misheard a dictated word, and inserted a word with a similar sound. Changes were often made in order to smooth out the differences between the Gospels. Since Matthew was the most widely used Gospel in the early church, manuscripts of Mark and Luke were often harmonized with Matthew.

The existence of errors of all kinds was known to Origen in the middle of the third century. In his commentary on Matthew, he wrote as follows:

> It is an obvious fact today that there is much diversity among the manuscripts, due either to the carelessness of the scribes, or to the perverse audacity of some people in correcting the text, or again to the fact that there are those who add or delete as they please, setting themselves up as correctors.[1]

We know that discrepancies between the Gospels were often seized on by opponents of Christianity in order to destroy the credibility of the evangelists. Writing between AD 177 and 180, Celsus, the first important pagan critic of Christianity, claimed that some Christians 'altered the original text of the Gospels three or four times, or even more, with the intention of thus being able to destroy the arguments of their critics.' In his reply Origen insisted that such alterations were only ever made by heretics 'who indeed dared to falsify the Gospels by introducing their own philosophical principles which were foreign to the meaning of the teaching of Jesus.' Origen may have had in mind 'heretical Gospels' (some of which will be discussed in *Chapter VII*), or he may have had in mind 'corrections' made by 'heretics' to the text of the four Gospels he accepted as authoritative.[2]

From time to time some scribes altered the wording of the text to make it suit their own doctrinal preferences. Two examples are worth noting at this point. Matthew 1:25 states that Joseph 'had no marital relations with her (Mary) until she had borne a son'. The Greek is ambiguous: it implies (but does not state explicitly) that following the birth of Jesus, Joseph had sexual intercourse with Mary. However, in the interests of the doctrine of the perpetual virginity of Mary which began to be accepted in some circles in the second century, one early Latin manuscript and one early Syriac manuscript remove all reference to 'marital relations' and simply state: 'Mary bore a son.'

Luke 24:51 records that while Jesus was blessing the disciples at Bethany late on Easter night, 'he withdrew from them and was carried up into heaven'. This reference to the Ascension on Easter night is out of line with Luke's second volume, Acts, which dates the ascension forty days after Easter (Acts 1:3-11). So perhaps it is not surprising that some manuscripts do not have the words, 'and he was carried up to heaven'.

Were these words added or omitted by later scribes? Many modern translators (e.g. NRSV, GNB) have concluded that these words were omitted from Luke 24:51 by scribes who wanted to avoid a contradiction with Acts. However, the manuscript evidence which supports the shorter simpler reading is not negligible and has persuaded the REB translators to follow this reading. In this case it is easy to explain later omission, but difficult to explain why, given the shorter simpler reading, some later scribes would have added an awkward reference to the Ascension taking place on Easter Day.

The large number of variations in the wording of manuscripts is not surprising when we bear in mind just how difficult it is to avoid slips when copying by hand an extended section of text. In the age of the printed page, errors can be corrected much more readily – though publishers have been known to print a draft of an author's camera ready copy, rather than the final version!

The 'carelessness' of scribes needs to be counterbalanced by drawing attention to their dogged fidelity. Often a simple error, or a phrase or sentence which does not make sense, has been copied over several centuries by scribes who have refused to 'tidy up' the text. Occasionally an explanatory comment or a pious observation written in the margin or between lines of text was incorporated into the text by a later scribe who believed that everything on the page in front of him was 'sacred' and should be included.

Manuscript Evidence

In the preceding paragraphs I have alluded to the basic principles which are used in assessing variations in the manuscripts. Before we look further at these principles and consider some more examples, we must look at the nature and extent of the manuscript evidence we have for the Gospels.

The translators of the 1611 Authorized Version (AV) based their work on the edition of the Greek text printed hurriedly by Erasmus in 1516 which came to be known as the 'Textus Receptus', the 'received text'. Erasmus used a mere handful of what are now recognized to be rather inferior Greek manuscripts. Occasionally he even included phrases from the Latin Vulgate translation which were not in the Greek manuscripts he consulted. For example, in Acts 9:6, at the time of Paul's conversion on the road to Damascus, the AV reads, 'And he trembling and astonished said, Lord, what wilt thou have me to do?' These words are not found in any Greek manuscript (though they are found in the parallel passage in Acts 22:10); they were taken by Erasmus from the Latin Vulgate translation.

Since the time of Erasmus large numbers of manuscripts of the Greek New Testament have been discovered. Handwritten copies are now said to total 5,487 – and that number does not include translations into other languages, or quotations of the text in the writings of the church fathers! Many of these manuscripts are from the early Middle Ages and are closely related to one another, but a large number date from the early centuries and are of great importance.

Most of the earliest manuscripts were written on strips of the pith of papyrus reeds pressed together. Papyri are not as fragile as photographs of fragmentary papyri might suggest, but they have survived the passing of the centuries only in dry climates: in rubbish dumps covered by dry sands in Egypt, in caves in Palestine, and under the volcanic ash of Mt Vesuvius in Italy. New Testament papyri have all been found in Egypt.

At the turn of the twentieth century only nine papyri with parts of the New Testament were known. There are now 98, known to scholars as P1 to P98. Not all 98 papyri are early or important. However the 45 earliest copies of parts of the New

Testament (all dating from before the beginning of the fourth century) were all written on papyrus. The discoveries of some of these papyri are undoubtedly among the most significant advances in our knowledge of earliest Christianity.

Two collections of papyri are particularly important. P45, P46 and P47 come from the Chester Beatty collection, published between 1933 and 1937. P45, a codex from the third century, contains parts of the four Gospels and Acts; P46, from c. AD 200, contains parts of the Pauline epistles; P47, from the end of the third century, has a large part of Revelation 9 to 17.

The Bodmer collection of papyri, published between 1956 and 1961, includes five which have parts of the New Testament. P66, from about AD 200, includes most of John's Gospel up to chapter 14. P75, which is from the third century, contains many parts of Luke and John, and is arguably the most important of all the papyri. The text of P75 is very closely related to the text of Codex Vaticanus, which dates from about 150 years later. Codex Vaticanus may even be a copy of P75. This magnificent Codex, which includes most of the New Testament, is an invaluable guide to the earliest forms of the text. So P75 confirms the value of Codex Vaticanus (at least in the Gospels) and takes us back 150 years earlier.

In recent years there have not been any comparable discoveries. Between 1979 and 1993 ten more New Testament papyri were published, but they are all very fragmentary. Only two are early: P90, from the second century, includes parts of John 18:36 – 19:7; P98, probably from the second century, contains parts of Acts 1:13-20.

Only a handful of papyri are thought to date from before AD 200: P4+64+67 (the fragments of Matthew and Luke discussed in *Chapter II*); P32 (part of Titus 1-2); P46 (noted above); P52, a fragment of John 18 from c. AD 125; P66, P90 and P98 (noted above).

Two hundred and ninety-nine Greek manuscripts written on parchment in capital letters (known as uncials, so-called from the 'inch' high size of the letters) have survived. Parchment, made from the skins of animals, is much more durable than papyrus, but it was more expensive to produce. Only five fragmentary parchment uncials date from the third century.

Two fourth-century uncials are particularly important. Codex Sinaiticus, which dates from the early fourth century, includes most of the Old Testament, the whole of the New Testament, and two early Christian writings, the letter of Barnabas and the Shepherd of Hermas (*see Plate 4*). This Codex was discovered in St Catherine's Monastery in the Sinai desert in 1844. Some of the missing pages of the Old Testament were found at the same monastery in 1975, though visitors to the British Museum in London (where most of the Codex has been since 1933) are kept in the dark about this important recent discovery. The text, written in four columns, has been 'corrected' by as many as seven later scribes.

Codex Vaticanus, in three columns, dates from the same period and also includes most of the Bible. It has been kept in the Vatican Library since the late fifteenth century; its earlier history is not known. It has been very highly regarded ever since it became generally available to scholars in 1889-90.

Codex Bezae, from the fifth century, contains most of the text of the four Gospels and Acts in Greek and in Latin on opposite pages. The Greek text is on the left, the Latin on the right. The Gospels are in the order Matthew, John, Luke, Mark: the two 'eyewitness' apostles have priority over Luke and Mark who were considered to be companions of apostles. This manuscript contains a large number of variations and interesting additions. The text of Acts is about one-tenth longer than that found in modern translations – i.e. this manuscript contains nearly three extra chapters of text! This longer form of the text is known as the 'western' text, though its use was not confined to the 'western' church: its origin continues to baffle specialists. It is now clear that this 'western' text form can be traced back well into the second century.

Two thousand eight hundred and eleven minuscule manuscripts have survived. They take their name from the small size of the letters, many of which are joined together. Although they date only from the ninth century when this style of handwriting began to be used, recent research has shown that about ten per cent of them have an early form of text which is as valuable as that of many papyri and uncials. Fragmentary papyri, such as the Magdalen College Oxford fragments of Matthew discussed in

Chapter II, occasionally hit the headlines, but unheralded painstaking research on the minuscules may yield more fruit in the long run.

Readers with mathematical minds will have noted that I have now referred to 3,208 of the 5,487 Greek manuscripts of the New Testament. The remainder are lectionaries in which the text is set out in line with the lessons appointed for the church year. Only about thirty date from before the ninth century, and only a few are important for reconstruction of early forms of the text.

In comparison with many classical writings, students of the New Testament are indeed fortunate. There is a gap of over 1,000 years between the date of the original writings and the earliest manuscripts of Euripides, Sophocles, Aeschylus, Aristophanes, Thucydides, Plato and Demosthenes.

The position is only a little better with the classical Latin writers. Virgil's writings are the best preserved; within a hundred years they were being used as 'sacred texts', consulted like an oracle. About 600 manuscripts have been preserved, but nearly all are very late. There is a gap of well over 300 years between the middle of the first century BC, when Virgil wrote, and the three more or less complete manuscripts of his writings which date from fourth and fifth centuries. These three manuscripts are said to be sufficient to establish the text of Virgil's writings. Only three small papyri fragments predate the major manuscripts, and two are merely writing exercises in which one line is repeated for practice! In contrast, the delightful love poems of Catullus, Virgil's near contemporary, are known through a single thirteenth-century manuscript which was subsequently lost.[3]

Assessing the Evidence

There is no shortage of manuscript evidence for the text of the Gospels, but how is it to be assessed? There is one principle which is fundamental: when confronted by variant readings, *the reading which best accounts for the others should be adopted*. Since scribes usually expanded and clarified the text, rather than the reverse, shorter and more difficult readings are usually preferable. In many cases it is possible to spot readily the ways in which later scribes have clarified an awkward text they were copying.

As soon as one begins to apply this principle it becomes apparent that a very early papyrus will not necessarily have precedence over a much later uncial or minuscule manuscript. An early papyrus may in fact have been copied many times before AD 200, whereas a sixth-century parchment uncial may have been copied only two or three times.

A second principle is equally important. A reading supported by dozens of manuscripts may be inferior to one supported by only one or two manuscripts: the same error or 'correction' may have been copied many times over, whereas the original reading may have been preserved in only one or two manuscripts.

A thorough appreciation of the style, emphases and idiosyncracies of each evangelist is invaluable: it is often possible to determine what an individual writer is most likely to have written. A detailed knowledge of the characteristics of an individual manuscript and of its relationship to other manuscripts is also important. In 1881 the British expert in textual criticism F. J. A. Hort formulated a principle which still has value: 'knowledge of documents should precede final judgement upon readings.'

Specialists differ in the weight they attach to these various factors. There are no absolutely hard and fast rules which can be applied in all cases. Assessing the evidence, known as the discipline of textual criticism, is an art not a science.

John 19:29 provides an interesting illustration of these principles. Most modern translations record that at the crucifixion of Jesus soldiers fixed a sponge soaked with wine 'on hyssop' and held it up to Jesus on the cross. The NEB, however, has 'on a javelin'. Only two late minuscule manuscripts have this reading; all other Greek manuscripts (including P66, and the great uncials Sinaiticus and Vaticanus) read 'on hyssop', a small bushy plant not well-suited for holding up a sponge. As we noted above, variant readings supported only by late manuscripts, or only by a few, should not be ruled out of court. However, the NRSV does not even refer to 'on a javelin' in a note!

Did the evangelist write 'javelin', or 'hyssop'? Which reading more readily accounts for the other? A scribe, aware both that hyssop was unsuitable for lifting up a sponge and that Roman soldiers were present, may have deliberately replaced 'hyssop' with 'javelin'. Perhaps the change came about by chance: the two

Greek phrases are similar, and two letters could easily have been overlooked. Compare ΥΣΣΩΠΩΠΕΡΙΘΕΝΤΕΣ 'placed it on hyssop' with ΥΣΣΩΠΕΡΙΘΕΝΤΕΣ 'placed it on a javelin'.

On the other hand, it is just possible that the evangelist's 'javelin' was deliberately replaced by 'hyssop'. Hyssop played an important part in Israel's Passover observance: 'Moses said, "Slaughter the passover lamb; take a bunch of hyssop, dip it in the blood that is in the basin, and touch the lintel and the two doorposts (of your house) with the blood in the basin" ' (Exodus 12:21-2). A scribe may have wanted to portray the crucified Jesus as the true Passover lamb, slaughtered for the deliverance of God's people, a theme emphasized in John 1:29, 36; 19:14, 36.

Or perhaps the evangelist himself wrote 'hyssop' in order to make this theological point. Whoever wrote 'hyssop' may have been quite unconcerned by the fact that hyssop could not be used to hold up a sponge soaked with wine. If so, then in this passage 'Gospel truth' was given priority over 'historical truth'.

Variant Readings in Key Passages

I shall now discuss several passages from the four Gospels where there are major variations in the manuscripts. It is important to note at the outset that these examples are by no means typical of every chapter of the Gospels. There is rarely doubt about the words the evangelists wrote; most of the variations are minor and the original wording can be reconstructed without difficulty.

My first example is the opening line of Mark's Gospel. Both the beginning and the end of any story or biography are important. So it is a surprise to find that there are important variations in the manuscripts both at the very beginning and at the close of the manuscripts of our earliest Gospel, Mark.

Mark probably intended his opening line to be a heading for at least the first section of his whole Gospel: 'the beginning of the good news of Jesus Christ, the Son of God' (NRSV). Other modern translations have similar wording. But some manuscripts (and some modern scholars) omit 'Son of God'. Unfortunately the opening of Mark is not found in any papyri. The words are missing in the original version of Codex Sinaiticus, but they were added by the first corrector of the manuscript!

If the longer reading (found in most manuscripts, including some weighty uncials) is accepted, Mark spells out the significance of Jesus for his readers with two titles he emphasizes at key points in his story: Jesus is the Christ, the Son of God. For Mark the two terms are closely related. They both recur on the lips of the high priest who questioned Jesus following his arrest: 'Are you the Messiah (Christ), the Son of the Blessed One (an indirect reference to God)?' (14: 61)

The longer reading is so apt that one wonders why 'Son of God' is not found in some manuscripts. The most obvious explanation is that a scribe's eye jumped over some key letters, but this is not entirely convincing. Surely a scribe would have been fully alert when copying the very first line of Mark. Since scribes often added Christological titles to references to Jesus, this may well have happened here. The editors of the most widely used edition of the Greek text of the New Testament duck the issue by including 'Son of God' in the text, but placed in square brackets!

ƀ

There is little doubt that the evangelist Mark did not write any words beyond 16:8, the reference to the fear of the women at their discovery of the empty tomb. Were the final lines written by Mark lost? Or did Mark intend to end his Gospel rather abruptly on this enigmatic note?

Mark 16:9-20, the so-called longer ending, is not found in several manuscripts (including the two oldest Greek manuscripts, Codex Sinaiticus and Codex Vaticanus). Some manuscripts which do contain the passage have conventional signs which indicate that copyists considered these verses to be a later addition. Most scholars accept that they are an early addition to what was felt to be an abrupt ending to the Gospel – a pastiche of other written or oral resurrection traditions.

Several manuscripts add after 16:8 two sentences known as the shorter ending of Mark:

And all that had been commanded them they told briefly to those around Peter. And afterward Jesus himself sent out through them, from east to west, the sacred and imperishable proclamation of eternal salvation. (NRSV)

These words seem to have been intended to supply the Gospel
with an ending, but it is hardly a tidy ending. Mark 16:8 stresses
that out of fear the women said *nothing* to anyone. The shorter
ending awkwardly allows the women to break their silence
immediately; they report (but only briefly!) to Peter and the disciples the words of the young man they had seen at the entrance
to the tomb. The shorter ending then refers to the eventual
spread of the Gospel message far beyond Galilee with phrases
which are certainly not Mark's.

One Old Latin manuscript concludes the Gospel with the
shorter ending; in all other manuscripts with the shorter ending
it is always followed immediately by the longer ending, i.e. Mark
16:9–20. Since the two endings do not fit together at all well,
their juxtaposition is a good example of the dogged determina-
tion of scribes to include everything which might possibly be
part of the original text.

Some modern translations follow their example. The REB, for
example, includes as part of the text of Mark both the shorter and
longer endings. Unless a rather complicated note is unravelled,
most readers of the REB will assume that *both* endings are part of
Mark's Gospel. The NRSV's solution is more satisfactory; both
the shorter and longer endings are printed as part of the text of
Mark, but the reader is alerted to their doubtful authenticity by
clear double brackets and by appropriate subheadings.[4]

The longer ending of Mark is found in 99 per cent of the
Greek manuscripts. Mark 16:9–20 was considered by nearly all
Christians down through the centuries to be part of the New
Testament. None the less, these verses were not part of the orig-
inal text of Mark's Gospel.

ɯ

In Codex Bezae there is a striking addition to Luke 6:4 :

> On the same day he (Jesus) saw someone working on the
> Sabbath and said to him: man, if you know what you are
> doing, you are blessed; if you do not know, you are cursed
> and a transgressor of the law.

This tradition is an enigma. This terse saying of Jesus and its narrative introduction is found in only one Greek manuscript. There is no close parallel either in the canonical Gospels or in apocryphal traditions. Some scholars have taken it as an authentic saying of Jesus. This possibility cannot be ruled out simply because the saying is not found elsewhere: as we shall see in *Chapter X*, there are a number of other 'isolated' sayings of Jesus found in early Christian writings, several of which may be authentic.

While this tradition is related indirectly to traditions in the Gospels in which Jesus seems to call in question some forms of Sabbath observance, only this passage turns on 'knowledge'. What is the 'knowledge' which allows the person to work on the Sabbath? Is it Gnostic thought, a second-century 'heresy' in which 'knowing' is a step on the path to 'finding'? If so, it would not be easy to account for the inclusion of an isolated Gnostic tradition in one copy of Luke.

Perhaps the person who is working on the Sabbath is being commended for his faith, i.e., for his knowledge of God which allows him to break the Sabbath. But if one does not have this knowledge, the traditional understanding of the Sabbath commandments still applies: the Law is not declared null and void for all and sundry.

Although this passage is not part of Luke's Gospel, it may well be an ancient oral tradition (perhaps even authentic) which circulated in some circles in the early church and was eventually included by a scribe.

ሠ

Luke's version of the Lord's Prayer (11:2-4) is shorter than the more familiar version which is included by Matthew as part of the Sermon on the Mount (6:9-13). In an 11th- and a 12th-century minuscule, instead of the words 'May your kingdom come', we read, 'May your Holy Spirit come upon us and cleanse us.' This reading is quoted as authentic in the fourth century by Gregory of Nyssa, and it may have been known earlier. This version of the prayer was probably used in some circles in the early church at baptisms.

Some scholars have even argued that these words were part of the text originally written by Luke the evangelist: they disappeared when most copies of Luke were assimilated to Matthew's

version of the Lord's Prayer which was used almost universally in
the early church. Defenders of their authenticity also note that
Luke emphasizes the gift of the Holy Spirit just a few verses later
in this chapter (11:13), and in many passages in Acts.

However, a reading which is not attested in any of the early
major manuscripts is unlikely to be original. These words seem to
have originated as an early scribe's comment on the significance
of the 'coming of the kingdom', perhaps as an explanatory comment in the margin of a manuscript. There are numerous marginal glosses elsewhere in the manuscripts, many of which found
their way into later manuscripts.

John 5:3-4 provides an interesting example of a gloss. The
following words are placed in a footnote in most modern translations:

> [In the five porticoes of the pool lay a multitude of invalids,
> blind, lame, paralysed] waiting for the disturbance of the
> water; for from time to time an angel came down into the
> pool and stirred up the water. The first to plunge in after this
> disturbance recovered from whatever disease had afflicted
> him.

These words are not in two early papyri P66 and P75, and not
in Codex Sinaiticus and Codex Vaticanus. They are included in
a large number of later manuscripts and eventually found their
way into the AV. I recall being very puzzled by these words at a
young age, so I was relieved when I eventually discovered that
they were not part of the text of John's Gospel.

※

John 7:53-8:11 is perhaps the most intriguing of the examples I
have chosen. The story of Jesus' refusal to condemn the woman
taken in adultery is placed in brackets in the NRSV, with a helpful note: 'The most ancient authorities lack 7:53-8:11; other
authorities add the passage here or after 7:36 or after 21:25 or
after Luke 21:38, with variations of text; some mark the passage
as doubtful.' REB prints the whole paragraph as an appendix at
the end of John's Gospel.

The passage is not found anywhere in P66 and P75 and the

great uncials, and it is certainly not part of the original text of John's Gospel. In style and vocabulary it is 'un-Johannine', and it clearly breaks the evangelist's story-line if it is included after John 7:52, as in many later manuscripts and the AV.

On the other hand, in its vocabulary and form, as well as in its teaching, it is similar to passages in the synoptic Gospels. Most exegetes accept that this tradition, with its familar words 'Neither do I condemn you. . .' has 'the ring of truth' and ought to be accepted as authentic to Jesus. It seems to have circulated widely in the early centuries as a piece of oral tradition which was incorporated into some manuscripts at various places.

Why, we may well ask, did it not find an early permanent home in the manuscript tradition of the Gospels? Early in the fourth century Augustine gives us a clue. He suspected that some anxious husbands had removed the account from manuscripts lest it be used by their wives in defence of adultery! In many early church circles with strict disciplinary conventions, this story ran against the grain, and was conveniently forgotten by some.

Unlike Mark 16:9-20, few today would want to omit this passage from the New Testament, even though it did not form part of the original text of John's Gospel. This passage reminds us of the radical nature of much of Jesus' teaching. It also reminds us that the writing of the Gospels did not bring an immediate end to the circulation of authentic oral traditions. The relationship between oral and written traditions will be one of our central concerns in the next chapter. Jesus' refusal to condemn the woman taken in adultery is 'Gospel truth', even though it is not part of the text of the written New Testament Gospels!

M

There is no shortage of manuscripts of the Gospels: their sheer numbers is something of an embarrassment. Although there are an enormous number of errors and 'corrections' of all kinds, it is not difficult to isolate most of them by application of the basic principles we have noted. However there are a number of residual passages in which a decision cannot be made with confidence. These passages should not be swept aside as of no significance: in a number of cases important historical or theological issues are at stake.

In recent decades important steps forward have been taken. The discovery of papyri which predate the great fourth-century uncial manuscripts has been a major advance. Even though the second and the third papyri are often fragmentary, they confirm the general reliability of the great fourth-century uncials which contain the full text of the Gospels. This is the case with the early codex discussed in *Chapter II*, the fragments of Luke and Matthew known as P4+64+67. An important corollary follows: discovery of further papyri is unlikely to alter this judgement radically. Hence the dating of the Magdalen College Oxford papyrus fragment, while of great interest, does not have major implications for the reliability of the textual evidence of the Gospels. With more exceptions than modern translations suggest, we may be confident that we have access to the Greek words written by the evangelists. Translation and interpretation of them is another matter.

CHAPTER V

BETWEEN JESUS
AND THE GOSPELS

'MIND THE GAP' is a familiar loudspeaker exhortation as train doors open at the platforms of many London Underground stations. 'Mind the gap' should also be ringing in the ears of readers of the Gospels. 'The gap' which has to be negotiated is the period of time between the crucifixion of Jesus and the writing of the earliest Gospel, Mark. Were traditions about the life and teaching of Jesus transmitted carefully by Peter and the other disciples? Or were the Jesus traditions adapted freely in the light of the needs and circumstances of the post-Easter Christian communities? Answers to these questions will obviously have an important bearing on the reliability of the Gospels.

In the first part of this chapter I shall consider what may for convenience be called the traditional approach. I shall then discuss the strengths and weaknesses of an alternative way of accounting for the gap between Jesus and the Gospels.

Mark and Peter

First we must establish the size of the gap. There is general agreement that Jesus was crucifed about AD 30. It is less easy to establish the date of the composition of Mark's Gospel. Most scholars attach at least some weight to the comments of Irenaeus (c. AD 180) on the origin of our earliest Gospel:

> Peter and Paul proclaimed the Gospel in Rome. After their death, Mark, the disciple and interpreter of Peter, transmitted his preaching to us in written form. (*Against Heresies* III.i.1)

Peter almost certainly died during Nero's intense persecution of Christians in Rome in AD 64/65. So according to Irenaeus, Mark's Gospel cannot have been written before this date. This conclusion is accepted partly because there is an alternative slightly later tradition which states that Mark was written *during* the lifetime of Peter. This sounds like an attempt to link Mark and Peter even more closely than the earlier tradition. So Irenaeus, who admits that there was a gap between the death of Peter and the writing of Mark's Gospel is more likely to be correct.

How long after Peter's death was Mark written? Here opinion is divided. Some date Mark shortly before the outbreak of the catastrophic Jewish war against Rome in AD 66. Others believe that Mark's Gospel was written shortly after the Romans captured Jerusalem and her temple in AD 70. For our present purposes we do not need to settle this issue. On the earlier date, there is a gap between Jesus and the Gospels of 35 years, and that is the approximate period of time we should keep in mind.

Peter was a towering figure in the early church. Does he stand behind Mark's Gospel? About 60 years before Irenaeus made the comments quoted above, Papias, bishop of Hierapolis, commented at length on the origin of Mark's Gospel. Today Hierapolis, about 100 miles inland from Ephesus, is one of the highlights of a visit to Turkey: its hot springs and its varied Graeco-Roman and early Christian archaeological remains delight the visitor. But not a single archaeological trace of Papias has been found.

However we do have literary evidence. Early in the fourth century Eusebius, the church historian quotes Papias at length:

And this is what the Elder said, 'Mark, who became Peter's interpreter, wrote accurately, but not in order, as many of the things said and done by the Lord as he had noted. For he neither heard the Lord nor followed him, but afterwards, as I said, he followed Peter who adapted his teaching to the needs (of his hearers) but not as a complete work of the Lord's sayings. So Mark made no mistake in writing some things just as he had noted them. For he was careful of one thing, to leave nothing he had heard out and to say nothing falsely.' (*Church History* 3.39.15)

Papias is citing an even older tradition, from the Elder. These words have been pored over many times. The precise nuance of several phrases is not entirely clear. However, we can be confident that the references to Mark's accuracy, carefulness and honesty are conventional rhetorical terms used to underline the general reliability of a writing.

Mark himself is not portrayed as an eyewitness: he is Peter's 'interpreter'. While this may mean 'translator' (from Peter's Aramaic into Greek), it probably refers to Mark's role as the person who transmitted and explained Peter's teaching. Perhaps the most interesting comment is that Mark wrote 'not in order'. While this may mean 'not in chronological order', it is more probably a rhetorical term which refers to Mark's lack of literary artistry. If this is the case, then Papias was mistaken. For recent studies have shown that Mark's Gospel is not an unsophisticated anthology of Jesus traditions, but a work of considerable literary skill and theological subtlety.

How much weight should be given to these intriguing comments? My own view is that while they cannot be taken at face value, they do give us some insights into the origin of Mark's Gospel. The reference to Mark as the author is surely an authentic tradition. The Mark named by Papias is the John Mark frequently mentioned in Acts as an associate of Paul. John Mark was not a prominent leader in the early church; he was neither a disciple of Jesus nor an apostle. So why was his name chosen if there were not good grounds for naming him as the author of a Gospel?

According to Papias, in his teaching Peter did not set out a full record of the actions and teaching of Jesus; he *adapted* the traditions to meet the needs of his hearers. At this point Papias partially anticipates some of the insights of modern scholarship to which we shall refer below.

It is difficult to accept a *close* link between Peter and the composition of Mark's Gospel. Galatians 2 reminds us powerfully that Peter and Paul were at odds with one another over crucial issues. Mark stands at the radical end of the early Christian spectrum, much closer to Paul than to the more conservative Peter. And as we have already noted, Mark is no mere anthologist of Peter's teaching; his own hand can be discerned clearly in the literary shaping and design of the Gospel.

The gap between Jesus and Mark's Gospel cannot be bridged readily by an appeal to Peter as the 'missing link'. If we read Papias's comments carefully, we find that he already concedes that there is a gap between Mark and the life of Jesus: Mark *expounded* Peter's teaching; Peter *adapted* the traditions about Jesus. Papias also accepts openly that Mark was not himself an eyewitness of the life of Jesus.

Eyewitnesses?

What role did eyewitnesses play in the 35-year period between Jesus and the writing of Mark? On the traditional view, the authors of Matthew's and John's Gospels were themselves disciples of Jesus and eyewitnesses of the events they record; Mark and Luke incorporated into their Gospels the memories of those who were eyewitnesses of the events of the life of Jesus. As we shall see, both Luke and John refer explicitly to eyewitness testimony.

Supporters of what I am calling the traditional view often insist that if some of the disciples were aged about 25 as they accompanied Jesus in the villages of Galilee, they would have been only 60 when Mark put pen to papyrus. In the often-quoted words of the British scholar, Vincent Taylor, the disciples were not 'translated to heaven immediately after the Resurrection . . . The hundred and twenty at Pentecost did not go into permanent retreat; for at least a generation they moved among the young, Palestinian communities, and through preaching and fellowship their recollections were at the disposal of those who sought information.'[1]

There is a further important consideration: we know from our own experience, or from the experience of others, that it is possible to recall several decades later the words and actions of a loved one whose memory has been cherished. So surely it is reasonable to suppose that our Gospels are based on the memories of those who witnessed the events and heard the teaching they contain.

This traditional way of bridging the 35-year gap seems sound and sensible. Why, then, has this explanation been spurned by nearly all students of the Gospels? Why has the word 'eyewitnesses' become like a red rag to a bull?

The first point to note is that even if we could establish that eyewitnesses did play a major role, we would not thereby have confirmed the reliability of the traditions. Even fleeting acquaintance with high-profile legal cases, such as the trial of O. J. Simpson, is enough to remind us that eyewitnesses do not always agree. Their reports are not necessarily taken at face value by judges and juries. Historians know full well that the observations of eyewitnesses have to be scrutinized with the same rigour as any other kind of evidence.

When we turn to the gospel traditions it soon becomes apparent that it is difficult to find the kind of vivid detail and local colour which we normally associate with eyewitnesses. There are exceptions, but they are exceptions which prove the rule. Mark notes that as a great storm buffeted the boat in which Jesus sought to cross the Sea of Galilee, Jesus was asleep in the stern 'on the cushion' (4:38). The five thousand present at the miracle of the multiplication of the five loaves and two fish sat on 'green grass' (6:39). As Jesus was arrested, 'a certain young man was following him, wearing nothing but a linen cloth. They caught hold of him, but he left the linen cloth and ran off naked' (14: 51-2).

In contrast to these examples, in most passages in the Gospels the kind of vivid local colour and extraneous detail which eye-witnesses provide is missing. The very terseness of the traditions suggests that they have been used and re-used in the life of early Christian communities.

As we have seen, Mark's Gospel was considered by Papias (and later in the early church) to have been based on Peter's preaching. When Mark records the healing of Peter's mother-in-law, we might have expected some lively, personal touches. There is hardly a wasted word:

> Now Simon's mother-in-law was in bed with a fever, and they told him about her at once. He came and took her by the hand and lifted her up. The fever then left her, and she began to serve them (1:30-1).

Our questions about the individuals and the local setting are unanswered: we are given a story of stark simplicity, a story 'worn smooth' by repetition.

There is one way we can check the extent to which eyewitnesses may have controlled the development of the Jesus traditions. With only a handful of dissenting voices, all scholars agree that Matthew has used and revised all but about fifty of Mark's 662 verses, and has added two sources: Q, which we shall consider in the next chapter, and some traditions (known as M) not found elsewhere in the Gospels. So whether or not Matthew's Gospel was written by a disciple of Jesus, on the traditional view we might have expected Matthew's revision and expansion of Mark to show traces of vivid eyewitness touches or 'control'.

But evidence of this kind is hard to find. Again and again Matthew abbreviates Mark's already terse accounts in order to focus more sharply on their key theological points. For example, Mark's account of the healing of a paralysed man at Capernaum includes the unforgettable description of the lowering of the paralysed man through a hole dug in the dried mud roof of the house (2:4). Although these vivid details might well suggest eyewitness testimony, Matthew omits the whole verse.

Almost without exception, the Q traditions are succinct sayings of Jesus which bear the hallmarks of transmitted oral tradition rather than eyewitness testimony. Some of the 'M' traditions do include vivid details, but many of them look more like later legendary expansions rather than direct reports of eyewitnesses. Matthew's addition to Mark's passion narrative of Pilate's wife's dream (27:19) and of the curious tradition of the earthquake and the opening of the tombs of the saints at the very moment Jesus died (27:51b -3) are good examples.

References within the Gospels themselves to the role of eyewitnesses must be taken very seriously. In his single-sentence preface to his Gospel, Luke notes that he has used as his model the work of his predecesors: they have based their accounts of the 'events that have been fulfilled among us' – on traditions transmitted by 'eyewitnesses and ministers of the word'. In a brilliant recent study of Luke's preface in its first-century Graeco-Roman and Jewish setting, Loveday Alexander has drawn attention to the ways in which the Greek word 'eyewitness' differs from modern usage. For us, an eyewitness is often invaluable in a legal setting: he or she is a passer-by who was present (usually by chance) at the time an incident took place. In contrast, the Greek word is hardly ever used in this sense. A better translation of Luke's reference to 'eyewitnesses' might be, 'those with personal/first hand experience: those who know the facts at first hand.'[2]

In his formal preface Luke notes that the eyewitnesses are also 'ministers of the word'. The latter are not a separate group. Although Luke has tried to avoid explicitly Christian language in his preface (perhaps in order to catch the attention of non-Christian readers), at this point his guard has dropped. 'Ministers of the word' is a reference to the role of the eyewitnesses in the proclamation of the Christian message. In other words, from Luke's perspective, eyewitnesses do not provide detached, 'neutral' reminiscence of the events of the life of Jesus; on the basis of their own personal experience of the events in question, they proclaim their significance. Eyewitnesses transmit 'interpreted tradition'. At this point, at least, we are not far from the alternative form critical approach to which we shall turn in a moment. Form critics emphasize that Jesus traditions were transmitted in order to sustain the life of the church rather than to provide bald reminiscence.

There is also an important reference to eyewitness testimony in John's Gospel. The evangelist records that immediately following the death of Jesus, a soldier pierced his side with a spear, 'and at once blood and water came out' (John 19:34). The next verse is placed in brackets in the NRSV in order to indicate that it is an 'aside' of the evangelist himself to his readers: 'He who saw this has testified so that you also may believe. His testimony is true, and he knows that he tells the truth.' Who is this person who has witnessed the death of Jesus? A few verses earlier (19:26-7) the evangelist has mentioned that 'the beloved disciple' stood by the cross. The 'beloved disciple' plays a special role in this Gospel: as Raymond Brown notes, 'he is more perceptive than any other follower of Jesus, and in a certain way here he anticipates resurrection faith.'[3] So the 'beloved disciple' is not simply affirming that Jesus did indeed die on the cross, his eyewitness testimony is intended to encourage the evangelist's readers to believe that the Jesus who died on the cross is *life-giving*. It is 'Gospel truth' not historical truth which the evangelist wishes to convey via the eyewitness testimony of the beloved disciple.

A similar point emerges in John 1:29-34. John the Baptist

affirms that he himself saw the Spirit descend on Jesus from heaven like a dove. He then stresses that he was told by 'the one who sent me' (i.e. God) that this person is 'the one who baptizes with the Holy Spirit'. 'And I myself have seen and have testified that this is the Son of God' (1:34). Once again we have eye-witness testimony, but it is appealed to by the evangelist in service of 'Gospel truth' rather than the historical accuracy of the record.

No doubt some of those who followed Jesus in Galilee and Jerusalem did pass on their experiences in the post-Easter period. But caution is necessary: appeal to the continuing role of eye-witnesses does not provide a guarantee of the historical reliability of the traditions. The traditions themselves rarely include the kind of detail we might expect of eyewitnesses. Paradoxically, vivid detail emerges most clearly in the later apocryphal gospels. And where the role of eyewitnesses is referred to explicitly within Luke's and John's Gospels, it is the *significance* of the events observed by eyewitnesses which is primarily in view.

Form criticism

We turn now to a rather different way of bridging the gap between the life of Jesus and the writing of Mark's Gospel, which was developed in the 1920s and 1930s. The approach known as form criticism rests on four basic principles, which, in their orig-inal formulation were often supported by detailed studies of the transmission of 'folklore' traditions in a number of cultural set-tings. (i) Traditions about the life and teaching of Jesus can be analysed according to their 'form'; (ii) they circulated orally in single pericopae (or paragraphs) in the early church; (iii) these traditions were retained by the early church only insofar as they were relevant to its own life; (iv) in the course of the transmission of the Jesus traditions, the early church placed its own stamp upon them, to such an extent that at many points we are in touch not with the life and teaching of Jesus, but with the Gospel of the early church. We shall now examine these principles one by one.

First, literary analysis of the 'form' of the traditions. Both the deeds and the words of Jesus were transmitted in set patterns, which strongly suggests that they were understood to be 'pro-

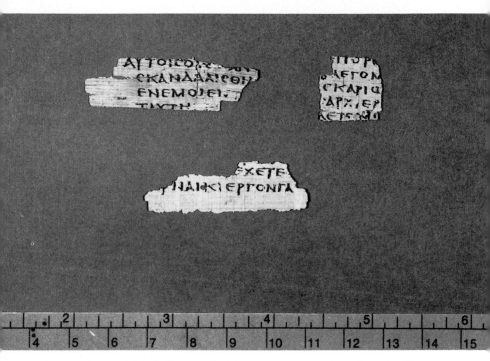

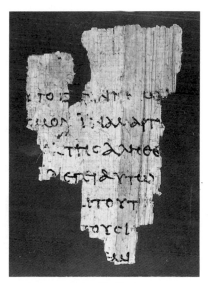

Plate 1. The Magdalen College Oxford fragments are part of Matthew 26. They may date from the end of the second century AD.

Plates 2&3. The earliest fragment of the New Testament from c. AD 125, featuring part of John's Gospel. As there is writing on both sides this is from a codex not a roll.

John 18: 31–4   John 18: 37–8

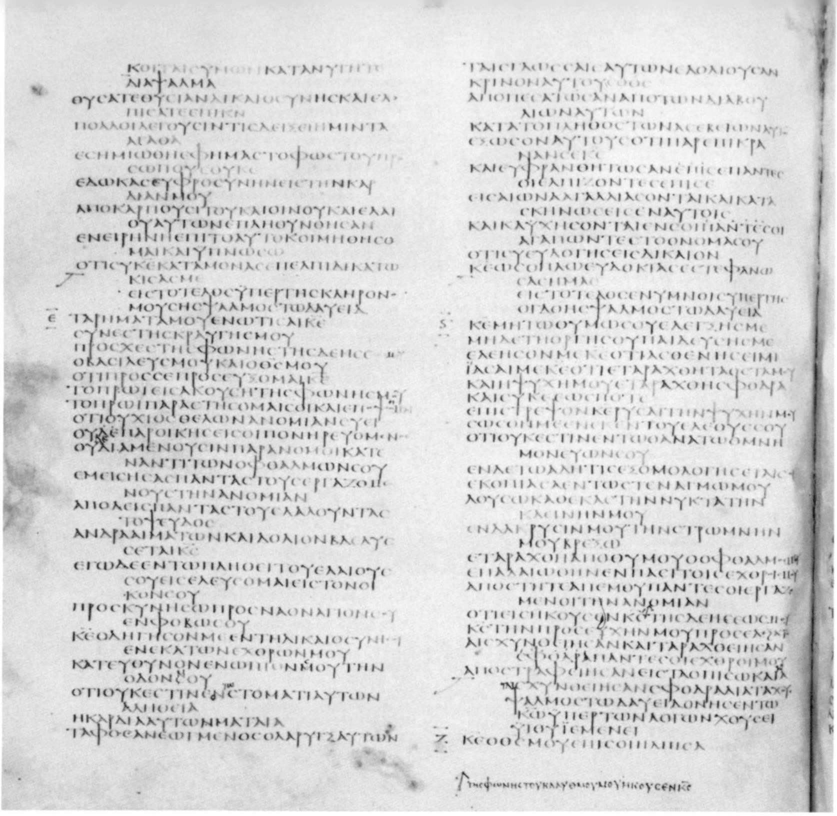

Plate 4. Codex Sinaiticus: a fourth-century codex of the whole Bible. It is written in a 'Biblical uncial' hand. The Magdalen College Oxford fragments are written in an earlier version of this style of handwriting.

Plate 5. Cave no. 7 at Qumran in Israel's Judean Desert. 18 fragments written in Greek were discovered here including 7Q5, the alleged fragment of Mark's Gospel.

Plate 6. An enlarged photograph of 7Q5, found in Cave 7 at Qumran. Is this from Mark 6?

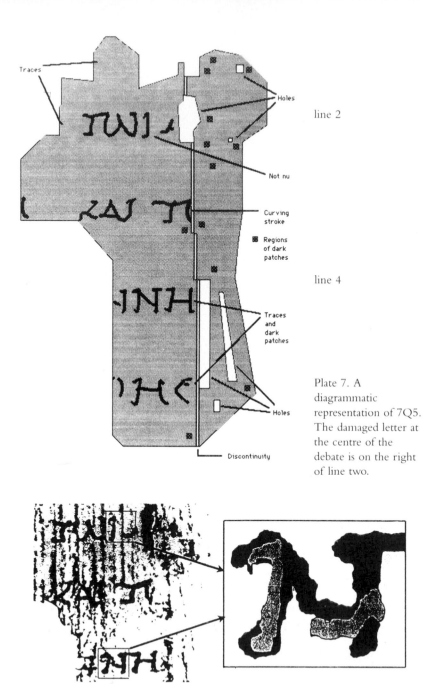

Traces

Holes

line 2

Not nu

Curving
stroke

Regions
of dark
patches

line 4

Traces
and
dark
patches

Plate 7. A diagrammatic representation of 7Q5. The damaged letter at the centre of the debate is on the right of line two.

Holes

Discontinuity

Plate 8. This diagram, in which the clear *nu* from line 4 (dark shading) has been superimposed on the damaged letter in line 2 (light shading), shows that the latter cannot be *nu*, thus undermining the theory that 7Q5 is part of Mark's Gospel.

Plate 9. Papyrus Egerton 2 ('The Unknown Gospel') from c. AD 150. Some sentences recall the New Testament Gospels; some are unrelated.

Plate 10. A close-up of the octagonal church at Capernaum (see overleaf).

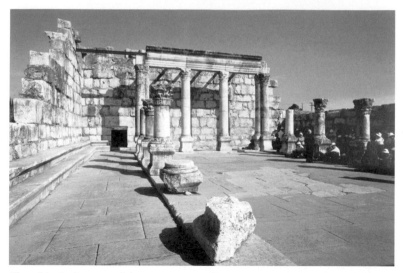

Plate 11. A close-up of the synagogue at Capernaum.

Plate 12. Capernaum. In the foreground is the fourth-century AD synagogue built over a first-century synagogue in which Jesus may have taught. In the background is the fifth-century octagonal church built over a first-century house which may have belonged to the apostle Simon Peter.

Plate 13. A *mikveh* (ritual bath) from the Palatial Mansion in Jerusalem. This recently excavated house is near the Temple.

Plate 14. The Celsus Library at Ephesus, erected c. AD 110. Copies of one or more of the Gospels may have found their way into this library a decade or so later.

Plate 15. This Latin inscription, found at Caesarea, is the only one which refers to Pontius Pilate. At the end of the second line *PILATUS* can be read easily.

Plate 16. The huge stones of Herod's temple are visible in today's Wailing Wall. Mark 13:2 records that the disciples of Jesus were amazed at the size of the stones of the Temple.

clamation' rather than 'reminiscence'. For example, some accounts of an incident in the life of Jesus are brought to a climax with a solemn 'pronouncement' of Jesus. In Mark 2:17 Jesus replies to his critics who were outraged at his conduct in eating with tax collectors and sinners: 'I have come to call not the righteous but sinners.' Nothing more needs to be said: the pronouncement of Jesus ends the report of the incident, and another report follows immediately. There are some fourteen 'pronouncement stories' in Mark which fall into this pattern.

Many accounts of healings or exorcisms in the Gospels end, not with a word of Jesus, but with a narrator's comment on the response of the bystanders. For example, following his account of the exorcism of an unclean spirit from a man at the synagogue in Capernaum, Mark notes that the bystanders 'were all amazed . . . At once the fame of Jesus began to spread throughout the surrounding region of Galilee' (Mark 1:27-8).

The sayings of Jesus have also been analysed according to their literary 'shape'. Some are riddles or proverbs, some are story parables, some are parables of comparison ('the kingdom of God is like . . .'). Some are 'wisdom' sayings, advice which can be appropriated in many different settings, advice which often ends with a reference to God's will and ways: 'No one can serve two masters; for a slave will either hate the one and love the other, or be devoted to the one and despise the other. You cannot serve God and wealth' (Matthew 6:24). Some are prophetic or apocalyptic sayings: 'For those who want to save their life will lose it, and those who lose their life for my sake, and for the sake of the gospel, will save it. For what will it profit them to gain the whole world and forfeit their life? . . . Those who are ashamed of me and my words in this adulterous and sinful generation, of them the Son of Man will also be ashamed when he comes in the glory of his Father with the holy angels' (Mark 9:35-8).

Although some scholars have used analysis of the 'forms' of the traditions to claim that some 'forms' are earlier or more reliable than others, this has turned out to be a blind alley. None the less, two more important observations are well-founded: the Jesus traditions are terse to a fault; all extraneous details have been worn away in the course of their transmission. They are 'proclamation' rather than 'reminiscence'.

Secondly, form critics claim that the Jesus traditions circulated in the early church orally and independently of one another. The Gospels can be likened to a tray of ice cubes: one sharp knock and the individual cubes tumble out of the tray and its divisions. The general point can hardly be denied. As we shall see in the next chapter, the same sayings of Jesus are found at different points in Matthew's and Luke's stories. There is also variation in the order of incidents. For example, in Mark Jesus visits his hometown synagogue once his ministry is well under way (6:1-6); in Luke, this visit takes place at the very outset of the teaching and healing ministry (4:16-30). Many incidents in Mark could be positioned without difficulty at many other points in his Gospel. So their present position has almost certainly been determined by the evangelist, rather than by genuine eyewitness reminiscence.

On the other hand, there are traditions whose position in the story must always have been fixed: for example, the baptism of Jesus by John at the outset of his ministry, and the major incidents in the passion narratives. And surely it is likely that traditions were linked together in clusters rather than used in splendid isolation. Such clusters would be expanded or contracted according to the circumstances. Many pericopae undoubtedly make a much greater impact and present a fuller portrait of Jesus when set alongside other pericopae.

In the ancient world, stories, myths and legends about a celebrated prophet or teacher, as well as his sayings, were often transmitted orally. Since it was time-consuming and often expensive to make copies of writings, memories were needed and used far more extensively than in today's print-dominated world. In some Jewish circles in the first and second centuries AD, publication of a teacher's words was forbidden: disciples were expected to learn the sayings by heart, and transmit them carefully to the next generation.

Papias, the bishop of Hierapolis whom we quoted above, commented on the importance of oral tradition: 'I supposed that things out of books did not profit me so much as the utterances of a voice that lives and abides' (as quoted by Eusebius, *Church History*,

III.39.4). While many of us would have difficulty recalling a dozen verses from the Sermon on the Mount without a printed page in front of us, in the first century such a feat would not have been at all unusual. So the conclusion that oral traditions were used over a 35-year period does not undermine the reliability of the Gospels.

On the other hand, form critics have assumed too readily that Jesus traditions were never recorded in writing before Mark wrote. There is increasing evidence for the wide use of writing in Palestine in the decades before the evangelists wrote. A Qumran document published in 1993, 'Some of the Works of the Law' (known as 4QMMT from its opening words in Hebrew), confirms that not all Jews at the time of Jesus shared the attitude to writing just noted. Parts of six copies of this document have been recovered, so it was treasured by the Qumran community. In this document, a teacher's sayings and legal rulings are recorded, perhaps even in his own life-time.

As we noted in *Chapter II*, pp.17ff. the codex was quickly adopted by Christian scribes. Its predecessor was a wax-coated wooden writing tablet which could be used many times over. It is now increasingly clear that these note books were used widely at the time of Jesus. It is certainly possible, or even probable, that followers of Jesus made notes of his teaching and written reports of his actions long before the Gospels were written. The terse nature of the Jesus traditions can be accounted for both by the use of oral tradition and also by the use of notebooks.[4]

❦

Thirdly, the form critical approach insists that Jesus traditions were retained and transmitted only in so far as they served the needs of the early Christian communities. Form critics related the various types (or 'forms') of Jesus traditions to the diverse needs of the early church – to missionary preaching, to catechetical instruction, to debate with opponents, or to worship. While this can hardly be denied, we need to bear in mind that we do not know as much as we would like about the earliest communities which transmitted the Gospel traditions, so reconstruction of their 'needs' must always be tentative. And some of the 'forms' sketched above seem appropriate for more than one setting in the life of the early church.

Many form critics appealed to the words of Martin Kähler, written in 1896: 'Just as the light of the sun is reflected in every drop of the bedewed meadow, so the full person of the Lord of the church's proclamation meets the reader of the Gospels in each little story.' In other words, each pericope (or paragraph) is itself 'Gospel', used in the early church to elicit and sustain faith. This valuable insight is directly related to one of threads which runs through this book: the relationship between the Gospel (Christian proclamation about the person of Jesus) and the written Gospels.

However, some form critics went a good deal further. They claimed that historical and biographical reminiscence were of no interest in the early church. The pre-Marcan traditions disclosed to followers of Jesus in the post-Easter church not so much who Jesus was in his earthly life, but who the Risen Lord is now. This distinction is artificial. Followers of Jesus would naturally have treasured his sayings and accounts of his actions. They must have been asked about the 'past' of the one proclaimed as Lord and Christ. As we shall see in *Chapter XIII*, Jewish and pagan critics objected not only to Christian claims about Jesus, but also to parts of the 'story' Christians told about the life of Jesus.

Ŵ

The fourth principle of form criticism is closely related. To what extent did the early church place its own stamp upon the Jesus traditions? There is no doubt that this has happened. Take Matthew 18: 20: 'Where two or three are gathered in my name, I am there among them.' During his lifetime Jesus could hardly have promised his disciples that he would be physically present at any gathering of two or three of them. In a post-Easter setting, however, the promise makes good sense: as Risen Lord, Jesus will be present spiritually with his followers. In Matthew's Gospel the disciples worship Jesus and call him Lord (e.g. 8: 2, 6-8, 21, 25; 14:30-3; 15: 22-5), both of which reflect the post-Easter church rather than the lifetime of Jesus.

There is also plenty of evidence which suggests that the early church did not read back anachronistically its own needs and convictions into the Jesus traditions. Two examples may be mentioned. First, we know that the deepest crisis in the life of the early church concerned the acceptance of non-Jews, without the requirement of circumcision. But the early church refused to attribute to the pre-Easter Jesus sayings which have resolved these issues. And secondly, we know that the Gospel proclamation of the early church focused on profound claims *made about Jesus.* In Matthew, Mark and Luke, Jesus proclaims good news *about God* rather than himself: there are only hints, for example, that Jesus himself is related to the coming of God's kingly rule. By and large the early church kept its present convictions separate from the traditions it preserved about the life of Jesus.

ꙮ

Appeal to eyewitness testimony is not a magic wand which guarantees the reliability of the Gospels as historical records. Not many of the traditions look like eyewitness accounts, and in any case the testimony of eyewitnesses must always be subject to rigorous historical scrutiny.

At the very point at which they refer explicitly to eyewitness testimony, Luke and John indicate that the traditions are 'faith' traditions, not mere records or 'neutral' eyewitness reminiscence. This is also one of the enduring achievements of the form critical approach: in the decades before Mark wrote, Jesus traditions were transmitted and used to sustain the faith and life of the church. In this respect the evangelists Luke and John are in agreement with the form critics.

I have noted that we should not dismiss out of hand the possibility that some Jesus traditions were written during the gap of 35 years between Jesus and the Gospels. However, in antiquity written traditions were not necessarily more accurate than oral traditions. Before the advent of the printed page, memories were sharp and keen. Children were trained to memorize carefully traditions passed on from earlier generations. In Jewish circles, special techniques were devised to ensure that the words of respected teachers were transmitted faithfully. So it is highly likely that traditions about the life and teaching of Jesus were passed on orally with care.

However, as soon as we place Matthew, Mark and Luke side by side in columns in a Synopsis we can see readily that Jesus traditions were not passed on without modification, adaptation

and development. The Lord's Prayer was surely treasured by his
followers, but the wording of the versions of that prayer differ
considerably in Matthew 6:7-15 and Luke 11:1-4.

*Traditions about Jesus were preserved primarily in the service of
'Gospel truth' rather than 'historical truth'.* So is it possible to use the
evidence of the Gospels to reconstruct the life and teaching of
Jesus? I shall return to this question in *Chapter XI.*

CHAPTER VI

Q: A LOST 'GOSPEL'?

RECOVERY OF a long lost source behind an important ancient writing will rarely be reported on the front page of *The Times*. But reconstruction of a source of a writing may open up many new unexpected vistas. This happened over 100 years ago in study of the Gospels. The new vistas are still being explored today.

Matthew and Luke share about 230 sayings of Jesus which are not found in Mark. For over a century the term 'Q' has been used to refer to these sayings. In 1861 the German scholar H.J. Holtzmann built on earlier studies and claimed that Matthew and Luke had drawn on two main sources: Mark's Gospel and a collection of the sayings of Jesus. The latter soon came to be referred to by German scholars as *Quelle* (source). In 1890 J. Weiss abbreviated *Quelle* to Q; this term quickly gained wide acceptance.

In the twentieth century the Q hypothesis has been the basis of nearly all serious study of the origin and development of the Gospel traditions. However, the term Q has been used in several ways, with resulting confusion. For some scholars Q is simply a short-hand way of referring to traditions shared by Matthew and Luke which are not found in Mark: Q traditions may have existed in a number of short written documents, or in collections of oral traditions. Some scholars see Q as no more than a cycle of *oral* tradition which circulated in the early church with a fairly fixed order.

Today most scholars who use the term assume that Q existed as a *written* document which disappeared shortly after it was incorporated by Matthew and Luke into their Gospels. They accept that with only a few exceptions Luke has preserved the original order of Q, though not necessarily the original wording. Hence it has become customary to refer to Q passages with the Lucan chapter and verse numbers. For example, Q 7:22 is a reference to the Q tradition which lies behind Luke 7:22.

Although most of the early supporters of Q believed that it was a collection of sayings in Aramaic (and therefore earlier and more reliable than traditions which circulated in Greek), this view is not now widely accepted. It was based partly on one interpretation of comments of Papias (the early second-century bishop whom we met in *Chapter V*): 'Matthew collected the oracles (*ta logia*) in the Hebrew language (i.e. perhaps Q in Aramaic) and each one interpreted (or translated) them as he was able.' However, since Papias also uses *ta logia* to include Mark's *narratives*, as well as sayings of Jesus, Papias was probably referring to Matthew's Gospel and not to Q. If so, Papias's phrase 'in the Hebrew language' may either be a reference to the Jewish stylistic features of Matthew's Gospel, or a mistake.

Several scholars have claimed that some Q traditions which differ considerably in Mathew and in Luke rest on the evangelists' differing, or even mistaken, translations of underlying Aramaic traditions. However, the linguistic evidence is not clear-cut, and Matthew's and Luke's knowledge of Aramaic is not demonstrable. On the other hand, there is some linguistic evidence which supports the conclusion that Q was composed originally in Greek. Since there is often close verbal correspondence in Matthew's and Luke's Q traditions, it is probable that they were both drawing on traditions in the same language, i.e. Greek.

Q was probably originally a little larger than the 230 or so verses shared by Matthew and Luke. Since both Matthew and Luke omit some Marcan material, why should we suppose that they have both incorporated Q in full? Hence some of the traditions found only in Matthew or in Luke ('M' or 'L') may have belonged originally to Q, though the precise extent of such additional Q traditions is far from clear.

Two examples will show just how difficult it is to be sure. First, Matthew 11:28-30, the familiar 'Come unto me all who are weary and heavy laden' passage. Perhaps these verses, which follow immediately after a section of Q traditions, originally belonged to Q, even though they are not found in Luke. On the other hand, if they did belong to Q, why did Luke omit this moving portrait of Jesus as 'meek and humble in heart'? Surely Luke would have included these words if he had known them, for he certainly wants to portray Jesus in this way?

Secondly, Luke 4:16-30, Luke's account of the visit of Jesus to his home town synagogue in Nazareth. These verses are at least partly independent of Mark. Did Luke include some Q traditions in this passage, even though there is no trace of them in the equivalent passage in Matthew? Since some of the non-Marcan traditions in Luke 4:16-30 cohere well with a number of Q traditions, several scholars accept this suggestion.

The Q hypothesis is important in current study of the Gospels for both historical and theological reasons. Many early supporters of the Q hypothesis believed that Q provided direct access to the authentic teaching of Jesus. They considered that the source on which both Matthew and Luke drew was early and reliable: it provided an impressive bridge between the life of Jesus and the writing of the Gospels.

However, not even Q escaped the attention of the form critics, whose assumptions were discussed in the previous chapter. They insisted that Q (and other Jesus traditions) were influenced by the life and faith of the early church. In the 1970s some scholars took a further step: like the four Gospels, Q was compiled in the light of distinctive theological concerns. Q was valued less as a 'pure' historical source, than as a collection of the sayings of Jesus made and shaped from a particular theological perspective.

Q still plays a role in discussion of the historicity of the Jesus traditions. Many believe that Jesus traditions which are found in several strands of the Gospel traditions (Mark, Q, traditions found only in Matthew or only in Luke ['M', 'L'], traditions behind John's Gospel) are more likely to be authentic than traditions less widely attested. This criterion, which is known as 'multiple attestation', will be discussed further in *Chapter XI*.

If we accept that Q existed either as a written document or as a fairly fixed collection of oral traditions, important issues arise. Since Q did not contain passion or resurrection traditions, did the Q community's understanding of the Christian faith differ markedly from Paul's and Mark's strong emphasis on the centrality of the death and resurrection of Jesus? Some scholars answer in the affirmative and note that the existence of Q provides still more evidence of the diversity of earliest Christianity.

Since Q contains about 230 sayings of Jesus and only one narrative, the story of the healing of the Roman centurion's servant in Matthew 8:5-13 = Luke 7: 1-10, its portrait of Jesus is in stark contrast to Mark's. Scholars who press this point note that followers of Jesus who treasured and compiled Q seem to have seen Jesus more as a teacher of aphorisms (short pithy sayings), riddles, proverbs and parables, than as one whose *actions* were as important as his sayings: a sage, rather than a prophet. Once again the extent of the diversity within early Christianity is at stake.

Did Q exist?

Five main arguments have been advanced in support of the view that both Matthew and Luke used Q as a primary source as well as Mark. Although some of these arguments are stronger than others, taken cumulatively they confirm that there are good grounds for accepting that both Matthew and Luke used Q.

(i) In verse after verse Matthew and Luke agree with one another very closely indeed. The following passages are good examples of close verbal agreement: Matthew 3:7-12 = Luke 3:7-9, 16-17; Matthew 4:1-11 = Luke 4:1-13; Matthew 11: 2-11, 16-19 = Luke 7:18-28, 31-35; Matthew 23: 37-39 = Luke 13: 34-35. In line after line of the Greek text (and even in an English translation) there is such close verbal correspondence that it is probable that Matthew and Luke are drawing on traditions from the same source. If both evangelists drew on oral traditions which had not been gathered together, very much greater divergence in wording would be expected. This observation is supplemented by an appeal to the generally agreed conclusion that Mark is our earliest Gospel: even though Matthew and Luke are two very different Gospels, they have both used Mark. Thus it is likely (so the argument runs) that where they agree closely in non-Marcan sections, they are both using a source, Q.

Although there is striking verbal agreement in many of the non-Marcan passages which Matthew and Luke share, in the following three passages (and in many others) it is not. Both

Matthew and Luke include the parable of the man who built his house on the rock (Matthew 7:21, 24-27 = Luke 6: 46-49), but the wording differs considerably. In Matthew 23:4, 6-7,13, 23, 25-27, 29-32, 34-36 = Luke 11:39-52 a large number of similar sayings are found in the same order; in some sayings the wording is very close, but in others there is considerable variation. Matthew and Luke both include what is clearly the same parable of the pounds, but their versions of the lengthy parable differ in numerous details (Matthew 25:14-30 = Luke 19: 11-27).

Supporters of Q account for the differences in the wording of non-Marcan traditions in two main ways. Since both Matthew and Luke often revise the wording of Mark quite extensively, we should not be surprised to find that they have also done so with the second main source which they have utilized. This is a plausible argument, and in some passages the evangelist's redaction of Q can be discerned with little difficulty. But why have the evangelists revised some Q traditions quite considerably, but not others? Many scholars suggest that the variations in some passages are so great that it is likely that Matthew and Luke drew on two different 'editions' of Q. In other words, Q was revised and even extended (perhaps more than once); it was utilized by Matthew and by Luke at different stages in its evolution. Some writers use the abbreviation Q^Mt and Q^Lk to refer to the versions of Q used by Matthew and Luke. Some such explanation seems necessary to account for the close verbal similarity in some passages, but differences in others.

(ii) Although Matthew weaves his sources together (especially in his five large discourses) and Luke places them in 'strips' or blocks, there are some significant agreements in the order in which the non-Marcan traditions are found in Matthew and Luke. These agreements in order cannot be coincidental and strongly suggest the use of a common source. For example, the following individual sayings or small units appear in Matthew in the same order: Luke 3: 7-9, 16-17; 4: 1-13; 6: 20b-21, 22-23, 29, 30, 32-35, 36, 37-38, 41-42, 43-44, 46, 47-49; 7: 1-10, 18-23, 24-26, 27, 28, 31-34, 35. John Kloppenborg has recently shown that in at least 85 per cent of the Q traditions it is possible to ascertain the common order, or to determine which evangelist disturbed the common order.[1]

This phenomenon seems to rule out the possibility that both evangelists are drawing on independent oral traditions. Why should so many traditions appear in both Gospels in the same order, especially when there is often no obvious reason for their juxtaposition? At the very least, Matthew and Luke seem to have drawn on a cycle of oral traditions with a fairly fixed order. Many scholars now believe that the phenomenon of order is so striking that it strongly suggests that Q was a written document.

(iii) In several passages in Matthew and Luke we find that essentially the same tradition is repeated; these repetitions are known as doublets. They occur where Matthew and Luke both use the Marcan form of a saying, but both evangelists also include a non-Marcan or Q form of essentially the same saying. The following two doublets are particularly striking (though there are many more). (a) 'He who has, to him will more be given. . .' Mark 4:25 = Matthew 13:12 = Luke 8:18; a similar saying is found at Matthew 25:29 = Luke 19:26 (Q). (b) 'If any man will deny me, he must deny himself . . .' Mark 8:34f. = Matthew 16:24f. = Luke 9:23f., with a similar saying at Matthew 10:38f. = Luke 14:27, 17: 33 (Q).

The presence of so many doublets is taken by many to confirm that Q was a written document rather than a set of oral traditions. If Matthew and Luke drew on oral traditions (so the argument runs), we might have expected that an oral Q tradition would have been conflated with the similar Marcan saying.

(iv) The Q material 'hangs together' as an entity. With the exception of the narrative noted above, the Q traditions are all sayings of Jesus. Although there is no evidence that Q survived beyond its incorporation into Matthew and Luke, the Gospel of Thomas, which was discovered in 1945, also consists of a collection of sayings of Jesus. The discovery of Thomas, which will be discussed in *Chapter VII*, suggests that other collections of the sayings of Jesus may have been made in the early church. This general line of argument is obviously less compelling than the preceding three, but its force should not be underestimated. Both in terms of content and literary genre, traditions which are found only in Matthew ('M' traditions) or only in Luke ('L') are much more disparate than Q traditions.

(v) The first three arguments just noted are not in fact

conclusive. The phenomena can be accounted for by rival hypotheses. Two have been championed recently: the Griesbach hypothesis (in which Mark was written as a 'Reader's Digest' version of Matthew and Luke) and the view that Luke has used Matthew as well as Mark. However, on close inspection, neither of these rival explanations of the non-Marcan material shared by Matthew and Luke is as plausible as the Q hypothesis. Gerald Downing (1992) has added fresh considerations in support of this conclusion.[2] He has shown that the two rival hypotheses involve complicated ways of working which are quite unlike the ways ancient writers handled their sources. On the other hand, Matthew and Luke use Mark and Q in ways which do bear comparison with well-established conventions in antiquity. This important observation strengthens the conclusion that the case for Marcan priority and Q is far stronger than the case for any other rival solution of the synoptic problem. Since both these hypotheses involve the claim that Luke used Matthew, this possibility needs to be looked at further.

Did Luke use Matthew?

If Luke used Matthew, there are major implications for our understanding of the origin, transmission and development of the Gospel traditions. On this view, the earliest form of the traditions must always lie behind Matthew's Gospel, not Luke's; hence Matthew becomes particularly important in historical reconstruction. If Luke has used Matthew, then he has used his major source extremely freely indeed: he is the first 'interpreter' of Matthew, which he has 'dismantled' in order to write his own very different Gospel. For several reasons, this alternative to the Q hypothesis is most unlikely.

If Luke has used Matthew, what has happened to Matthew's five impressive discourses? On this view, a small part of Matthew's Sermon on the Mount in chapters 5-7 reappears in Luke 6: 20-49, but the rest of the material is either scattered (apparently haphazardly) right through Luke's Gospel and set in very different contexts, or it is omitted completely. For example, Matthew's second discourse in chapter 10 reappears in no fewer than seven different chapters in Luke!

While attempts have been made to account for Luke's rather odd treatment of the Matthean discourses, they have convinced few. Michael Goulder, an able and enthusiastic defender of Luke's use of Matthew, recognizes that Matthew's fifth discourse poses particular difficulties for his hypothesis. He has to concede that Luke has carefully separated the Marcan and non-Marcan parts of Matthew 24–25. The former are included in Luke 21, the latter are isolated (by marking a copy of Matthew with a pen!) and included in Luke chapters 12–13, 17, and, we may add, 19. This is a tortuous explanation of Luke's methods, to say the least.

If Luke has used Matthew, we would expect him to have adopted some of the expansions and modifications Matthew makes to Mark. But hardly a trace of them can be found in Luke. Where Matthew and Mark have the same tradition, Luke opts for Mark's version and ignores Matthew's; and at the same time he rearranges Matthew very considerably. Why did Luke find Matthew so unattractive, when in almost all other parts of early Christianity it became the favourite Gospel?

Peter's confession at Caesarea Philippi provides a good illustration of this point. At Luke 9: 18-21, Mark 8:27-30 has been used, but there isn't a sign in Luke of the major addition Matthew makes to Mark at 16: 16-19. Here several striking sayings of Jesus addressed to Peter, including the words 'On this rock I will build my church', have been ignored.

Why, then, does Luke omit so many of Matthew's numerous expansions of Marcan material? This point has often been pressed by those who deny that Luke has used Matthew. Goulder replies as follows. Luke has a 'block policy': 'when he (Luke) is treating Marcan matter he has Mark in front of him, and he has made it his policy not to keep turning up Matthew to see what he has added. . . Luke does not include the additions because he had decided on a policy which involved letting them go.'[3] This leads to the suggestion that once a Marcan block has been dealt with, Luke sometimes comes back to Matthew's additions to Mark: some of the additions are transferred to other contexts, some are ignored unintentionally, some are re-written.

Where Matthew and Luke contain similar non-Marcan traditions, most scholars accept that it is very difficult to decide which evangelist has the earlier form of the tradition. But scholars who claim that Luke has used Matthew must accept that it is *always* Luke who has changed Matthew's earlier form of the tradition. Their attempts to defend this view often look like special pleading.

For example, if Luke has used Matthew, then he has *abbreviated* Matthew's earlier and fuller version both of the Beatitudes (5:1-12) and of the Lord's Prayer (6:9-13). Why should Luke wish to do this? In both cases it is very difficult indeed to discover plausible reasons; it is much less difficult to suppose that while Luke has retained Q traditions with few changes, Matthew has expanded them.

One final point sums up several of the above observations. If we accept that Luke has used Mark, then with the help of a synopsis we can readily discover the changes of various kinds which he has made to Mark. On the whole he has retained the order of Mark's traditions and has considerable respect for their content, especially when he is quoting sayings of Jesus. If Luke has also used Matthew, we would expect him to have modified his second source in broadly similar ways. But this is by no means the case.

The cumulative force of the arguments for the existence of Q set out above is very impressive, but the case for Q falls short of absolute proof. Even the strongest supporters of Q accept that the hypothesis is less securely established than the conclusion that Matthew and Luke have both used Mark. As we noted, some of the phenomena can be accounted for by rival hypotheses. However, once the rival hypotheses are subjected to critical scrutiny, they turn out to be much less satisfactory than the Q hypothesis. So Q remains a valid working hypothesis for serious study of the Gospels.

Was Q a 'Gospel'?

Were Q traditions brought together simply as an anthology or summary of the sayings of Jesus? Or do they contain a distinctive theological perspective? In what sense, if any, is it appropriate to refer to Q as a 'Gospel'?

These questions have always been prominent in Q studies. Behind them lurk even more crucial questions. Just how diverse

was earliest Christianity? Does the existence of Q suggest that
some followers of Jesus were committed solely to his teaching?
Did they know nothing about his crucifixion and resurrection?
Or did they not attach any theological significance to whatever
they did know?

At the turn of the century several writers accepted that Q
must have included an account of the death and resurrection of
Jesus as well as a collection of his sayings. In their passion and resurrection narratives Luke and Matthew share no more than a few
phrases which are not found in Mark, so it is impossible to sustain this view.

In his influential study of Q in 1908, Harnack insisted that Q
was a source of unparalleled value. It had been compiled without
any discernible bias, 'whether apologetic, didactic, ecclesiastical,
national or anti-national'. Mark had exaggerated apocalypticism
and subordinated the 'purely religious and moral element' of
Jesus' message.[4] Q, on the other hand, was a relatively complete
account of 'the message of Jesus' which expressed clearly the very
essence of Christianity for twentieth-century men and women.
As we shall see, echoes of this long-abandoned view can be
found in Burton Mack's 1993 book, *The Lost Gospel*.

Harnack's theological presuppositions were challenged in the
1920s and 1930s by Karl Barth and Rudolf Bultmann, who
insisted that proclamation of the Cross and the Resurrection, not
the teaching of the historical Jesus, was at the heart of the earliest Christian Gospel. Harnack's confidence in Q as 'the message of Jesus' was also challenged by the work of the first form
critics. They insisted that since all the Gospel traditions have
been shaped by the faith and the needs of the post-Easter communities, not even Q provides *direct* access to the teaching of
Jesus.

So what was the relationship of Q to the proclamation or
'Gospel' of the earliest post-Easter communities? M. Dibelius
(1919), B. H. Streeter (1924), and T. W. Manson (1937) all saw
Q as a *supplement* to the early Gospel of the Cross and
Resurrection of Jesus. Q traditions were used as ethical guidance
and encouragement for those who had accepted proclamation of
the significance of the death and resurrection of Jesus.

Although this general view held sway for some time, it was

strongly challenged by H. E. Tödt (1956). In his view the community did not develop a theology of the cross, but was convinced that Jesus, who has re-established fellowship with his followers as the risen one, is also the one who, as the coming Son of Man, will be ultimate guarantor of that fellowship. In other words, Q did contain a rich Christology, even if it was rather different from Mark's.

Other scholars followed his lead and showed that Q traditions had been arranged and shaped in the light of christological concerns. In 1973 I drew attention to the importance of the accounts of the baptism and temptations of Jesus which stood at the beginning of Q; together with Matthew 11:2-6 = Luke 7:18-23 (and related passages) they confirm that for the Q community the promises of the prophet Isaiah were being fulfilled in the actions and words of Jesus.[5] The 'past' of Jesus (including his rejection by those to whom he was sent), as well as his soon-expected parousia, was important to the Q community.

In the 1950s the ways the four evangelists re-shaped and arranged the traditions at their disposal were studied intensively. It soon became possible to show that 'redaction' of earlier traditions had been carried out in accordance with particular theological emphases. Discussion of Q from this perspective was pioneered by D. Lührmann (1969) and has been continued by a number of scholars. Attention is focused on the ways originally separate traditions have been linked together in Q and on sayings which have been 'created' by the Q community in order to clarify or interpret earlier traditions. Separation of original tradition and later redaction is obviously much more difficult and hypothetical than it is in the case of Matthew's and Luke's redaction of their sources, but that has not deterred scholars from trying to discern the primary purposes of the compiler(s) of Q.

At present opinion is divided. Two main approaches are being keenly debated. M. Sato (1988) argues that the literary genre of Q is comparable with Old Testament prophetic writings; many individual Q traditions are prophetic in form and in emphasis. D. R. Catchpole (1992) and C. M. Tuckett (1995) are both reluctant to separate Q traditions into two or more layers, and also see Jesus portrayed in Q more as a prophet than as a sage.[6]

John Kloppenborg (1987) argues that the formative component of Q consisted of a group of six 'wisdom speeches'. This stratum was subsequently expanded by the addition of groups of 'prophetic' sayings which adopted a critical and polemical stance with respect to Israel; the temptation story (Matthew 4:1-11 = Luke 4:1-13), which was the final addition to Q, gave it a more biographical cast. Whereas for Kloppenborg prophetic traditions in Q are a later secondary development, for Sato the prophetic traditions are primary.

Kloppenborg's general approach has been taken several steps further by Burton Mack (1993).[7] Mack claims to be able to disentangle three quite different strata, Q^1, Q^2 and Q^3. The original 'Q people' revered Jesus as a Cynic-like sage. 'Cynics were revered for their begging, voluntary poverty, renunciation of needs, severance of family ties, fearless and carefree attitudes, and troublesome public behavior. Standard themes in Cynic discourse included a critique of riches, pretension, and hypocrisy, just as in Q^1.' Mack does not claim explicitly that Q^1 puts us directly in touch with the historical Jesus who was a Cynic sage, but he does repeatedly emphasize that it is an earlier and more historical portrait of Jesus than the portraits set out in the 'narrative Gospels'.[8] Although Mack does not discuss in what sense Q may be seen as a 'Gospel', he believes that Q^1 is a preferable form of 'Gospel' for American culture today than Mark's or Paul's Gospel with their focus on the crucifixion and resurrection of Jesus. With Q^2 the rot sets in: traditions are added which portray Jesus as a prophet who pronounces judgement on Jewish religious leaders. Q^3 provides a 'little window' into the Q community after AD 70, in the wake of the disastrous Jewish war against the Romans.

There are serious difficulties with this form of reconstruction. While it is certainly the case that there are both wisdom and prophetic sayings among the Q traditions, it is by no means clear that one is earlier and more historical than the other. There is in fact no reason why some sayings in both categories should not go back to Jesus. The division of Q into three strata rests on questionable assumptions about the development of earliest Christianity. It is simply not possible to relate individual Q sayings to historical and social conditions in Galilee between about AD 40 and 75 in the way that Mack does.

A very different and much more convincing approach is taken

by the doyen of modern Q studies, James Robinson (1992).[9] Although Robinson does not reject attempts to uncover 'layers' within Q traditions, he concentrates on the final form of Q. This starting point is very much in line with current studies of the Gospels which concentrate on the form of the text which has come down to us, rather than on hypothetical earlier layers or sources. Robinson shows that Q interprets John the Baptist from a Christian perspective. On his reconstruction, Q included an account of the temptations of Jesus as Son of God, and an account of his baptism, with the declaration by the heavenly voice (God) that Jesus is 'my beloved Son'. Robinson emphasizes (as I did myself in 1973)[10] that Q7: 18-23 (i.e. Luke 7:18-23) is a central passage in Q. Here both the actions and the words of Jesus are set out as the fulfilment of a cluster of passages in Isaiah. The climax is the claim that words of Jesus are proclamation of the good news ('Gospel') to the poor: Isaiah 61:1 is clearly alluded to, as it is in the opening beatitude 'blessed are the poor' (which may have stood near the beginning of Q).

Robinson draws attention to several ways in which Q is similar to Mark, though of course without claiming that Q contained passion and resurrection narratives. Perhaps his most interesting point is that some of the Q traditions themselves suggest that the term 'Gospel' is an appropriate way of referring to Q. Although the noun 'Gospel' is not used, as we have just seen, the verb 'to preach the good news' (or 'Gospel') is found in Q7:23.

A further step is taken by the evangelist Matthew, who carefully incorporates Q into different parts of his Gospel. The evangelist uses the noun 'Gospel' in two quite different ways. In important summary passages in 4:23 and 9:35 the term 'Gospel' refers to Jesus' own proclamation of 'the good news of the kingdom' (4:23 and 9:35), i.e. it refers to the 'Gospel *of* Jesus'. Later, in 24:14 and 26:13 Matthew uses the noun 'Gospel' to refer to his own full written account of the life, death and resurrection of Jesus, the 'Gospel *about* Jesus'. In 24:14 we read, 'this Gospel of the kingdom will be proclaimed throughout the world, as a testimony to all nations.' In 26:13 it is clear that 'this Gospel' includes *narratives* about Jesus.[11]

So was Q a 'Gospel'? Obviously not in the sense in which Paul and Mark used the term to refer to the Gospel *about* Jesus. But if

we have in mind Matthew's use of the noun to refer to the words
of Jesus as 'proclamation of good news', then Q may be seen as
a 'Gospel of Jesus'.

However, as we shall see in *Chapter VIII*, it was Mark's use of
the noun 'Gospel' in 1:1, and Matthew's use of the same noun
in 24:14 and 26: 13 to refer to narratives of proclamation *about*
the life, death and resurrection of Jesus which won the day. It was
this usage which was influential on the emergence in the second
century of the titles, 'The Gospel according to' Matthew, Mark,
Luke and John.

What significance, if any, was attached to the death and resurrection of Jesus by those who transmitted Q? Some will insist that
we can consider only what we have, namely Q itself: hence we
must conclude that the circle of followers of Jesus who used Q
traditions was uninterested in the death and resurrection of Jesus.
Others will recall that if Matthew and Luke both knew traditions
other than Q (i.e. primarily Mark), so too may those who transmitted and used Q. In both cases an argument is constructed on
the basis of silence.

Crucifixion was the most detestable form of death known in
the ancient world. Hence it is inconceivable that the crucifixion
of Jesus at the hands of the Romans was ignored by *any* of his
followers in the gap between his death and the incorporation of
Q into Matthew's and Luke's Gospels. There is no evidence for
the survival of Q (or a so-called Q community) beyond the writing of Matthew and Luke about AD 80.

CHAPTER VII

OTHER GOSPELS: PETER, EGERTON, THOMAS AND 'SECRET MARK'

IN THE EARLY centuries of the Christian era there was no shortage of 'Gospels'. Only four became part of the collection of writings which were eventually acknowledged as authoritative for the faith and life of the Christian church. The failure of the other 'Gospels' to gain acceptance has given them an aura of fascination: was unjustified 'censorship' used?

Some of these writings called themselves Gospels; others were referred to as Gospels only at a much later period. Some are broadly similar to the four New Testament Gospels in form and content; others bear little or no relationship to them: they are not narrative acccounts of the life and teaching of Jesus, and their theological perspective is well out of line with any of the varied stances of the New Testament writers.

Until two decades ago there was general agreement that the 'other' Gospels, usually referred to as the apocryphal Gospels, were invaluable sources for the student of the early church in the second to fifth centuries – and, in some cases, even later. Most accepted without further ado that they contain little more than a pastiche of traditions from the canonical Gospels in elaborated and reinterpreted form. Hence they were considered to be of little or no value for the serious student of the life and teaching of Jesus, and of no value at all for the life and faith of the Christian church today.

In recent years, however, their cause has been championed vociferously by some scholars. Several apocryphal Gospels have been singled out as historical sources of great value. Since they are alleged to be independent of the New Testament Gospels, they are said to provide an important alternative route back to the historical Jesus.

With some recent writers there is also a theological agenda: in the words of Raymond Brown, one of the most distinguished scholars of our generation, there is 'a simplistic tendency to regard extracanonical works as the key to true Christianity as contrasted with a narrow-minded censorship represented by the New Testament.'[1]

In this chapter the four writings which have been most prominent in recent discussion will be considered. Do they contain 'Gospel truth', understood *either* as reliable historical information *or* as the content of Christian proclamation?

The Gospel of Peter

Until the discovery in 1886-7 in Akhmîm in Egypt of a single eighth- or ninth-century Greek manuscript, the text of the Gospel of Peter was unknown. The manuscript contains 60 verses which are broadly similar to parts of the passion and resurrection traditions of the New Testament Gospels. The fragment starts in mid-sentence with a reference to the trial of Jesus. Presumably in contrast to Pilate who had washed his hands of Jesus, '. . . the Jews, neither Herod nor any of his judges' refused to wash their hands (cf. Matthew 27:24-5). Later, at 11:46, Pilate says, 'I am clean of the blood of the Son of God', thus underlining even more strongly than Matthew, the Roman Pilate's innocence in contrast to Jewish responsibility for the death of Jesus. Following an account of the discovery of the empty tomb, the Gospel of Peter ends with these words (14:60): 'But I, Simon Peter, and my brother Andrew took our nets and went to the sea. And Levi, the son of Alphaeus was with us, whom the Lord . . .' An account of a resurrection appearance of Jesus to the disciples probably followed.

We do not have any quotations from the Gospel of Peter in ancient writers. However, one, or possibly two pieces of further evidence have recently come to light. In 1972 a papyrus fragment (POxy 2949) from the end of the second century, or early in the third, was published; it contains some 16 words which correspond with the Gospel of Peter 2:3-5. The differences in wording are so marked that it is clear that the text of the Gospel of Peter changed considerably between the second and the eighth centuries. In

1993 a possible further fragment (POxy 4009) was published. Like 14:60 quoted above, it uses the first person singular ('I said to him . . . he said to me'), but since it does not overlap with the main fragment, certainty is not possible.[2] This minimal and mainly very late textual evidence is in sharp contrast to the manuscript evidence for the canonical Gospels discussed in *Chapter IV*.

In the early part of the fourth century the church historian Eusebius reports that Serapion, who became bishop of Antioch about AD 190, had doubts about the Gospel of Peter. Serapion had discovered that the Christian congregation at Rhossus, about 30 miles north west of Antioch, had taken up heretical views on the basis of this Gospel. Without carefully examining the Gospel of Peter, Serapion had said, 'If this is the only thing that seemingly causes captious feelings among you, let it be read.' Later, however, on hearing serious rumblings of heresy, Serapion had studied the Gospel more closely. He discovered that 'the most part indeed was in accordance with the true teaching of the Saviour, but that some things were added, which we also place below for your benefit.'[3]

The heresy is referred to as docetism, the view that in his earthly life Jesus was not fully human: he only *appeared* to be human. Unfortunately no further details of the heresy are given. Although shortly after the Gospel of Peter was discovered some writers claimed that it contained docetic 'heretical' teaching, this view has been generally abandoned. Serapion does not say explicitly that the Gospel was docetic, rather that docetists used it. Although some passages can be interpreted in a docetic manner, this is not the most plausible interpretation of them. So the Gospel of Peter need not be dubbed 'heretical', a term that is in any case misleading with reference to the second century.

In some places the traditions in the Gospel of Peter correspond closely with the comparable traditions in the canonical Gospels; in places there are significant variations and additions, and some omissions. Unlike any New Testament writing, the resurrection of Jesus is *described* in legendary fashion with a strong emphasis on the eyewitness character of the report: the soldiers guarding the tomb of Jesus 'saw three men coming out of the tomb, with the two supporting the other one, and a cross following them, and the head of the two reached up to heaven, but that of the one being led out by the hand surpassed the heavens. And they heard a voice from the heavens saying, "Have you preached to those who have fallen asleep?" And from the cross there was heard an answer, "Yes" (10:39-42).'

Several passages seem to be later developments of traditions in Matthew's Gospel; there are less extensive echoes of traditions in Luke and John, and probably none at all of Mark. As examples of later developments, the following may be noted: Herod is described (inaccurately) as having jurisdiction in Jerusalem, and as the one whom Pilate must ask for the body of Jesus; when crucified, 'the Lord was silent as having no pain'; the darkness at midday caused many to go around with lamps, thinking it was night; the centurion sent to guard the tomb receives a name, Petronius; the stone rolls away from the tomb itself; two references to Sunday as 'the Lord's Day' (9:35; 12:50) seem to reflect early second-century developments. These features (and others) strongly suggest that the Gospel of Peter was composed after the New Testament Gospels by someone who knew at least three of them. The author may not have had a copy of Matthew in front of him as he wrote, but he knew this Gospel very well.

In a series of publications J. D. Crossan has put forward with great ingenuity and detailed arguments a very different account of the origin and importance of the Gospel of Peter. Crossan accepts that parts of it reflect later developments, but claims that once the later traditions have been removed, the earliest stratum (which he calls the Cross Gospel) is in fact the only source used by Mark, and then by Matthew and Luke, and finally John. In a recent book, Crossan lists the 'Cross Gospel' as a primary historical source, composed by the fifties AD, possibly in Sepphoris in Galilee.[4]

An attempt to find very early historical traditions in a fragmentary writing which has survived almost exclusively in one eighth-century manuscript is rash, to say the least. At the one point where comparison of the second century and the later form of the text is possible, there are major variations. So it is very unlikely that the textual traditions remained stable over such a long period. This is in sharp contrast to the much greater stability of the canonical Gospel traditions over this period.

Crossan's views have been severely criticized for further reasons. Several scholars have shown that the traditions isolated as the earliest stratum of the Gospel of Peter show clear knowledge of Matthew's Gospel.[5] If the canonical evangelists used the 'Cross Gospel' as their major source, why did they make such little use of its vocabulary and word order? And why did they leave out so many details which would have added colour to the passion narratives? For example, if Mark copied from the 'Cross Gospel' the reference to the centurion at 15:44-5, why did he not include his name, Petronius?[6]

The Gospel of Peter gives us fascinating insights into the ways passion and resurrection traditions developed in the second century, but as a historical source it is valueless. Even if it should not be dubbed 'docetic' or 'heretical', the only theological themes which might stimulate Christian reflection today are already found in the canonical Gospels. There is no sign of any fresh 'Gospel truth' in the Gospel of Peter.

The Egerton Gospel

In 1935 the publication of the four papyrus fragments known as Papyrus Egerton 2, or *The Egerton Gospel*, created a considerable stir (*see Plate 9*). The editors dated them to the middle of the second century and noted that they were from 'unquestionably the earliest specifically Christian manuscript yet discovered in Egypt'.[7] This pre-eminent place was lost later in 1935 with the publication of a fragment of John's Gospel (John Rylands papyrus 457, known to New Testament scholars as P52), thought to be 25 or so years older (*see Plates 2 and 3*).

In 1987 an additional few lines, known as PKöln 255, were published. Since the new fragment fits neatly on to the bottom of Fragment One, it is from the same manuscript. Suddenly it became possible to fit together two pieces of a large jigsaw puzzle, most of whose pieces are still missing.

In the translation of Fragment One set out below, the words in brackets are not in the surviving text and are therefore no more than a good guess; the words in italics come from PKöln 255.[8]

Fragment 1 verso:

1. [And Jesus said] to the lawyers [punish] every person who acts [against the law] and not me. For [if] . . . [he keeps] . . . how he does it.

2. He turned to [the] leaders of the people, and said this word: 'Search the Scriptures, in which you think you have life. They bear [witness] to me.

3. Don't [think] that I have come to accuse [you] before my Father. Moses is the one who accuses you, in whom [you] have hoped.

4. And when they [said], 'We know full well that God has spoken to [Moses]. But we do not know [where you have come from]', Jesus answered and said [to them]: 'Now [your] unbelief accuses [you] *in the things* written *by him* . . . *For if* [you had believed Moses] *you would have believed* [me]. *For this* [has been written] *about me in your fathers* . . .

The words in 2b–4 echo phrases in John 5:39, 45, 46 and 9:29. The correspondence is striking, but the text of John's Gospel is not being quoted carefully.

Fragment 1 recto (i.e. the reverse side of the above):

5. . . . . . [that they] should . . . together [carrying] stones, so that they might [stone] him.

6. And the [rulers] placed their hands on him to arrest him and hand him over to the crowd. And they were not [able] to arrest him for the hour of his handing over had not yet [come].

7. The L[ord] himself went away [from them] and escaped from [them].

8. And behold a leper came [to him] and said, 'Teacher Jesus, as I was wandering with lepers and eating [with them] in the inn, I also contracted lep[rosy]. So if [you wish] it, I shall be cleansed.

9. The [said to him], 'I wish it, be cleansed.' [And immediately] the leprosy left him.

10. *And Jesus* [said] *to him, Go, show yourself to the* [priests], *and offer sacrifices* [for your] *cleansing as* [Moses] *commanded,* [and] *sin no more . . .*

The opening lines continue the narrative recorded on the other side of the fragment. Once again there are echoes of John's Gospel: 5:46; 7:30 and 8:20; 10:31. The story of the leper has close links to Mark 1:40-5, but some of the phraseology is reminiscent of Matthew's and Luke's accounts of this incident. The final phrase 'sin no more' recalls John 5:14, where it concludes a quite different miracle tradition. This mixture of synoptic and Johannine phraseology is baffling.

Fragment Two is shorter. On one side several phrases recall passages in Mark, especially Mark 7:6-7 and 12: 14. Once again there are also Johannine phrases. To complicate matters still further, the tradition on the other side does not echo the canonical Gospels at all; it seems to be part of a rather fanciful tale more akin to traditions found in later apocryphal Gospels such as the *Infancy Gospel of Thomas*. Fragment Three contains only a handful of words. Fragment Four contains only one partly legible letter.

What is to be made of these fragments? Ever since their initial publication, most scholars have concluded that the Egerton Gospel is later than the New Testament Gospels, and dependent on them: the author seems to have drawn on his memory of a number of passages in all four Gospels.

In recent years several scholars have challenged this consensus and insisted that Papyrus Egerton 2 is independent and earlier than the canonical Gospels, and perhaps even used by them. In a recent book (1991) J. D. Crossan champions Egerton's cause and suggests that it could be as early as the fifties AD.[9]

This view has not gone unchallenged.[10] At numerous points the phraseology of Papyrus Egerton 2 seems to be either dependent on or secondary to the comparable traditions in the canonical Gospels. For example, the use of the plural in v.10 (above), 'the priests', is historically inaccurate and secondary to Mark 1:44. It is very difficult to imagine how traditions in the canonical Gospels could have developed from these fragments. It is less difficult to envisage their author writing down Jesus traditions

from memory on the basis of knowledge of the canonical
Gospels.

The Gospel of Thomas

The Gospel of Thomas is the most controversial of the early
Christian writings considered in this chapter. Scholars take dia-
metrically opposite views on its importance for Christian origins.
For some, Thomas is a 'fifth Gospel' independent of the canonical Gospels; its earliest form is said to be even earlier than Mark.
It is therefore invaluable for reconstructing both the teaching of
the historical Jesus and the development of Jesus traditions in the
first century.

For others, Thomas is a second-century adaptation of sayings
of Jesus taken from the Gospels, an adaptation undertaken by
gnostic groups deemed to be 'heretical' by 'orthodox' church
leaders. On this view, Thomas sheds light on the development of
one strand of 'heretical' Christianity in the second century, but is
of no value at all for first-century questions.

Scholars defending either of these two views often sound like
politicians: they claim that they represent majority opinion, and
they largely ignore the strongest points made by their opponents.
The issues at stake are important, complex and fascinating.

The story starts at the beginning of this century with the publication of three fragmentary Greek papyri from Oxyrhynchus in
Egypt, known as POxy1, POxy654, and POxy655. These
papyri, which do not come from the same manuscript, all date
from the third century AD. Since they all contain sayings of Jesus,
their publication immediately attracted attention. Do they contain authentic sayings of Jesus? Or are they mere shadows of the
canonical Gospels? It did not prove possible to link them with
any known apocryphal Gospel, though there were plenty of sug-
gestions.

Their origin and significance remained a mystery until the
publication of the Gospel of Thomas in 1957, when it quickly
became clear that all three fragments came from this long lost
writing. The Coptic text of the Gospel of Thomas had been discovered in 1945 in upper Egypt, along with a large number of
Christian writings known as the Nag Hammadi Library. Two

years later the first Dead Sea Scrolls began to appear, and they have featured regularly in newspaper colour supplements and in radio and television programmes. In contrast, until recently, the Nag Hammadi Library has remained the preserve of specialists, but for the student of early Christianity its writings are almost as important as the Dead Sea Scrolls.

The Gospel of Thomas contains 114 sayings of Jesus, nearly all of which are introduced by the phrase, 'Jesus said'. Most of the sayings are terse, many are enigmatic. There are no narratives, only a minimal amount of dialogue, and little indication of a social setting. About half are similar to sayings of Jesus in the canonical Gospels; the other half are 'new'.

Do the sayings of Jesus which are not found elsewhere go back ultimately to Jesus and provide fresh examples of his teaching? The following are examples of 'new' sayings.

'Jesus said, "Be passers-by".' (logion 42)

'Jesus said, "The one who has become rich should reign. And the one who has power should renounce [it]'." (logion 81)

'Jesus said, "Whoever is near me is near the fire, and who-ever is far from me is far from the kingdom".' (logion 82)

'The kingdom of the [Father] is like a woman who was carrying a [jar] full of meal. When she had travelled far [along] the road, the handle of the jar broke and the meal spilled out after her [along] the road. She was not aware of the fact; she had not understood how to toil. When she reached home, she put the jar down and found it empty'." (logion 97).

'Jesus said, "The kingdom of the Father is like a man who wanted to assassinate a member of court. At home, he drew the dagger and stabbed it into the wall in order to know whether his hand would be firm. Next he murdered the member of the court'." (logion 98).

Now some examples of sayings similar to those included in the canonical Gospels:

'Jesus said, "A city built upon a high hill and fortified

cannot fail. Nor can it become hidden".' (logion 32; cf. Matthew 5:14)

'Jesus said, "Blessed are the poor, for yours is the kingdom of heaven".' (logion 54; cf. Matthew 5.3=Luke 6:20)
'Jesus said, "The harvest is plentiful but the workers are few. So plead with the lord to dispatch workers for the harvest".' (logion 73; cf. Matthew 9:37=Luke 10:2).

Are these sayings (and others like them) dependent on the Gospels, or do they come from early independent oral traditions which are perhaps closer to the original words of Jesus?

There is certainly some evidence which seems to point towards this latter possibility. Many of the sayings in Thomas are shorter and apparently less theologically developed than their parallels in the four Gospels. Parables of Jesus, for example, are found without the interpretations or elaborations provided by the evangelists. Thomas's version of the parable of the sower is a good example.

'Jesus said, "Listen, a sower came forth, took a handful (of seeds), and scattered (them). Now some fell upon the path, and the birds came and picked them out. Others fell upon the rock, and they did not take root in the soil, and they did not send up ears. Others fell on thorns, and they choked the seed; and the grubs devoured them. And others fell upon good soil, and it produced a good crop: it yielded sixty per measure and a hundred and twenty per measure".' (logion 107).

The versions of this parable in Mark 4:3-8, Matthew 13:3-8 and Luke 8:5-8 are more elaborate. Whereas in the verses which follow in all three Gospels the parable is interpreted allegorically, in Thomas no explicit interpretation is added.

In the light of evidence along these lines, bold claims have recently been made about Thomas. In 1993 the American *Jesus Seminar*, which has attracted wide media interest in North America, published some of its work as *The Five Gospels: The Search for Authentic Words of Jesus*.[11] The fifth Gospel is Thomas.

The preface to this book, which includes a lively fresh translation of all five Gospels, notes that Thomas is 'free of ecclesiastical and religious control, unlike other major translations'. Because it is 'not bound by the dictates of church councils', Thomas can be given the same status as the New Testament Gospels.

J. D. Crossan believes that the first layer of Thomas was composed by the 50s AD, some twenty years *before* the first version of Mark's Gospel, which he assumes to be 'Secret Mark' (see below, pp. 93-5)! Thomas is not only independent of the canonical Gospels, much of its collection of the sayings of Jesus is 'very, very early'.[12]

Conclusions along these lines have recently been trumpeted confidently by several American scholars as if they were 'Gospel truth'. What is the truth about Thomas? It turns out to be much more complex than the simplistic answers just mentioned.

Thomas and Gnosticism

In its present form, Thomas is a Gnostic writing, as are most of the writings in the Nag Hammadi Library. Gnosticism was one of the main threats to 'orthodox' Christianity in the second and third centuries. Although Gnosticism flourished in several different forms, there were some common features. For Gnostics, the world is an evil place, created by an evil God, Yahweh, who had turned away from the one true God. Gnostics saw themselves as descendants of the one true God, as sparks of divine light trapped in this evil world. Christ the Redeemer was sent to remind Gnostics of their true nature. He shares with them secret knowledge (gnosis) which enables them to break free from this evil world and return to the true God. In such a schema neither the first-century Jewish context of Jesus, nor his death and resurrection, is of importance.

Although Thomas does not set out a Gnostic myth along these lines, it is now generally agreed that in its present form this collection of sayings of Jesus is Gnostic. In his highly respected edition of Gnostic writings, Bentley Layton notes that Thomas presupposes the structure of the Gnostic myth known in a more coherent form in the Hymn of the Pearl, which comes from the same 'school' as Thomas. 'Once the myth had been recognized or reconstructed by the ancient reader (of Thomas), it would

have provided a framework within which the other more traditional sayings could be interpreted.'[13]

The opening and closing words of any writing are particularly
important. In the canonical Gospels, they underline some of the
distinctive emphases of the evangelists. The Gospel of Thomas is
no exception: its first and last sayings make clear its close links
with a Gnostic world view.

Since the words 'the Gospel according to Thomas' were
appended at the end, probably secondarily, the first logion of
Thomas functioned as a title or key to the whole collection:

> These are the secret sayings which the living Jesus uttered
> and which Didymus Jude Thomas wrote down. And he
> said, 'Whoever finds the meaning of these sayings will not
> taste death.'

The sayings which follow are words of the 'living' Jesus, not Jesus
of Nazareth, a first-century Jewish prophet. For the readers of
Thomas, it is the esoteric, timeless *words* of the living Jesus, not
his death and resurrection, which are the key to salvation.

Thomas closes with these words (logion 114):

> Simon Peter said to them, 'Mary should leave us, for
> females are not worthy of life.' Jesus said, 'See, I am going
> to attract her to make her male so that she too might
> become a living spirit that resembles you males. For every
> female (element) that makes itself male will enter the king-
> dom of heaven.'

This is hardly a good example of political correctness! Mary is to
undergo transformation from her present 'worldly' nature to a
higher spiritual nature. As in many Gnostic writings, there is a
misogynist streak: the female role in bearing more 'imprisoned
spirits' is deprecated.

Some sayings in Thomas seem at first sight to be devoid of
Gnostic ideas, and represent sound common sense which is not
far from some forms of Christian piety common today. Logion
110, for example: 'Jesus said, "Let one who has found the world,
and has become rich, renounce the world."' This saying seems to

be an encouragement to resist the snares of wealth and worldly values. Logion 56, however, confirms that in Thomas (and even in this apparently straightforward saying) there is a radical rejection of the created world: 'Jesus said, "Whoever has become acquainted with the world has found a corpse, and the world is not worthy of the one who has found the corpse."'

Logion 52 differentiates sharply Gnostic Christianity from the forms found in the New Testament writings:

> His disciples said to him, 'Twenty-four prophets have spoken in Israel, and they all spoke of you.' He said to them, 'You have abandoned the one who is living in your presence, and you have spoken of those who are dead.'

The number twenty-four is the key to this dialogue. In Jewish tradition the Scriptures contained twenty-four books, so here we have polemic against Christians who claim that Jesus is the fulfilment of the Scriptures. This sharp rejection of the Scriptures is reminiscent of Marcion whose influential views were rejected as heretical in AD 144. Although Marcion was not himself a Gnostic, like many Gnostics he believed that the God of Jesus was not the creator God of the Scriptures. This dialogue underlines just how far Thomas is from 'mainstream' first- and second-century Christianity.

Thomas and the Four Gospels

There is now general agreement that in its present form Thomas is a Gnostic writing. Once the Gnostic 'overlay' is removed, what is left? Very early forms of the Jesus tradition, or a set of sayings which are largely dependent on the New Testament Gospels and quote or elaborate selected sayings?

Scholars who insist that Thomas does not draw on the New Testament Gospels note that many of the sayings in Thomas which have parallels in the canonical Gospels are shorter. Since they often lack the theological elaborations and interpretations found in the New Testament Gospels, many of them are earlier and more likely to go back to Jesus of Nazareth. Thomas's version of the parable of the sower quoted above is a striking example.

However, 'short' does not necessarily mean 'earlier'. In passage after passage Matthew abbreviates Mark's traditions in order to set out his own rather different portrait of Jesus. Perhaps Thomas has similarly abbreviated and adapted passages in the Gospels.

The parable of the lost sheep in logion 107 illustrates these points. Here a shorter version of the parable in Matthew 18: 12-14 and Luke 15: 3-7 is shorn of any context and is introduced, as usual in Thomas, by 'Jesus said'. There is no sign in Thomas of the concluding theological interpretation of either evangelist. At first sight the version in Thomas seems to be independent of both Matthew and Luke, and more likely to represent the original words of Jesus.

However, matters are not so simple. In Thomas, the opening words of the parable liken *the kingdom* to a shepherd who has lost one of his hundred sheep. The kingdom is the realm of Gnostic believers, from which one sheep has strayed. The shepherd searches for it, not because it is lost, but because it is *large*. This motif is found in several parables in Thomas: the wise fisherman has selected a *large* fish from his catch (logion 8); the mustard seed puts forth a *large* plant (logion 20); the woman bakes *large* loaves from leaven (logion 96). Gnostics saw themselves as an elect, élite minority: 'Jesus said, "Blessed are those who are solitary and superior, for you will find the kingdom; for since you come from it, you shall return to it"' (logion 49). In Thomas's version of the parable of the lost sheep, the *large* sheep represents the Gnostic believer who has strayed from the kingdom from which he or she has come. In order to turn the parable into esoteric Gnostic teaching, Thomas may well have taken this parable from Matthew or Luke, abbreviated it, and stripped it of its context and interpretation.

Scholars who defend the independence of Thomas note that there is hardly a trace of the order of the sayings of Jesus in the synoptic Gospels. Why, they ask, would Thomas dismember the order of the canonical Gospels? This argument would be strong if we could be certain that there is no order at all in Thomas. If there are some signs of groupings of sayings according to catchwords or themes, then Thomas would have had a motive for abandoning the order of sayings in the canonical Gospels. In fact there are some such links between sayings in Thomas. And elsewhere the sayings may well have been arranged according to a logic which is not clear to us, in view of our ignorance of Gnostic patterns of thought. Christopher Tuckett makes a further important point: since it is clear that Thomas has revised the wording of many sayings which have parallels in the Gospels, why should the order not also have been changed radically?[14]

The final bone of contention is whether or not it is possible to discern in Thomas traces of the evangelists' own shaping or redaction of sayings of Jesus. If it is, Thomas would seem to have drawn on the Gospels in their final form – not simply on earlier oral traditions which found their way into the Gospels. Both sides agree that there are some phrases which fall into this category, though they differ in their explanations.

Those who maintain that Thomas is basically independent of the canonical Gospels insist that such sayings are few in number and most readily accounted for as late assimilation of some sayings to the canonical text. They envisage that the original Greek version of Thomas incorporated sayings of Jesus on the basis of oral tradition rather than the written Gospels. At the point when Thomas was translated into Coptic, or during the transmission of the Coptic text of Thomas, some sayings were modified, perhaps unconsciously, in the light of the phraseology of the written Gospels.

This is a strong point. However, it is not a knock-down argument. There are a number of such phrases – perhaps too many to be accounted for as later assimilations.[15] There is one piece of evidence which is particularly striking. Logion 5 reads, 'there is nothing hidden which will not be manifest'. This saying is preserved in the Greek fragment POxy 1, where it closely parallels verbal changes Luke 8:17 makes to Mark 4:22. As several scholars have noted, Thomas seems to presuppose Luke's finished Gospel here: the link with Luke predates the translation into Coptic and cannot be laid at the door of the Coptic translator.[16]

One more general point is relevant. Sayings of Jesus in the Gospel of Thomas have counterparts in all four Gospels, in Q, in 'M' and in 'L' traditions. While it is just possible that Thomas drew solely on many strands of oral traditions from diverse branches of earliest Christianity, it is perhaps more likely that some traditions have been drawn from the canonical Gospels.[17]

From this sketch it will be apparent that the arguments are complex. The evidence does not all point clearly in one direction. Perhaps Thomas drew on an early harmony of the Gospels; this would largely account for the absence of the synoptic order of sayings of Jesus in Thomas. We know that shortly after AD 150 Tatian composed a harmony of the four Gospels. It now seems probable that there were even earlier harmonies.[18]

At least some of the sayings included in Thomas were drawn (but perhaps only indirectly via a harmony) from the written Gospels. Other sayings may have come from the oral tradition: it did not die out once the Gospels were written. This conclusion sounds like a classic compromise between two extremes. None the less it may be closer to the truth than either of the alternatives.

Thomas and Gospel Truth

Thomas does not provide a new royal path back to the historical Jesus. We have only one copy of the full text, written in Coptic about AD 350.   Since there are differences in wording and order between the Greek and Coptic versions, the text of Thomas was fluid. We know that an earlier version was composed in Greek no later than the end of the second century. How much earlier must remain an open question. In addition, there is a further major obstacle in the path of those who wish to use Thomas to reconstruct the teaching of Jesus. In its present form, Thomas is a Gnostic writing. Removal of the Gnostic veneer will never be easy.

About half of Thomas's sayings of Jesus have no close parallels in the canonical Gospels. How many of them may possibly go back to Jesus of Nazareth? Earlier in this chapter mention was made of the recent publication of the American *Jesus Seminar* which has published a translation of Thomas alongside the canonical Gospels. The *Jesus Seminar* is enthusiastic in its advocacy of the value of Thomas for students of the teaching of Jesus, but after critical scrutiny, only five of Thomas's logia are deemed to have good claims to be authentic. The five logia are the five listed above on p.85. While the historian must always be grateful for new scraps of evidence, these five sayings hardly mark a dramatic advance.

But what about the sayings of Jesus in Thomas which do have

counterparts in the New Testament Gospels? Are the versions in Thomas more likely to be original? If they are not simply revised versions of sayings from the canonical Gospels, then this is at least possible. But enough has been said to confirm that there are no easy answers. Reconstruction of a non-Gnostic Greek version of Thomas is problematic, to say the least – and even then we may still be a hundred years after the time of Jesus. In the quest for historical truth, Thomas must not be ignored, but the obstacles are much more formidable than in the case of the four New Testament Gospels. Hence to dub Thomas a 'fifth Gospel' is surely misleading.

Thomas is even less help if we are considering it as a possible resource for Christian theological reflection today. Apart from some 'New Age' enthusiasts, who wants to be a Gnostic?

The 'Secret Gospel of Mark'

This writing may be either a forgery from the end of the second century, or even a twentieth-century forgery; it may contain a hint that Jesus was a homosexual – a hint which Mark the evangelist may have 'censored'. This is a heady mixture, to say the least.

In 1973 Morton Smith published a previously unknown letter of Clement of Alexandria (written c. AD 200). The letter commented on the origin of Mark's Gospel and included some twenty lines of Greek alleged to come from the 'Secret Gospel of Mark'. Smith himself claimed to have discovered Clement's letter in 1958 at the ancient monastery of Mar Saba, twelve miles from Jerusalem.

The plot now thickens. No other scholar has even seen the original manuscript which was found copied onto the back page and inside cover of a seventeenth-century book. On the basis of the photographs published by Smith, some scholars accepted that the letter was a genuine letter written by Clement; some were not persuaded. Twenty years later the manuscript is still not available for general scholarly perusal; this has led an increasing number to doubt whether it comes from antiquity. The distinguished Jewish scholar Jacob Neusner has recently dubbed it 'the forgery of the century'.[19]

Clement is known to have been rather gullible in his acceptance of traditions about apocryphal writings which are obviously spurious. However, in spite of this, and in spite of the possibility of forgery either in the second or the twentieth century, some scholars are still willing to take Clement's letter seriously.

The letter claims that Mark wrote a 'secret Gospel' as well as a 'public Gospel'. The 'Secret Gospel of Mark' was carefully guarded by the church at Alexandria, but none the less Carpocratian heretics got hold of it and produced their own version. Although Clement himself believes that 'Secret Mark' was an expanded version of what we know as Mark's Gospel, a few scholars have claimed that 'Secret Mark' was the original version which was then 'censored' to produce Mark's Gospel.

One of the two additional traditions found in 'Secret Mark' is very brief: 'And after the words, "And he comes into Jericho" (i.e. Mark 10:46), the Secret Gospel adds only, "And the sister of the youth whom Jesus loved and his mother and Salome were there, and Jesus did not receive them." '

The other tradition is rather more controversial. Clement states that the following passage occurs after Mark 10:34:

And they come into Bethany. And a certain woman whose brother had died was there. And, coming, she prostrated herself before Jesus and says to him, 'Son of David, have mercy on me.' But the disciples rebuked her. And Jesus, being angered, went off with her into the garden where the tomb was, and straightway a great cry was heard from the tomb. And going near Jesus rolled away the stone from the door of the tomb. And straightway, going in where the youth was, he stretched forth his hand and raised him, seizing his hand. But the youth, looking upon him, loved him and began to beseech him that he might be with him. And going out of the tomb they came into the house of the youth, for he was rich. And after six days Jesus told him what to do and in the evening the youth comes to him, wearing a linen cloth over his naked body. And he remained with him that night, for Jesus taught him the mystery of the kingdom of God. And thence, arising, he returned to the other side of the Jordan.[20]

Although the Carpocratian heretics interpreted this scene in terms of homosexuality (as did Morton Smith), Clement denies that the 'Secret Gospel' contains the words 'naked man with naked man'. J. D. Crossan correctly stresses that there is no evidence in the above passage that Jesus and the youth are engaged in anything shocking, adding, 'And I prefer to let the Carpocratians alone in salivating over the incident.'[21]

Less easily set aside is the relationship of this passage to Mark's and John's Gospels. There are obvious similarities with John's account of the raising of Lazarus, though there are more parallels with Mark's vocabulary than with John's. So could this possibly be an early form of John 11? As with the Gospel of Peter, a few scholars claim that here we have traditions which are independent of, and earlier than, the canonical Gospels. Most of those who have looked closely at the evidence, however, conclude that 'Secret Mark' is based on Mark's and John's Gospels.[22]

ʊ

From our discussion of these four writings, a clear pattern has emerged. In each case the manuscript evidence is problematic, though for different reasons. In comparison, the manuscript evidence for the New Testament Gospels is extremely good. The claims that these writings contain independent valuable historical evidence for the life and teaching of Jesus do not stand up to scrutiny. Of the four writings, only the Gospel of Thomas is at all likely to contain any genuinely 'new' historical traditions. And Thomas provides us with no more than a handful of sayings with good claims to authenticity.

In comparison with the four New Testament Gospels, the four rivals we have considered have little to offer. This is so, whether we are searching for historical evidence or for 'Gospel truth'. None of these writings contains traditions which might stimulate reflection today on the Christian Gospel.

CHAPTER VIII

ONE GOSPEL AND
FOUR GOSPELLERS

For the apostle Paul there is only one Gospel, a proclaimed *oral* message of good news about the significance of the death and resurrection of Jesus. The Gospel was not a personal discovery made by Paul after a quest for truth; it was God's self-disclosure in the person of Jesus. For Paul there was only one set of Scriptures which acted as the foundation documents for Christian communities, 'the law and the prophets' (Romans 3:21), the writings Christians eventually called the Old Testament.

One hundred and thirty years after Paul's day matters were very different. Irenaeus supported vigorously the church's acceptance of four *written* Gospels, no more, no less. In several passages Irenaeus spoke of the one Gospel in four forms: one Gospel, four Gospellers (i.e. four evangelists). Irenaeus likened the four written Gospels to four pillars holding up the one Gospel, 'the pillar and base of the Church'. By the time Irenaeus became Bishop of Lyons (c. AD 178), an equally radical step beyond Paul was being taken: 'the writings of the evangelists and the apostles' were being set alongside 'the law and the prophets' as Scripture (*Against Heresies* I. 3. 6; III. 12. 9).[1]

How and why did the early church come to accept four written narratives about Jesus as both Gospel and Scripture?

First steps

Although for Paul the focal point of the Gospel is the death and resurrection of Jesus, there are hints in his writings that the Gospel has a narrative element. In Galatians 4:4 Paul refers to God's sending of his Son, Christ Jesus, who was born of a woman, born under the law as an ordinary Jew. For Paul the Gospel includes narratives of what Jesus said and did during his last meal with his disciples (I Corinthians 11:23-6). And the Gospel also includes narratives of what happened on the third day (I Corinthians 15:3-7).

The seeds of the later emergence within Christian communities of a second set of authoritative Scriptures can also be found within Paul's letters. In some passages the Scriptures are referred to and interpreted in the ways used by other learned Jews of the time. But in other passages Paul interprets the Scriptures in the light of his distinctive Christian convictions about God's new revelation in Jesus Christ.

In what is probably his earliest letter, Paul cites a 'word of the Lord' as the basis of his teaching (I Thessalonians 4:15). In I Corinthians 9:9, 13, 14 a command of the Lord is set alongside the plain teaching of the law of Moses: both are equally helpful and authoritative. In I Corinthians 7:10, 12, 25 Paul carefully differentiates his own opinions from the authoritative teaching of the Lord.

In other early Christian circles the words of Jesus were gathered together in small oral collections of sayings which were later incorporated into the Gospels in larger discourses (e.g. Mark 4:1-32; 13:1-37; Matthew 5-7; 10; 13; 18; 23-5). As we saw in *Chapter VI*, about 230 sayings of Jesus, known for a century as Q, were collected together and probably written down before Matthew and Luke used them.

Matthew's Gospel, which circulated much more widely than the other three, is particularly important both for the development of the term 'Gospel' and also for steps towards accepting a written account of the life and teaching of Jesus as 'Scripture'. In Matthew's Sermon on the Mount six paragraphs of sayings of Jesus all have the same structure: 'You have heard that it was said (by God) to the men of old (i.e. in Scripture) . . . but I say to you . . .' (5:21-48). The antithetical pattern implies that Jesus is not simply confirming the teaching of the Old Testament law. On the other hand Matthew is not using sayings of Jesus to contradict God-given Scripture. For Matthew the demands of Jesus surpass those of the law without contradicting it: taken as a whole Matthew 5, together with 6:1-18, confirms that purity of motive rather than mere outward observance is primary.

Matthew uses the term 'Gospel' in two ways. In 4:23 and 9:35 it refers to Jesus' own oral proclamation of good news. In 24:14 and 26:13 Matthew uses the noun 'Gospel' to refer to his own written account of the Jesus story. For the evangelist the sayings and actions of Jesus recorded in his Gospel are to be prominent in the missionary proclamation and catechetical instruction of the Christian communities for which he writes (28:18-20). So Matthew's Gospel itself provided strong encouragement to its readers to set this Gospel alongside the law and the prophets as 'Scripture'.

There is explicit evidence just a few decades later at the end of the first century and the beginning of the second that this was beginning to happen. In a letter written c. AD 96 to the church at Corinth, Clement, bishop of Rome referred to both 'Scripture' and 'the words of the Lord Jesus' as of equal value (I Clement 13:1ff.; 46:2f., 7f.). Already in the Epistle of Barnabas 4:14, perhaps written just before the end of the first century, the phrase 'many are called but few are chosen' from Matthew 22:14 is introduced by, 'as it stands written', a phrase often used in early Christian writings to introduce quotations from the Old Testament Scriptures. Here Matthew's Gospel is implicitly given the same authority as the Scriptures.

In an early second-century letter to the Smyrneans, Ignatius of Antioch notes that neither the prophecies, nor the law of Moses, nor 'the Gospel' (most probably Matthew, which he has quoted just a few paragraphs earlier) has persuaded his opponents (5:1). A similar juxtaposition of 'the Gospel' with the Scriptures is found at 7:2; here Ignatius urges his readers to 'pay attention to the prophets and especially to the Gospel in which the Passion has been made clear to us and the resurrection has been accomplished' (7:2).

From the same period, a letter attributed wrongly to Clement of Rome introduces a quotation of words of Jesus (probably Luke 16:10a-11) with, 'For the Lord says in the Gospel' (II Clement 8:5).

So by the early decades of the second century written accounts of the life of Jesus were beginning to be known as 'Gospels'. Christian communities emphasized that their claims were in line with Scripture, and hence not novel. At the same time, however, they acknowledged that in some ways the teachings of Jesus and the story of his life were both 'new'. Christians found themselves holding together 'new' and 'old' in a delicate balancing act.

Second-century options

By the middle of the second century Jesus traditions were being used in four different ways. First, many traditions continued to circulate orally. In several of the writings just referred to, there are quotations from or allusions to sayings of Jesus which almost certainly come from oral tradition rather than written Gospels. Papias (whom we met on pp.50-2) mentioned that he had asked carefully what the disciples of Jesus had said about 'the commandments given to the faith by the Lord and derived from truth itself'. He then adds, 'For I did not suppose that information from books would help me so much as the word of a living and surviving voice' (as quoted by Eusebius, *H.E.* III. 39. 3-4).

Papias's preference for oral tradition was by no means unusual. For many Christians in the second century oral traditions of the actions and sayings of Jesus were the life-blood of their faith. For some, oral traditions continued to co-exist alongside one or more written Gospels. No doubt as the decades passed, there was a gradual tipping of the balance from oral to written traditions, but it is not entirely clear how and when that happened.

U

For the second option we turn to Marcion. In AD 144 Marcion was rejected by the Christian community in Rome, and his large financial contribution was returned. Marcion, however, did not meekly submit: he went his own way and founded numerous strong churches which were a thorn in the flesh for 'mainstream' Christians for several generations.

Marcion drew a sharp distinction between the Supreme God of goodness whom Jesus came to reveal, and the inferior God who created the material universe and who was the God of Israel. In this and in some other respects Marcion echoed the teaching of Gnostics.

Marcion drew attention to alleged contradictions within the Old Testament. Since it portrayed the inferior Creator-Judge, and not the Father of Jesus, it was in effect rejected. Its place was taken by a 'bible' of two parts: 'Gospel' and 'Apostle'. Marcion seems to have been the first person to link together explicitly as equally authoritative a written Gospel (his own edited version of Luke) and a collection of ten edited letters of Paul (the Pastorals were not included).

Some scholars have claimed that Marcion was the founder of the canon of the New Testament: the church later followed his example and drew up its own list of canonical writings. There is some truth in this view, but it should be noted that Marcion formed his own collection from writings which the church had for some decades placed alongside the Old Testament Scriptures.

There is no clear evidence that Marcion selected Luke from an existing collection of four Gospels. Matthew, with its strong emphasis on the story of Jesus as the fulfilment of the Scriptures, would not have suited his purposes. He may not even have known Mark. Luke's Gospel may have been chosen partly because it was associated with Paul, whom he regarded as the only faithful apostle of Christ. Even Luke's Gospel had to be edited radically in order to serve Marcion's purposes. Passages which referred to the Old Testament roots of Jesus were considered to have been interpolated into the text by 'false apostles'; they had to be removed in order to recover the original pure Gospel of Jesus Christ. Hence Marcion's Luke began as follows: 'In the fifteenth year of Tiberius Caesar (3:1) God descended into Capernaum, a city of Galilee (4:31).' For Marcion true Christianity was a totally new religion which had nothing to do with Judaism.

At the other end of the theological spectrum at this time stand various Jewish-Christians groups, some of whom had their own individual Gospels. These Gospels have survived only in short quotations in much later Christian writings. The origin, number, date and theological perspective of the Jewish-Christian Gospels have been disputed for a very long time.

In a learned study published in 1992, the Dutch scholar A. F. J. Klijn brought some clarity to an immensely complex subject.[2] Klijn concludes that during the second century three Jewish-

Christian Gospels were written at different places: the Gospel according to the Ebionites (east of the Jordan); the Gospel according to the Nazoreans (Beroia in Syria); the Gospel according to the Hebrews (Egypt). The latter two were composed according to the same general principles as the canonical Gospels; the Gospel according to the Ebionites was an attempt to harmonize Gospel traditions on the basis of existing Gospels.

The precise relationship of these writings to the canonical Gospels is not clear, but there are some close links with Matthew's Gospel. The three Jewish Christian Gospels included Jesus traditions chosen and adapted in order to be congenial to Jewish Christians who stood rather closer to Judaism than most other Christian groups.

Marcion's preference for his own version of Luke, and the preference of some Jewish Christians for their own version of Matthew, can be seen as part of the same trend to opt for only one Gospel.

✤

The third option was to weave passages from the four written Gospels into one. This was done about AD 172 by Tatian, whose *Diatessaron* (= 'through [the] four [Gospels]') enjoyed widespread popularity in many circles over a very long period. At an early point it was translated into Syriac, Latin, Armenian and Georgian. In Syriac-speaking churches it was '*the* Gospel' for over two hundred years. Unfortunately Tatian's *Diatessaron* has survived only in short quotations in many languages: reconstruction of it is not for the faint-hearted.

Our knowledge of this influential writing is gradually increasing. Tatian followed John's Gospel for chronology, and used the content of Matthew extensively. He carefully removed duplications and contradictions. By abbreviating the text and adding clarifying words or phrases he was able to turn virtually the entire text of the four Gospels into one comprehensive writing.

Why did Tatian undertake such an ambitious project? Tatian, like other Christians of the time, was troubled by the attacks of critics of Christianity who poked fun at the discrepancies in the Christians' foundation documents. Half a century later Origen was well aware of the problem. He conceded that if the disagreements could not be solved, 'one has to give up one's historical trust with respect to the Gospels.' Origen also noted that the historical discrepancies were so severe that there were only two options: *either* to give up the attempt to establish the truth of (all four) Gospels and at random choose one of them, *or* 'to accept that the truth of these four (Gospels) does not lie in the literal text.'[3] Origen opted for the latter solution and looked for the deeper truths behind the literal text.

Tatian took another path. He believed that truth takes shape in unity and harmony, and therefore sought to set out one complete history in which the discrepancies of the sources were resolved. By using what he took to be sound historical methods, he aimed to produce not a fifth Gospel, but rather what his *Diatessaron* became for many, *the* Gospel.[4]

This was an attractive option. It appealed to many Christians in diverse settings over a long period of time. Eventually, however, the 'four-Gospel' canon won the day. The importance of this outcome both for the modern historian and for Christian theology today can hardly be over-estimated. I shall return to this point at the end of this chapter.

❦

The fourth option was to accept four Gospels, no more, no less. This seems an obvious decision to us today. In the middle of the second century, however, it was by no means certain that this would be the outcome. There were a number of rival Gospels: the Gospel of Peter (*see pp. 78-81*); the Gospel of Thomas (*see pp.84-93*); the Jewish-Christian Gospels discussed earlier in this chapter; Justin Martyr's harmony of Matthew, Mark and Luke; Marcion's truncated Gospel of Luke; several Gospels which had won support in Gnostic circles.

And to complicate matters, in some circles there were doubts about Mark, Luke and John. Only Matthew was above suspicion and used very widely, partly because it was thought to have been written by one of the twelve disciples of Jesus, and partly because of its comprehensive nature, and its carefully arranged and easily memorable five discourses of Jesus. Little is heard of Mark in the second century, perhaps because it was only a 'secondary' Gospel, dependent, it was thought, on Peter. There were similar doubts about Luke: he was dependent on Paul, who was not himself a follower of Jesus during his earthly life. For many, John's Gospel was even more problematic. Justin Martyr, Tatian's teacher, paid little or no attention to John, probably because it had been 'hijacked' by Gnostic circles. John was also under a cloud because of its enthusiastic use by a very different 'heretical' group, the followers of Montanus who was a very influential charismatic prophet. Montanists believed that the promise of the coming of the Paraclete-Spirit in 14:26 and 15:26 had been fulfilled in the person of their leader, Montanus.

Why four Gospels?

During the course of the second century Matthew, Mark, Luke and John gradually came to be accepted by more and more churches as the only accounts of the life of Jesus which were to be accepted as authoritative. No doubt the way 'heretics' regularly appealed to their own favourite Gospel(s) prompted many churches to clarify their reasons for accepting four, no more, no less. No doubt 'on the ground' experience over a long period played a part: Matthew, Mark, Luke and John fed the life and faith of the church in ways that others did not.

In the latter half of the second century three steps were taken which greatly encouraged general acceptance of the 'four-Gospel canon'. I shall discuss the three steps before setting out the main criteria by which the church decided which writings were 'in' and which 'out'.

For the first step, we must return to the Magdalen College fragments of Matthew discussed in *Chapter II*. There I argued that their real significance turns out to be something of a surprise. The fragments are part of what may well be the earliest surviving four-Gospel codex. They provide impressive physical evidence that no later than c. AD 200 the four Gospels were being bound in one volume. Although only fragments have survived, the codex was a most handsome production. The style of writing is formal and meticulous. An immense amount of very skilled planning lies behind its production. It is highly likely that this codex represents a relatively advanced stage in a tradition with deep roots.

We are so used to books today that it is difficult to appreciate the importance of the adoption of the codex–book. The roll was hallowed by centuries of use. The invention of the codex by the Romans was not an immediate success. And yet every one of the 42 papyrus fragments of the Gospels which have come to light is from a codex. Until the end of the third century the roll was still preferred by non-Christians for their writings. Christians took to the codex with enthusiasm. Why?

There must have been a compelling reason why Christians, perhaps early in the second century, broke with convention and started to use only the codex and never the roll for copies of the Gospels. T. C. Skeat's explanation, which I find convincing, is that Christians adopted the codex because it could contain the texts of all four Gospels. No roll could do this. Once the codex began to be used for the four Gospels, it was found to be convenient for single Gospels (which continued to circulate in the second century), and for other Christian writings.[5]

The four-Gospel codex and the four-Gospel canon are like chicken and egg: the need to encourage the use of four Gospels led to the adoption of the codex; binding four Gospels into a codex discouraged use of rival Gospels.

❧

About AD 185 Irenaeus took a rather different step which also strongly influenced acceptance of the four-Gospel canon, when he wrote a lengthy, formal defence of it. Irenaeus insisted that there are four Gospels 'since there are four directions of the world, and four principal winds . . . The four living creatures (of Revelation 4:9) symbolize the four Gospels . . . and there were four principal covenants made with humanity, through Noah, Abraham, Moses and Christ' (*Against Heresies* III. xi.8).

Although Irenaeus refers in this quotation (and elsewhere) to *Gospels* in the plural, for him there is 'one Gospel in fourfold form, held together by one Spirit.' Appeal to the four points of the compass seems bizarre to us, but for Irenaeus the fourfold pattern of the Gospel is so fundamental that it can be likened to the facts of nature. In this carefully argued discussion Irenaeus does not seem to be defending an innovation, but rather to be providing theological grounding for a well-established convention. This is made more likely by the fact that in his association of the four Gospels with the four living creatures of Revelation, Irenaeus is probably drawing on an earlier source.[6]

⚜

A third step was taken at about the same time. The earliest detailed list of New Testament writings, the Muratorian Fragment (or Canon), was drawn up. Its importance for our appreciation of the ways some early Christian writings were accepted as authoritative and some not can hardly be overestimated.

In 1740 the distinguished Italian scholar Muratori published an eighth-century codex which included copies of several Christian writings in Latin. Among them was a list of the books of the New Testament, together with intriguing comments about many of them. The Latin text has been copied (and perhaps even composed) very carelessly; in places it is almost unintelligible.

The Muratorian Fragment provides invaluable information about the books considered to be authoritative by the church in Rome towards the end of the second century. Although this dating and suggested origin have been disputed, it is now accepted by most scholars.[7] A reference to the 'very recent' composition of the *Shepherd* of Hermas 'while Pius was occupying the episcopal chair' points to a date in the second half of the second century.

The author refers first of all to four Gospels, the third and fourth of which are named as those of Luke and John. The opening lines, which referred to Matthew and Mark, are missing. Line 1 may be a reference to Mark's dependence on Peter.

1. at which however he was present, and so he set it down.
   The third book of the Gospel: according to Luke.
   This physician Luke after the ascension of Christ,
   when Paul had taken him with him as a legal expert,
5. composed it in his own name
   in accordance with Paul's thinking. He himself, however, did not see the Lord in the flesh and therefore, as far as he was able to follow events,

he began to tell the story from the nativity of John.
The fourth of the Gospels, that of John, one of the disciples.

10. When his fellow-disciples and bishops encouraged him,
John said, 'Fast with me from today for three days,
and whatever may be revealed to each one,
let us relate it to one another.' The same night
it was revealed to Andrew, one of the apostles,

15. that while all were to revise it, John in his own name
should write down everything. Thus, though different
beginnings are taught in the various Gospel books,
yet that makes no difference to the faith of believers,
since by the one primary Spirit,

20. everything is declared in all (the Gospels)
concerning his nativity, his passion, his resurrection,
his life with his disciples,
and concerning his two comings,
the first in humility when he was despised, which is past,

25. the second, glorious in royal power,
which is still in the future. It is no wonder, then,
that John should so constantly
mention these particular points in his letters,
saying about himself, 'What we have seen with our eyes

30. and heard with our ears and
our hands have handled, these we have written.'
For in this way he claims to be not only an eyewitness and
hearer, but also a writer in order of all the wonderful deeds
of the Lord.

Two points are of particular interest. The detailed comments on
the role of John's fellow disciples in the composition of the
fourth Gospel is striking, as is the emphasis on its conformity
with the other three Gospels. The author of the Fragment was
particularly concerned to encourage second-century Christians
to accept John's Gospel and to show that the fourth Gospel had
the backing of the whole apostolic circle. Since many Gnostic
writers made considerable use of the fourth Gospel, mainstream
Christians were suspicious of it.

In lines 16-20 the Fragment acknowledges that the four
Gospels have different openings, but stresses that by the guidance

of the one Spirit everything of importance for the faith of believers is included in all four Gospels. The author may well have
known that opponents of Christianity seized on the differences
in the Gospels to discredit them. The reference to the different
beginnings of the four Gospels is also found in Irenaeus.

The author stresses that 'by the one primary Spirit' the central
tenets of the one Gospel are found in all four Gospel writings, in
spite of their differences. Although expressed in rather less
sophisticated terms, the Fragment makes essentially the same
point as Irenaeus: there is one Gospel in fourfold form. Both the
Fragment and Irenaeus refer to the 'one Spirit' who holds
together and inspires the four Gospel writings.[8]

Criteria

Although the main lines of the canon were settled by AD 200, it
was not until AD 367 that the first list of early Christian writings
which exactly corresponds to our New Testament was drawn up.
In the fourth century the criterion of alleged apostolic authorship was crucial in discussions on the boundaries (or 'canon') of
authoritative writings. However, there is evidence in the
Muratorian Fragment which confirms that this criterion was
important much earlier: the Christian writings which are to be
accepted as authoritative are referred to collectively as 'the apostles' (line 80). But appeal to apostolic authorship could not be
used as the sole way of determining which Gospels were to be
accepted as Scripture, and which were not. From the middle of
the second century (and perhaps even earlier) several Gospels circulated under the name of an apostle. Which were 'true' and
which were 'false'?

Appeal was often made to conformity with 'the rule of faith'
('the Gospel', to use the terminology I have adopted in this
book) which was the foundation stone of the church's convictions. In the second century there was much greater diversity
within the Christian tradition than there was later: the terms
'orthodoxy' and 'heresy' can be used only with great care, and
are perhaps better avoided. None the less even in the second
century Christian writers knew that certain views were unac-
ceptable, and they knew that their opponents based their views

on writings which should not be accepted. Line 67 of the Muratorian Fragment stresses that 'gall cannot be mixed with honey', and rejects vigorously the writings of Valentinus the Gnostic leader, a book of Psalms from the circle of Marcion, and the writings of Montanus, the founder of the Montanists.

In later centuries a third criterion became important: continuous acceptance and use of a writing by the church at large. Towards the end of the fourth century Augustine noted that in deciding which writings to accept as canonical, the Christian reader 'will prefer those that are received by all Catholic Christians to those which some of them do not receive. Among those, again, which are not received by all, let him prefer those which the more numerous and the weightier churches receive to those which fewer and less authoritative churches hold' (*De doct. chr.* ii. 12). However this criterion by no means settled matters. Who could decide which were 'the more numerous and weightier churches'? And in the second century at least, it was not always clear just which of the diverse strands of Christianity would prevail as 'catholic Christianity'.

The Muratorian Fragment (lines 75-80) refers to yet another criterion: the date of a writing. The *Shepherd* of Hermas, it notes, does not have the same authority as other early Christian writings because it was written 'quite recently, in our own times . . . after the time of the apostles'. This criterion was not appealed to frequently in antiquity – after all, 'heretics' could easily make similar claims. However, it is often prominent in modern discussion of the canon: none of the Gospels which were 'passed over' was written as early as the four which were accepted. I believe that this is an important point. But one must also bear in mind that some of the Jesus *traditions* incorporated in later writings such as the Didache, and the Gospel of Thomas, may well antedate the writing of the four canonical Gospels.

⚘

From the middle of the first century Christians began to cite Jesus traditions alongside references to Scripture (the Old Testament). In the second century we begin to see individual Gospel writings used in the same way. In the middle of the second century Justin mentions that in the context of Christian worship 'the memoirs of the apostles (i.e. the Gospels) and the writings of the prophets' should be read 'as long as time allows' (*I Apology* 1.67).[9] The reading of the Gospels *in worship* was a major step towards accepting them as 'new' Scriptures, alongside what came to be known later as 'the Old Testament'. In the Muratorian Fragment (lines 77–80) there is a similar reference to the reading of authoritative texts in the context of worship: the term 'prophets' is used to refer to the Old Testament, the term 'apostles' is juxtaposed as a reference to the Christian writings the Fragment accepts as authoritative. Although it was a long time until a concept of a 'closed canon' of New Testament writings emerged, boundaries of acceptability were being drawn by the end of the second century.

In the second half of the second century the 'four-Gospel canon' began to emerge. It was by no means as natural a process as we might imagine today. We have seen in the comments of Irenaeus and the Muratorian Fragment a strong insistence that though there are four written Gospels, there is only one Gospel, and one Spirit: 'one Gospel in fourfold form' to quote Irenaeus's important terminology.

This conviction is also clearly expressed in the titles given to the four Gospels. It is not clear exactly when this happened. As soon as a Christian community began to use two or more Gospels, it would be necessary to distinguish them. That was done no later than the closing decades of the second century by the use of the phrase, 'the Gospel *according to* Matthew', 'the Gospel *according to* Mark . . . Luke . . . John' as titles on manuscript copies.[10] Note that the titles were not 'the Gospel *of . . .*' *There is only one Gospel, and four Gospellers (Evangelists).*

If Tatian's *Diatessaron* had won the day, matters would have been very different. One 'historically accurate' written Gospel would have been *the* expression of the one-Gospel message of the church. Plurality of theological convictions would have been severely restricted. By removing discrepancies, contradictions, and repetitions, Tatian thought he was providing the Christian faith with a more secure historical foundation. If he had been totally successful, today we would have *less* historical evidence for the life and teaching of Jesus of Nazareth. For as we shall see in *Chapter XI,* Jesus traditions which are attested in *several strands* of the evidence are particularly valuable.

By opting for four written Gospels instead of one, many Christians in the second half of the second century decided to live with the historical complications which ensued, even though critics were throwing the discrepancies in their faces. They were convinced that the historical difficulties did not undermine the one Gospel of Jesus Christ, inspired by the one Spirit. They also accepted that the significance of Jesus Christ could be understood in a variety of ways.

Today John's association of Christ with Creation (John 1:3) sometimes seems to sit a little awkwardly alongside the less sophisticated ways Matthew, Mark and Luke spell out the significance of Jesus. 'Christology from above' and 'Christology from below', to use the standard theological jargon, are uneasy bedfellows. The decision to hold Matthew, Mark, Luke and John together in the four-Gospel canon ought to prompt serious theological reflection today.

CHAPTER IX

JESUS: THE ARCHAEOLOGICAL EVIDENCE

Archaeological discoveries fascinate many people. I am no exception: every time I walk to my local commuter station I pass a recently excavated fourth-century Roman villa. I often wish the excavations could be extended under the adjacent busy road where there are likely to be more remains of the villa. If a Roman villa on the edge of London still weaves a spell and stirs the imagination, how much more so with archaeological discoveries from the Palestine of the time of Jesus. So it is no surprise to find that reports of archaeological finds regularly excite the media. All too often, however, exaggerated claims are made. Sober scholarly assessment sometimes tells a different story.

Archaeology seems to offer an easier path to 'Gospel truth' than literary evidence, but this is an illusion. Artefacts or foundations of buildings uncovered by the archaeologist's spade, brush and vacuum cleaner have to be dated, interpreted and set in a social context. And these tasks are no easier than in the case of literary evidence.

Many of the most important recent discoveries from the time of Jesus have been unspectacular and have not caught the attention of the media. Discoveries of some first-century pottery and a handful of coins from Galilee or Jerusalem are not likely to feature in newspaper colour supplements, but they can often bring a fresh perspective on aspects of the political, cultural and religious world in which Jesus lived and taught.

In recent years two important steps forward have been taken by archaeologists working in Galilee and Judaea. In the past the key question has often been, 'Does this discovery prove (or disprove) the reliability of the Gospels?' Archaeologists now hope

that their work may lead to a better appreciation of the *social*
world of Jesus and his followers. So archaeologists often work
hand in hand with social anthropologists. This development is
full of promise for the future.

The second step forward is so simple that one wonders why
it was often ignored in the past. Until recently archaeologists
and specialists working with literary evidence managed to live
largely separate lives. Now they both realize that they need one
another's expertise. No longer will scholars writing major books
on Jesus of Nazareth ignore the site reports of archaeologists
working in Galilee. No longer will archaeologists attempt to
interpret their finds without considering the relevant literary
evidence most carefully. In exploring the social world of Jesus,
one needs a spade in one hand and a text in the other.

I have selected examples of several different kinds of archaeological discoveries. I shall follow broadly the life of Jesus – from
Nazareth to his burial. The most important discovery of the
twentieth century, the Dead Sea Scrolls, has already been discussed in *Chapter II*.

Galilee

What was life like in Nazareth where Jesus grew up? Were the
villagers simple peasants dependent both economically and cul-
turally on the neighbouring capital city of Sepphoris? To what
extent were the inhabitants of Nazareth aware of the heavy hand
of Rome? And how close were the religious ties with Jerusalem
and its temple to the south? These questions are high on the current agenda of archaeologists working in Galilee. Steady progress
has been made in recent years, and further advances can be
expected.

Today Christian tourists to Israel will almost certainly be taken
to Nazareth, even though there are very few significant first-
century remains to be seen. In spite of intensive searches, there
is as yet no trace of the synagogue at Nazareth to which so much
importance is attached in Luke 4:16-30. Recent estimates put
the population of Nazareth at the time of Jesus at about 500.
Nazareth was a satellite village of Sepphoris, about 5 km to the
northwest – less than an hour's walk away.

Visitors to Israel must place Sepphoris high on their list of priorities. Work there has been gathering pace in recent years. At last visitors are being given the assistance they need in order to appreciate the site fully. Sepphoris has a Roman theatre, an extensive Jewish quarter, a superb large Roman villa with a mosaic which depicts the 'Mona Lisa of Galilee', several streets almost as fascinating as the streets of Pompeii, and a number of eye-catching mosaics. Digging still continues; perhaps only a quarter of the city has been excavated. Dating and interpreting the rich finds will continue for decades.

Did Jesus visit Sepphoris? How would Sepphoris have been perceived from Nazareth – as a cosmopolitan city to be avoided by a loyal Jew, as a fortified Roman base to be despised, or as a market town with a largely Jewish population and deep Jewish roots?

When Joseph took Mary and the child Jesus to Nazareth, Herod Antipas (the Rome-sponsored ruler) was recruiting workmen to rebuild and expand his capital Sepphoris. Some of the workmen may well have come from Nazareth. When Josephus mentions that Herod fortified Sepphoris as 'the ornament of all Galilee' (*Antiquities* xviii. 27), he may have had in mind both the splendour and the strength of its buildings, as well as its hill-top location with extensive views over fertile Galilee.

The well-preserved Roman theatre seated about 5,000 people. In his excellent guide *The Holy Land*, the distinguished New Testament scholar Jerome Murphy-O'Connor writes:

> The most natural explanation of Jesus' use of *hypokritēs* ('stage actor') in criticism of the religious leaders of his day (e.g. Mark 7:6) is that he went to this theatre, the nearest one to Nazareth. The word, which has no Semitic equivalent, would not have been part of the vocabulary of a village artisan.[1]

If this is correct, perhaps many sayings of Jesus should be interpreted against a Graeco-Roman rather than a Jewish background, and an urban rather than a village setting. A great deal hangs on the dating of the theatre, but unfortunately archaeological opinion is divided. Several specialists believe that the theatre was built in time for possible visits by Jesus; others date it up to one hundred years later. The latter view seems to be gaining ground.

Excavations have uncovered nearly thirty Jewish ritual baths (*miqva'ot*) in a number of houses in one part of the city. Some of them date from the time of Jesus. This evidence, as well as evidence for strict burial outside the city precincts, strongly suggests that at the time of Jesus Sepphoris had a large Jewish population which sought to observe the Jewish law faithfully.

About twenty years after the rebuilding of Sepphoris, Herod Antipas moved his capital to a site on the Sea of Galilee and named it Tiberias after the Roman emperor (cf. Luke 3:1). Archaeological work continues there, but very little of it has yet been published.

The Gospels do not record that Jesus ever taught or healed in Sepphoris or Tiberias, the two leading Galilean cities of his day. Since Matthew 11:20-4 = Luke 10:12-15 (Q) refers to unsuccessful visits to places in Galilee, the failure of the Gospels to mention visits to Sepphoris and Tiberias is not likely to be due to Jesus' lack of success there. It is much more probable that Jesus deliberately avoided both cities, for they were the power bases of the despised Herodian family and the ruling elite of the day.[2] They posed a direct threat to Jesus and his followers.

❦

Mark records that Jesus moved from Nazareth and set up base in Capernaum (1:9, 21). Capernaum is mentioned in several other passages in the Gospels (e.g., Mark 2:1; 9:33; Matthew 4:13; 8:5 = Luke 7:1-10, and in John 2:12; 4:46; 6:17, 24, 59). This large fishing village was used by Jesus as his headquarters in Galilee.

Excavations there have unearthed a splendid fourth-century synagogue (*see Plates 10 and 12*). The remains are so substantial that they are unlikely ever to be removed in order to allow full excavations underneath. There is evidence that the white limestone synagogue was built over the black basalt foundations and walls of a first-century synagogue, the one visited by Jesus (Mark 1:21; Luke 7:5; John 6:59).

Rather extensive remains of houses have been uncovered. Capernaum was planned carefully with 40 x 40 metre blocks, each with three or four one-storey houses with rooms opening

on to common courtyards. About 100 metres from the synagogue is a first-century house which since 1968 has been claimed
by some to be Simon Peter's house in which Jesus healed the
fever which had struck Peter's mother-in-law (Mark 1:29) (*see
Plates 10 and 11*). Early Roman pottery and coins under the floor
confirm that it existed in the first century. From the graffiti
scratched by Christians in the plaster of the house after it was
rebuilt as a church in the middle of the fifth century, it is clear
that in the fourth century, if not earlier, this house was revered as
Peter's. Was this wishful thinking by Christian pilgrims? Or is it
possible that the graffiti reflect an accurate tradition which survived from the first century? This must remain an open question.

There is new archaeological evidence which indicates that
Romans lived in Capernaum in the first century.[3] So Capernaum
was not isolated from the presence of an occupying power. The
centurion who asked Jesus to heal his very ill servant was a
Roman, but neither Matthew (8: 5-13) nor Luke (7:1-10) tells
us why he was there.

As a result of a prolonged drought in 1985, the level of Lake
Galilee dropped alarmingly. There was one happy outcome: not
far from Capernaum the timbers of a boat appeared. Study of the
timbers (which included carbon 14 testing) and of the cooking
pot and lamp found in the boat confirmed that it came from the
time of Jesus, so it was quickly dubbed the 'Jesus boat'.

Plenty of archaeological evidence confirms that at the time of
Jesus Capernaum was a thriving commercial and agricultural
centre, partially supported by fishing. About 1,000 people lived
there, not the 12-15,000 suggested by some earlier scholars!
Capernaum was on an important trade route, only 5 kilometres
from the border between Herod Antipas's territory of Galilee and
Perea, and his brother Philip's territories on the other side of the
Jordan. As Mark 2:14 notes, there was a customs office there.
Capernaum would have been a natural place for Jesus to choose
as the base for an itinerant preaching and healing ministry.

Jerusalem

Between 1969 and 1983 extensive archaeological excavations
were carried out in part of Jerusalem known as the Herodian

quarter, just to the south and east of the Temple mount. These were the first excavations of a first-century residential area in Jerusalem. The site was opened to the public in 1987. The remains are very clearly displayed, with excellent background information.

The remains of six luxurious houses, as well as a large number of artefacts, were discovered. Coins found there, as well as signs of destruction by fire when Jerusalem fell to the Romans in AD 70, confirm that these buildings near the Temple existed at the time of Jesus. The everyday life of wealthy Jerusalem families, probably aristocratic priestly families, was revealed for the first time.

At least one and often two or more ritual baths (*miqva'ot*) existed in each house for purification from uncleannness (*see Plate 13*). The owners obviously kept the Jewish law meticulously. The houses contain numerous floor mosaics and decorated wall frescoes which are very similar in design to those found in many parts of the Graeco-Roman world. Geometric and floral patterns abound: biblical commands against images led the owners of the houses to avoid mosaics depicting people or animals (and, of course, gods and goddesses). The frescoes recall the decoration found in many houses at Pompeii. So right in the heart of Jerusalem the cultural influence of the Graeco-Roman world made a strong impact, even among families which maintained their distinctive Jewish way of life.

The lifestyle of the wealthy owners of these houses may well have caused outrage to the Galilean prophet Jesus when he visited Jerusalem. The contrast between these houses and the houses in Capernaum from the time of Jesus could hardly be more stark. At this point archaeology forces one to return to the literary evidence with two key questions in mind. Did Jesus challenge the religious and political establishment in Jerusalem and call in God's name for the renewal of Israel? If so, did this confrontation cause his downfall? I shall return to these questions in *Chapter XIV.*

Mark 14:3-9 records that in the house of Simon the leper in Bethany (a village very close to Jerusalem) a woman poured very costly perfume over the head of Jesus. Mark attaches great significance to this action: Jesus is reported to have said, 'she has anointed my body beforehand for burial. Truly I tell you, wherever the Gospel is proclaimed in the whole world, what she has done will be told in remembrance of her' (14:8-9). The Greek verb used to describe the way the woman opened the small bottle of perfume has long puzzled readers, for it means 'smash' or 'break'. If she 'smashed' the alabaster jar, then surely fragments would have fallen into the costly ointment.

Archaeologists now seem to have solved this particular puzzle. Small perfume flasks with very long narrow necks have been discovered in first-century tombs on the edge of the Valley of Hinnom, Jerusalem's refuse tip. They would have been ideal for storing expensive perfume; inexpensive pottery jars were normally used for storing perfume for everyday use. The woman in Simon's house may have snapped off the neck of an alabaster jar cleanly before pouring the valuable perfumed ointment over the head of Jesus.

ꮤ

In 1990 on the southern outskirts of Jerusalem a spectacular discovery was made. During preparation of a leisure park a cave with twelve burial boxes for bones of deceased persons (ossuaries) was found. Six ossuaries had been ransacked by ancient tomb robbers; the other six had not been disturbed. One bears an inscription on the long side of the ossuary, 'Yehosef bar Qayafa', Joseph son of Caiaphas; on the shorter side is an apparently abbreviated form, 'Yehosef bar Qafa.' Was this the burial box which contained the bones of the high priest Caiaphas who handed Jesus over to the Romans? (cf. Matthew 26:3, 57; John 18:13-14) The ossuary contained the bones from six different people, including a male aged about 60. The unusually elaborate decoration on the ossuary and the inscriptions both suggested that the bones of Caiaphas may have been placed in this very ossuary. Josephus refers to a 'Joseph who was called Caiaphas of the high priesthood' (*Antiquities* xviii. 35), so Caiaphas may have been a family name or a nickname. The inscription 'Joseph son of Caiaphas' does not necessarily mean that Caiaphas was Joseph's father; it may well refer to Joseph of the family of Caiaphas, as the reference in Josephus suggests.

The discovery was reported in two articles in the September/

October 1992 issue of the responsible magazine *Biblical Archaeology Review* which has a wide circulation in North America. A year later I saw the 'Caiaphas' ossuary on display in Washington DC, accompanied by an excellent video. Since such artefacts are rarely allowed to leave Israel, this was an unexpected treat. However, after careful linguistic study, the distinguished Cambridge scholar William Horbury has raised doubts about the original interpretation of the inscriptions on the ossuaries. He concludes that on the linguistic evidence now available, the identification with the high priest Caiaphas cannot be classed as probable.[4]

ᴍ

The Gospels do not give detailed information on the precise way in which Jesus was crucified. But Luke 24: 39 implies that the hands and feet of Jesus were nailed to the cross, and John 20:25, 27 refers explicitly to the nailprints in his hands. These two references were combined in later Christian piety in which devotion to the 'five wounds of Jesus' (his two hands, two feet and side) became popular. Since there was no archaeological evidence for the custom of nailing hands or feet to a cross, some doubted the accuracy of the Gospels at this point.

In 1970, however, an Israeli archaeologist published an account of the discovery of a first-century ossuary from Jerusalem. It contained the bones of a young man who, as the inscription on the ossuary stated, was named Yehohanan and had been crucified. The right heel bone had been pierced by an iron nail and there was said to be evidence of nails piercing the wrist or forearm. The bones of the lower leg had been broken by a blow. According to John 19:32 this was done to the fellow victims of Jesus, but not to Jesus himself. Traces of wood were found on either side of the bones and it was a natural inference that the nail had secured the victim to a cross.

This discovery provided for the first time *archaeological* evidence for the crucifixion in Palestine of a near-contemporary of Jesus. Two details found in John's Gospel – the very Gospel which was widely thought to be the least likely of the four to contain accurate historical information – seemed to be confirmed: the breaking of the bones of a crucifixion victim and nailing to a cross. Needless to say this evidence was used to refute the view that the Gospel narratives are irresponsible fabrications. Some earlier writers had suggested that the fourth evangelist had invented the reference to the breaking of the bones of the two crucified with Jesus, but not the bones of Jesus himself, in order to make the death of Jesus conform precisely to Old Testament passages such as Exodus 12:46 or Psalm 34:20.

In 1985 much more rigorous investigation uncovered a number of errors in the original report. The leg bones do not seem to have been deliberately broken while the young man was alive on the cross; bone-breaking may have occurred during the course of putting the bones into the ossuary. There is clear evidence that Jehohanan's feet were nailed to the upright, with an olive wood plaque between the head of each nail and the foot. However, there is no evidence for *nailing* the arms or wrists, which would have been tied to the crossbar.[5]

In spite of the need to revise aspects of the original report, this discovery provides important archaeological evidence for crucifixion at the time of Jesus. It should remove scepticism about the accuracy of Luke's and John's references to the nailing of Jesus to the cross.

ꙮ

This reference to the crucifixion of Jesus brings us finally to the Turin Shroud. All four Gospels record that Joseph of Arimathea asked Pilate for the body of Jesus and wrapped it in linen. Ever since the Middle Ages some have claimed that a four-metre-long piece of linen in the cathedral at Turin is in fact the very cloth in which the body of Jesus was wrapped. The history of the shroud can be traced from the middle of the fourteenth century, but nothing certain is known about any earlier history.

Does this cloth date from the first century? For many Christians the shroud offered tangible proof of the reliability of the Gospels – 'Gospel truth'. Those who were doubtful about the cloth's authenticity stressed that even if scientific study could confirm beyond reasonable doubt that the cloth dates from the first century, how could we ever be sure that it provided a link with Jesus of Nazareth? Many others who died violently in the first century would have been wrapped in linen for burial.

'Believers' in the shroud pointed to two pieces of evidence.

Traces of pollen grains from plants which grow in and near Palestine have been found on it; however, one of the pollens common there, that of the olive tree, is missing. Much more puzzling is the startling image which appears when the shroud is photographed, a phenomenon noticed when the shroud was first photographed in 1898.

The church authorities in Turin finally granted scientists permission to submit very small sections of the cloth to three different laboratories in order to test radioactive carbon 14 particles. This is a well-tried method for dating fragments of living material. In order to carry out 'blind' testing, other small pieces of cloth known to belong to the first century and to the Middle Ages were sent to the laboratories along with the fragments of the Shroud. In 1988 the results were announced. All three laboratories gave the same answer: the cloth was made between AD 1260 and 1390, to a 95 per cent degree of certainty.

On hearing that news, I confidently expected that no more would be heard of the Turin Shroud. Not a bit of it. In 1994 at least three more books on the Shroud were published. One audaciously questions the validity of the scientific tests carried out independently in internationally renowned laboratories in Zurich, Tucson and Oxford. Another accepts the carbon 14 dating, but claims that the church commissioned Leonardo da Vinci to fake an image on a shroud in order to hoodwink the gullible. The third has a very different Vatican conspiracy theory: the Vatican agreed to carbon 14 dating to put a stop to persistent reports that the Shroud proved that Jesus survived crucifixion. Just for once, I am refusing to give bibliographical details: I do not wish to supply even a whiff of the oxygen of publicity to books which spurn scientific and historical scholarship.

The story of the Turin Shroud confirms the attachment many people have to objects said to be associated with Jesus. For them seeing is believing. At the end of the first century readers of John's Gospel were reminded that this is a false trail: 'Blessed are those who have not seen and yet have come to believe' (John 20:29). In other words, 'Gospel truth' does not reside in first-century shrouds or stones.

The examples of archaeological discoveries I have discussed in this chapter sound warning bells. Extravagant media claims may be undermined by more careful patient research. Even cautious conclusions may well have to be revised in the light of further research. For every two steps forward, there may be one backwards.

However, in the past 50 years there have been a series of discoveries which have withstood critical appraisal and revolutionized our understanding of the religious, cultural and political world of Jesus. In recent years, the pace of genuine advance, especially in Galilee, has undoubtedly quickened. Aided by technological developments and further inter-disciplinary co-operation, it will continue to do so.

In the future new discoveries from the time of Jesus will probably be on a small scale, not dramatic enough to catch the attention of the media. I hope my prediction proves to be incorrect. It is based in part on the results of 'Operation scroll', launched in 1993 by the Israel Antiquities Authority. The Judaean desert, including the area near Qumran, was scoured very thoroughly once more, but the harvest was meagre.

Small-scale discoveries will continue to shed new light on the social world of Jesus and his followers. They may well help us to read the literary evidence for the life of Jesus more sensitively.

CHAPTER X

JESUS TRADITIONS
OUTSIDE THE GOSPELS

WHERE IS THE evidence, and how reliable is it? The first step in our quest for Jesus of Nazareth must be to locate and assess the evidence. The historian will naturally want to consider carefully Jesus traditions *outside* the Gospels as well as the evidence of the Gospels themselves. There are snippets of information in pagan and Jewish writings. Since this evidence comes from 'neutral' writers, it may seem to some to be more valuable than evidence from the four evangelists who wrote from their own distinctive Christian perspectives. However, the pagan and Jewish writers whose comments are set out below had their own axes to grind. Their evidence is neither less 'biased' nor any easier to interpret than that of the evangelists. In the final pages of this chapter I shall turn to Christian evidence outside the Gospels.

Pagan Evidence

The great Roman historian Tacitus was born about AD 56; we do not know when he died. His *Annals* were intended to cover the history of Rome from AD 14 to 68. Only about half of this ambitious history has survived. Unfortunately the section of the *Annals* which covered AD 29 to 32, and which might have referred to the trial and crucifixion of Jesus, has not survived. The earliest manuscript dates from the eleventh century! In marked contrast with the early strong evidence for the text of the Gospels which was discussed in *Chapter IV*, the textual evidence for the *Annals* is limited.[1]

In his account of the outbreak of the great fire of Rome in AD 64, Tacitus tells us – all too briefly – about the Christians who were blamed by the Emperor Nero for the fire in order to squash rumours that he himself was responsible.

> They got their name from Christ, who was executed by sentence of the procurator Pontius Pilate in the reign of Tiberius. The pernicious superstition, suppressed for the moment, broke out again, not only throughout Judaea, the birthplace of the plague, but also in the city of Rome . . . (*Annals* 15:44)

There is no reason to doubt the genuineness of these negative comments. Although they are brief, they are invaluable. Tacitus does not say that Jesus was *crucified* by Pilate, but his readers would naturally assume this. He states that the execution of Christ was only a temporary set-back and implies that the Christ-movement began before his execution.

The reference to Pilate as 'procurator' is important. In an inscription discovered in 1961 at Caesarea Maritima (on the coast of Israel), Pilate is referred to as 'prefect', not 'procurator', during his term of duty in Judaea (*see Plate 15*). Tacitus may have slipped in his reference to Pilate as 'procurator', or it is possible that that the two terms were almost interchangeable.

Tacitus was a close friend of Pliny the Younger, governor of Bithynia in Asia Minor AD 111-113. One of Pliny's letters written to the Emperor Trajan in about AD 111 is of special interest. He passes on to the Emperor information he has gleaned about Christians:

> They meet on a certain fixed day before sunrise and sing an antiphonal hymn to Christ as a god, and bind themselves with an oath: not to commit any crime, but to abstain from all acts of theft, robbery and adultery, and from breaches of trust. . . (*Letter* 10:96)

Pliny's references to early Christian worship, and to Christ as a god, are striking, but neither in this letter nor in Trajan's reply is there any reference to the life and teaching of Jesus.

Writing about AD 120 Suetonius may refer briefly to Christians in his life of the Emperor Claudius: 'He (Claudius) expelled the Jews from Rome because of the riots they were causing at the instigation of Chrestus.' 'Chrestus' is probably a spelling variant for 'Christus'. If so, then Suetonius (or an earlier source) states that 'Christ' encouraged (directly or indirectly) Jews or Jewish-Christians to riot in Rome in AD 49. While this comment is of great interest to students of earliest Christianity in Rome, we are not much further forward in our quest for information about Jesus of Nazareth.

Later in the second century the satirist Lucian of Samosata mentions that Christians worshipped 'that great man who was crucified in Palestine because he introduced this new cult into the world.' Lucian also notes that Christians 'worship that crucified sage of theirs and live according to his laws' (*Peregrinus* 11). By the latter part of the second century at least some educated pagans knew a little about Christianity: Jesus a 'sophist' or sage was crucified in Palestine.

These extremely meagre comments are all that we have from pagan writers. Why are we not told more? As it happens, few Roman writers provide information on the history of the Roman empire in the east. From the point of view of a Roman historian, Jesus of Nazareth and his followers were of no interest. Judaea was an obscure corner of the empire and the execution of a troublemaker was of no consequence.

Josephus

The most important references to Jesus outside the New Testament are found in the writings of the Jewish historian Josephus (born in Jerusalem in AD 37, died c. 100). In AD 66 he was prominent in the Jewish resistance against the advancing Roman armies in Galilee and was taken prisoner. He later 'changed sides' and supported the Roman cause. The Flavian Roman Emperors Vespasian and his sons Titus and Domitian became his patrons. Hence he is often known by his Roman name, Flavius Josephus. His most extensive work, *Jewish Antiquities*, was written in AD 93-4. Since it includes a brief reference to Jesus as the brother of James, a long paragraph about Jesus, and an extended account of the life and death of John the Baptist, it is of considerable importance in any quest for the life and teaching of Jesus of Nazareth. We shall defer discussion of Josephus's comments on John the Baptist until *Chapter XIV.*

Before we look at the other passages, two important points must be noted. In one respect, Josephus is not unlike the New Testament evangelists: he also wrote from a distinctive 'biased' point of view which has to be kept constantly in mind. Josephus wrote in an apartment in the Emperor's house in Rome, so naturally he sets out a 'pro-Roman' point of view. He hoped that fellow Jews would read his writings and be more sympathetic both to Roman conduct during the Jewish war, and to his own decision to switch sides. He also hoped that his Roman readers would gain greater respect for Jewish history, culture and religion. However, his writings were later largely ignored by his fellow Jews who considered him to be a 'traitor'. They were preserved through the centuries by Christians who recognized the importance of the comments of a Jewish historian on Jesus and John the Baptist. As we shall see, at some point Josephus's comments on Jesus were interpolated by Christians.

The textual evidence for the writings of Josephus is much inferior both in quality and quantity to the evidence for the Gospels set out in *Chapter IV* . Only a dozen manuscripts of the *Antiquities* have survived. The most reliable three Greek manuscripts date from the thirteenth, fourteenth and fifteenth centuries. Two earlier manuscripts from the eleventh century are much less satisfactory. A Latin translation made in the fifth or sixth centuries is especially important. We do not have a single papyrus fragment of the *Antiquities*, and only one papyrus fragment of the *Jewish War* which contains 38 complete words and 74 words in part.

ᴜ

Josephus refers in passing to Jesus in a comment on the stoning of James in AD 62. He notes that Ananus the high priest, a Sadducee, acted rashly:

He convened the judges of the Sanhedrin, and brought before it the brother of Jesus the so-called Messiah, James by name, and also some others. When he had accused them of transgressing the law, he handed them over to be stoned.' (*Antiquities* xx. 200)

This brief comment is most unlikely to be a later Christian interpolation. A Christian would have referred to James as 'the brother *of the Lord*' (as in Galatians 1:19; cf. I Corinthians 9:5), and
would not have referred to Jesus as 'the *so-called* Messiah'. James
is a common name, so some further identification would be
expected, normally in the form, 'James, son of X'. Here, however, James is identified with reference to his better-known
brother, Jesus. This single Greek sentence does not tell us very
much, but it provides further confirmation from outside the
Gospels that James was known as the brother of Jesus, and that
Jesus was recognized by some as the Messiah.

Josephus implies that Jesus is well known: he probably intends
his readers to recall that he had earlier said rather more about
Jesus. There is in fact an earlier extended, but rather problematic reference to Jesus in *Antiquities* xviii. 63-64. Although this
passage is found in all the manuscripts of the writings of Josephus
which have survived, and although it is quoted in full by the
Christian historian Eusebius early in the fourth century, in its
present form it cannot be attributed to pro-Roman Jewish historian Josephus. The passage refers to Jesus as a wise man, but adds
a comment which can only have been written by a Christian, 'if
one ought to call him a man'. Jesus is referred to as 'the Christ'
and he is said to have 'appeared alive again on the third day' to
his followers in fulfilment of the prophets.

Although in the past many scholars have written the whole
paragraph off as a later interpolation by a pious Christian scribe,
opinion has changed recently. Once the obviously Christian
additions are removed, the remaining comments are consistent
with Josephus's vocabulary and style. It is possible that later
Christians not only interpolated this statement, but also removed
some negative comments about Jesus of which they disapproved.
This paragraph is preceded by a reference to two riots during
Pilate's term of office, so there may well originally have been a
reference to the trouble Jesus caused. Perhaps Josephus referred
to Jesus as 'the so-called Christ', as he did in his comment on the
death of James, the brother of Jesus.

The whole paragraph reads as follows in the Greek manuscripts which have survived; words and phrases I take to be
Christian additions are placed in square brackets:

About this time lived Jesus, a wise man [if indeed one ought to refer to him as a man]. For he was one who did surprising deeds, a teacher of those who delight in accepting the unusual. He brought trouble to many Jews, and also many from the Greek world. [He was the Messiah-Christ.] On the accusation of our leading men Pilate condemned him to the cross, but those who had loved him from the first did not cease to do so. [For on the third day he appeared to them again alive, just as the divine prophets had spoken about these and countless other marvellous things about him.] And to this day the tribe of Christians, named after him, has not died out.

Once the obvious interpolations are removed, this paragraph gives an ambivalent or even a mildly hostile assessment of Jesus – one which can be attributed to Josephus with confidence. Jesus is portrayed as a 'wise man', a teacher and a miracle-worker who impressed rather gullible people. The Gospels suggest that Jesus accepted the faith of non-Jews only with great reluctance, but for the benefit of his Roman patrons Josephus might well have exaggerated the numbers of Gentiles who were attracted to Jesus. The extent to which Jewish leaders were involved in the arrest and trial of Jesus is a much disputed issue. I shall return to this passage in *Chapter XIII*, when negative portraits of Jesus both within and outside the Gospels will be considered.

Further Jewish evidence

The handful of scattered references to Jesus in writings of the rabbis are even more difficult to assess. The earliest rabbinic document in written form is the Mishnah which was compiled from earlier traditions about AD 200. It does not contain any references to Jesus, though this is hardly surprising since it contains sixty-three tractates of religious law with very few historical references of any kind. Commentaries or supplements to the Mishnaic traditions (known as Gemaras) were set alongside the Mishnah itself in the Palestinian and Babylonian Talmuds which were completed c. AD 350 and 500 respectively.

In this supplementary material there are two passages which

may reflect a fairly widespread rabbinic assessment of Jesus. In
b. Sanh. *43a* an anonymous tradition is introduced with the for-
mula, 'It is said', an indication that it is a *baraitha*, an old tradition:

> On the eve of Passover Yeshu was hanged. For forty days
> before the execution took place, a herald went forth and
> cried, 'He is going forth to be stoned because *he has prac-
> tised sorcery and enticed and led Israel astray*. Anyone who can
> say anything in his favour, let him come forward and plead
> on his behalf.' But since nothing was brought forward in his
> favour, he was hanged on the eve of Passover. Ulla retorted:
> 'Do you suppose that he was one for whom a defence could
> be made? Was he not a *deceiver*, concerning whom scripture
> says (Deuteronomy 13:8), "Neither shalt thou spare neither
> shalt thou conceal him?" With Yeshu however, it was dif-
> ferent, for he was connected with the government.'

Two possible links with John's Gospel are worth noting.
According to the synoptic Gospels Jesus shared a Passover meal
with his disciples and was crucified the following day. But John
19:14 and the passage above locate the crucifixion on the eve of
Passover.

In *b. Sanh.* *107b* a similar accusation against Jesus is noted:

> One day he (R. Joshua) was reciting the Shema when Jesus
> came before him. He intended to receive him and made a
> sign to him. He (Jesus) thinking it was to repel him, went,
> put up a brick and worshipped it. 'Repent', said he (R.
> Joshua) to him. He replied, 'I have thus learned from thee:
> He who sins and causes others to sin is not afforded the
> means of repentance.' And a Master has said, 'Jesus the
> Nazarene *practised magic and led Israel astray.*'

The reference to 'worshipping a brick' has baffled interpreters
and there is no satisfactory explanation. These lines are noteworthy for the initial welcome which seems to have been extended
to Jesus: only after a misunderstanding is Jesus criticized. These
two rabbinic traditions are very difficult to interpret in detail, and

even more difficult to date with any confidence.

The accusation in the final sentence is also prominent in the preceding passage. Since it is found in a wide range of early anti-Christian polemical writings, it may be an early stock criticism of Jesus, even though this form of the tradition was not committed to writing until about AD 500. I shall discuss its significance further in *Chapter XII*.

In the Middle Ages a Jewish polemical writing known as *Toledoth Jeshu* was popular and existed in many different versions. It probably goes back to the end of the third century, and it may have even earlier roots. Although some of its traditions about Jesus are polemical versions of traditions in the Gospels, some may well be independent. Unfortunately a modern critical edition of the texts in English is not available, so it is difficult for non-specialists to make an assessment of this material.

With the exception of Josephus, why do Jewish writings say so little about Jesus? The earliest rabbinic writing, the Mishnah, contains religious law; it does not include explicit polemic against 'heretical' Jewish groups, let alone an apostate daughter religion, Christianity. The later rabbinic writings stem from a period when Christianity had become dominant, so it is not surprising to find scattered polemical references to Jesus and his followers. But by and large the later rabbis ignored Christianity, perceiving it to be an alien Gentile religion. They were more concerned with pressing internal matters.

Christian Evidence outside the Gospels

Mark's Gospel, the first to be written, probably dates from just before the fall of Jerusalem in AD 70. As we saw in *Chapter V*, during the gap between the crucifixion of Jesus in c. AD 30 and the writing of Mark's Gospel, traditions about the life and teaching of Jesus were transmitted orally. Paul's letters, which were written between c.49 and 56, provide earlier *written* evidence than the Gospels.

Paul's first letter to the Corinthians includes an account of words Jesus spoke to his disciples at a meal (perhaps a Passover meal) on the night when he was betrayed: 'This is my body which is for you . . . This cup is the new covenant in my blood'

(I Corinthians 11:23-5). Paul also refers to a summary of the evidence concerning the death and resurrection appearances of Jesus: 'Christ died . . . he was buried . . . he was raised on the third day . . . he appeared to Cephas (Peter), then to the twelve . . .' (I Corinthians 15:3-7). In both cases Paul emphasizes that he *received* these traditions, i.e. they were earlier oral traditions which he is now committing to writing. There is no reason to doubt that a version of the account of the Last Supper goes back to Jesus himself, though *exactly* what Jesus said and meant is difficult to determine. Some scholars have argued that the 'credal' summary quoted by Paul at the beginning of I Corinthians 15 may go back to the very early post-Easter Aramaic-speaking circle of followers of Jesus in Jerusalem; this conclusion is possible, but it cannot be affirmed confidently.

Paul does not refer to any other events from the life of Jesus. His letters say nothing at all about the healings and exorcisms of Jesus. In I Corinthians, however, Paul does refer to a few sayings of Jesus. In 7:10 he insists that married couples should not separate and that a husband should not divorce his wife; he notes that this instruction is not his own, it comes from 'the Lord'. This verse is related closely to the sayings of Jesus recorded in Mark 10:11-12, though the correspondence in wording is not exact. Paul feels free to modify Jesus' absolute prohibition of divorce: if divorce does take place, the wife should not remarry; divorce is permissible if one partner is an unbeliever.

In I Corinthians 9:14 Paul reports that 'the Lord commanded that those who proclaim the Gospel should get their living by the Gospel', clearly a version of words of Jesus recorded in Matthew 10:10b = Luke 10:7b. But in the very next verse Paul stresses that he has not made any use of this provision, i.e. that he has not felt bound by that command of Jesus. As in I Corinthians 7, Paul uses sayings of Jesus to support his argument, but he adapts the teaching of Jesus in the light of the circumstances.

In addition to these explicit references to Jesus traditions, Paul alludes to a number of sayings of Jesus. Some scholars have made long lists of allusions and have concluded that Paul was deeply dependent on the teaching of Jesus. Others accept only a handful of allusions. The latter conclusion is preferable. In many cases it is difficult to be certain that the phrase or sentence comes from

Jesus, rather than from a Jewish or Greek source. How do we decide that there is a definite allusion to a saying of Jesus, and not just a coincidental correspondence of a few words?

While the evidence just sketched is important, Paul's failure to refer more frequently and at greater length to the actions and teaching of Jesus is baffling. It does seem likely that in his initial missionary preaching Paul referred to the story of Jesus and explained why Jesus had been put to death. In his letters Paul is writing to established Christian communities, not setting out all he knows about the life of Jesus. While it is possible to account for Paul's partial silence along these lines, in a number of places in his writings Paul fails to refer to a saying of Jesus at the very point where he might well have clinched his argument by doing so.

In I and II Peter, and also in James, there are similar problems over allusions. Long lists of possible allusions can be drawn up, but in very few cases can we be confident that the writer is referring to words of Jesus.

Oral traditions about Jesus circulated both before and after the New Testament Gospels were written. Some of those traditions found their way into the four 'other' Gospels we looked at in *ChapterVII*. A few appear in the fragmentary Jewish-Christian Gospels we considered briefly in *Chapter VIII*. As we saw, it is often difficult to decide whether Jesus traditions in these 'other' Gospels have been taken from oral tradition or from the canonical four. Similar problems arise in other Christian writings from the second and later centuries, as the following two examples illustrate.

The Didache is a fascinating writing from about AD 100. In a discussion of the eucharist we read, 'The Lord said, "Do not give what is holy to the dogs (9:5)".' This could derive from oral tradition, or it could be a citation of Matthew 7:6. If the latter, Matthew's more general advice to avoid wasting the words of Jesus on stubborn hearers is reinterpreted radically in terms of sharing the eucharist with non-Christians.

In his letter to Polycarp (c. AD 110) Ignatius writes: 'be wise as the serpent, and pure as the dove.' This seems to be an allusion to Matthew 10:16, though both Matthew and Ignatius may be referring independently to a well-known proverb.

The German scholar Joachim Jeremias assessed critically the references to sayings of Jesus outside the Gospels over many years and concluded that 18 such sayings were in all probability spoken by Jesus.[2] The evidence has been reassessed recently by his former pupil and colleague, Otfried Hofius, who concludes that only nine of these sayings have strong claims to authenticity.[3]

The nine sayings are as follows:

1. In 1905 one damaged page of a tiny parchment book was discovered with writing on both sides. The 45 lines of Greek text in microscopic script have still not received the attention they deserve. The tiny book was probably used as an amulet – a charm hung around the neck to ward off evil. The text includes an account of a discussion between Jesus and a Pharisaic chief priest named Levi, who criticizes Jesus and his disciples for ignoring regulations for walking in the temple court. Levi speaks to Jesus as follows:

Who gave you leave to [trea]d this place of purification and to look upon [the]se holy utensils without having bathed yourself and even without your disciples having [wa]shed their f[eet]?

In his response Jesus echoes anti-Pharisaic polemic found in Matthew 23 and concludes:

But I and [my disciples], of whom you say that we have not im[mersed] ourselves, [have been im]mersed in the li[ving . . .] water which comes down from [. . . B]ut woe unto those who . . . (P.Oxy 840)

This passage is similar to discussions concerning purity regulations in Mark 7, but it does not seem to be directly dependent upon any of the New Testament Gospels. If in its original form it is an authentic tradition, it would provide further evidence that Jesus took a radical stance concerning purity regulations.

2. In a sermon in Syriac, we read: 'As you are found, so you will be led away hence.' (*Liber Graduum* III, 3.)

3. Logion 8 of the Gospel of Thomas:

And Jesus said: A man is like a wise fisherman, who cast his net into the sea and drew it up from the sea full of small fish. Among them the wise fisherman found a good large fish. He threw down all the small into the sea. He chose the large fish without trouble. He who has ears to hear, let him hear.

4. At the beginning of the third century, Clement of Alexandria quotes the following saying of Jesus: 'Ask for great things, and God will add unto you the little things' (*Stroma.* I, 24, 158).

5. In the middle of the third century Origen quotes the following saying, which is also referred to by six other early Christian writers: 'Be approved money changers.'

6. In Codex Bezae an additional short tradition is added to the text of Luke 6:4: 'On the same day he (Jesus) saw someone working on the Sabbath and said to him, "Man, if you know what you are doing, you are blessed; if you do not know, you are cursed and a transgressor of the law." '[4]

7. Gospel of Thomas logion 82: 'Whoever is near me, is near the fire; whoever is far from me, is far from the kingdom.'

8. Jerome (c. AD 400) claims that he found the following words in the Gospel of the Hebrews (now lost): 'And never be joyful, save when you look upon your brother in love.'

9. A papyrus fragment (P.Oxy 1224), probably part of an apocryphal Gospel, contains two sayings which are similar to Matthew 5:44 and Luke 9:50. A third saying which is not related to the canonical Gospels may be authentic: '[He that] stands far off [today] will tomorrow be [near you].'

Otfried Hofius notes that the first five of these nine sayings may be related in some way to the canonical Gospels, so perhaps only the last four have strong claims to be independent 'new' sayings of Jesus. Hofius concludes, surely correctly, that the four New Testament Gospels contain nearly all that was known about the life and teaching of Jesus in the second half of the first century. A thorough search of all early Christian writings for possible references to words of Jesus confirms the value of the canonical Gospels as evidence for the life and teaching of Jesus.

In this chapter we have looked in several fascinating nooks and crannies. For the historian every phrase from outside the Gospels is gold, but there isn't much of it. In comparison with other writings, the canonical Gospels contain rich veins of evidence, difficult though it is to extract it.

One important result has emerged. The comments about Jesus in pagan and Jewish writings are very terse, but none the less, their concentration on the *death* of Jesus is striking. Tacitus, Lucian, Josephus and the rabbinic tradition *b. San.* 43a all refer to the violent death of Jesus. In contrast, with the exception of I Corinthians, in the Christian traditions or writings we considered, Jesus is portrayed as a teacher. Undoubtedly Jesus was a teacher who was put to death. How did that happen? That question will dominate the later chapters of this book.

CHAPTER XI

JESUS TRADITIONS INSIDE THE GOSPEL

THE SEARCH FOR historical evidence for the actions and teaching of Jesus must include every alley, as well as every main street. Christian writings which did not become part of the New Testament should not be neglected, as they often have been in the past. On the other hand, some of the claims made in recent years about their value as historical evidence have been exaggerated. Archaeological evidence often helps us to read the literary evidence more perceptively. The same is true of the comments of pagan and Jewish writers.

Perhaps the most important evidence of all does not even mention Jesus. I have in mind the Dead Sea Scrolls and other Jewish writings from the time of Jesus. They are the backdrop against which the Gospels must be read. For example, the Dead Sea Scrolls help us to appreciate just how thoroughly Jewish the teaching of Jesus is – and yet how different it is in some respects. And almost every page of the writings of Josephus reminds us of the political and social tensions of the world in which Jesus lived.

Even when full attention has been given to the different kinds of evidence outside the Gospels, it is the Gospels themselves which provide most of the historical evidence for the life of Jesus. In making that point I am not giving the Gospels a privileged position simply because they are part of the New Testament. As a Christian, but not as a historian, I do give them a privileged position because of their role as foundation documents for the Christian faith. As a historian, I must examine their evidence critically in the same way as all the other kinds of evidence.

In this chapter we shall consider how the historian can make use of these 'faith writings' effectively. First we must visit one of the finest libraries of antiquity.

What is a Gospel?

In AD 110 a magnificent library was erected in Ephesus as a memorial to Gaius Julius Celsus, Roman governor of the local province from about AD 105–107. The library of Celsus, as it is now known, has been partially reconstructed by archaeologists (*see Plate 14*). Today it is one of the most striking monuments in ancient Ephesus. The library contained 12,000 scrolls which were kept in rows of niches in the walls of the inner chamber. Galleries, not unlike those in modern libraries, provided access to the upper niches. Celsus's son donated an enormous sum of money for the maintenance of the library, and for the purchase of new works. Within a generation of the opening of the library, Christianity began to attract the interest (and often criticism) of the chattering classes of the area. So copies of some of the Gospels probably found their way into the library. The arrival of the Gospels would have given the librarians a headache.

Where should they be put? They were in codex (book) form and the library had been built to house thousands of *rolls*! As we saw in *Chapter VIII*, by the middle of the second century (or perhaps even earlier) the four Gospels were being bound together in a codex. The codex which contained the Oxford, Barcelona and Paris fragment of the Gospels was a most handsome production. The formal style of handwriting would have been well known to the librarians at Ephesus. The technical skill used in its lay-out and design would have drawn their appreciative comments. Clearly the codex should not be consigned to a backroom, but where could shelf space be found?

The acquisitions librarian at Ephesus was faced with an even more serious problem. In which section of the library should the Gospels be put? Next to the histories, or the novels, or the biographies, or the religious treatises? The librarian's decision would arouse particular expectations in the minds of readers. When we borrow a novel from our local library, we don't read it as if it were a biography. When we pick up any piece of writing, a provisional decision about its literary genre must be made before we can begin to appreciate it.

Although authors regularly adapt or extend existing genres which are familiar to their readers, they are able to do this only if they are confident that communication with their readers will still be possible. If an author were to invent a totally new genre, readers would be baffled and communication would be impossible.

If we are to take the genre of the Gospels seriously, they must be set in their first-century literary context. Consideration of early readers' comments on the Gospels is fruitful and points us in the right direction. Writing about AD 155, the Christian Justin Martyr referred to the Gospels as 'memoirs of the apostles'[1]; his use of this phrase is almost certainly intended to recall Xenophon's *Memorabilia*, 'memoirs' about Socrates, i.e, a biography. While the evidence is a little less clear, it is probable that three decades earlier Papias viewed Mark's Gospel as 'memoirs' which were 'not artistically arranged', and seems to have believed that Matthew had gathered together the sayings of Jesus in a more polished or finished form. Hence within two generations or so of the composition of the Gospels, at least some readers considered them to be 'memoirs', a type of biography.[2]

Was this early assessment of the genre of the Gospels correct? That question can only be answered by comparing their form and content with their closest relatives among ancient writings. For several decades earlier this century it was generally accepted that Justin was mistaken in referring to the Gospels as 'memoirs'; some even suggested that Justin had been misled by his education in the Greek rhetorical tradition.

Rudolf Bultmann and several other influential New Testament scholars insisted that in terms of their genre the Gospels are *unique*, they are not to be read as biographies, whether ancient or modern. The Graeco-Roman biographies do not provide an analogy to the genre of the Gospels. The proclaimed Gospel message of the Risen Christ was central to Christian faith, not the story of 'gentle Jesus meek and mild', not indeed the historical Jesus at all. The Gospels may tell us a few things about the life and teaching of Jesus, but this is, as it were, incidental or even contrary to their original intention.

These claims were built partly on a surprisingly inaccurate assessment of ancient biographical writing. It is true that the

Gospels differ markedly from most modern biographies. They are not concerned with precise chronology, they do not describe the personal appearance of Jesus; they neither attempt to unravel the development of the personality of Jesus, nor to set him in the historical context of his own day. These are all part of the expectations with which a modern reader approaches a biography, but they were not hallmarks of ancient biographical writing. The Gospels must be read against the backdrop, not of modern biographical writing, but of their own times. It then becomes clear that the evangelists are concerned with both the *story* as well as the *significance* of Jesus.[3] They tell the story in order to persuade their readers of the truth of his significance.

If the evangelists had this dual aim, does it not mark them off from ancient biographers? Not at all. Ancient biographers often wrote with several different intentions, including apologetic and polemic. Some wrote in order to uphold (or to challenge) a system of beliefs or values personified in the subject of the biography.[4] So too with the evangelists, whose accounts of the life and teaching of Jesus were 'foundation documents' for the newly emergent Christian communities.

The Gospels, then, can be seen as a special kind or sub-set of ancient biographical writing. Primarily as a result of the term by which they became known, they form a distinct family within ancient biographies. For Justin Martyr's term, 'memoirs' (a term which recalls ancient biographies) quickly lost out to the term 'Gospels', a term not used by non-Christians to refer to written records. In one very important passage Justin refers to the 'memoirs of the apostles' and adds an explanatory comment: they are 'Gospels'.[5]

Librarians at Ephesus would have been entirely justified in trying to find room for a codex of the Gospels as close as possible to the biographies which always had plenty of readers. With the partial exception of Luke, the style and language used by the evangelists would have seemed unsophisticated to many of those who frequented the library at Ephesus. But the scribe who penned the Oxford-Barcelona-Paris codex wanted the Gospels to be taken seriously by Christians and non-Christians alike.

Discussion of the literary genre of the Gospels is not an antiquarian pursuit. The conclusion that they formed a sub-set of ancient biographical writing is important for the historian who is assessing their evidence. The Gospels are not theological treatises whose every phrase is packed with religious significance. In recent decades the Gospels have often been treated as if they were treatises. For example, scholars have assumed too readily that every change made by Matthew to Mark was in the service of Matthew's distinctive theology; Matthew's changes were often purely stylistic.

The Gospels are not novels, tales invented to delight readers, often with an element of titillation thrown in for good measure. Only the story of the beheading of John the Baptist falls into that category (Mark 6:17-29 = Matthew 14:3-12). In antiquity there was little appreciation of the modern commonplace that fiction is instructive about the human condition.

The Gospels are not histories, either in the ancient or the modern sense. They have often been assumed to be histories, with disastrous consequences. The evangelists did not intend to set down *records*, accurate in every detail of what happened between AD 30 and 33.

The Gospels are biographies. They tell the story of the career of Jesus in order to persuade the reader of his significance. Like many ancient biographies, they give prominence to character portrayal of Jesus, and of all the other participants in the story. In ancient biographical writing there was a deeply-rooted conviction that a person's actions and words sum up the character of an individual more adequately than the comments of an observer. The evangelists rarely intrude into their narratives in order to explain directly to the reader the significance of what has been said or done.

Finally, the Gospels are a distinct family of biographies. They quickly became known, *not* as 'lives', or 'memoirs of the apostles', but as 'Gospels'. As such they are first and foremost Christian proclamation of the 'good news' (Gospel) about Jesus Christ, the Son of God (cf. Mark 1:1).

Criteria

Given that the Gospels have this distinctive character, how does the *historian* assess their evidence? What are the appropriate methods to use in reconstruction of the actions, teaching and intention of Jesus?

Before I set out basic principles or methods which must govern a search for the authentic sayings and actions of Jesus, it may be helpful to compare the Gospels to an archaeological site with three levels. The most accessible level is the Gospels as they now stand; here we can readily discern the emphases of the evangelists. The middle level is the period between the life of Jesus and Mark's written Gospel, the period of at least 35 years when Jesus traditions were transmited orally. The bottom level is the life of Jesus himself. Once we have reached the bottom level (admittedly with greater or lesser certainty) we may attempt to answer the question, Who was Jesus of Nazareth?

We must first of all start at the top level and look carefully at the ways the evangelists have modified the traditions they incorporated into their Gospels. In the case of Matthew and Luke, it is not difficult to do this. With the use of a synopsis which sets out the text of the Gospels in columns, we can observe the ways Matthew and Luke abbreviate, clarify and modify Mark's Gospel.

The four evangelists often *re-interpret* their traditions by placing them in a particular context. In Luke 15:3-7, for example, the parable of the lost sheep is the first of a trilogy of parables used to explain why Jesus 'welcomes sinners – who include tax collectors – and eats with them' (Luke 15:1-2): *they* are the 'lost sheep'. Luke himself is probably responsible for bringing these three parables together as a reply to the complaint of the scribes and Pharisees about the outrageous conduct of Jesus. Matthew, on the other hand, has placed the same parable of the lost sheep in a very different setting and so has given it a quite different interpretation. In Matthew 18: 12-14 the parable is used to encourage Christians in the evangelist's day to search out the 'lost sheep' who has strayed from the community. In Matthew the 'lost sheep' is not a sinner or a tax collector, but a Christian disciple.

In Matthew 11:2-6 John's disciples are told by Jesus to go and tell their imprisoned leader that they have seen evidence of the fulfilment of Scripture: the blind are regaining their sight, the lame are walking again, the lepers are being made clean, the deaf are hearing, the dead are being raised to life, the poor are hearing the good news proclaimed to them. In the preceding two chapters Matthew has re-ordered Marcan (and other) traditions to make sure that examples of all these actions of Jesus have been given. In their original context in Mark and Q they were not set out as the fulfilment of Scripture, but they are in Matthew. This is stated explicitly in 8:17: 'This (i.e. the healing activity of Jesus) was to fulfil what was spoken by the prophet Isaiah, "He took our infirmities and bore our diseases".'

The evangelists frequently re-interpret earlier traditions by including them as part of their 'Gospel' story of Jesus. For example, the 'Gospel' framework plays an important role in the parable of the vineyard, Mark 12:1-12. Here it is difficult to disentangle the original parable of Jesus from the later version Mark used. In the original parable Jesus referred to God's relationship to his people Israel; he may well have *implied* that he himself was God's son who was sent to obtain 'the fruit of the vineyard,' i.e. Israel. In its present context as part of Mark's 'Gospel story' the parable sums up the *evangelist's* understanding of the significance of Jesus: he is God's beloved son. This is the very phrase spoken by the voice from heaven at the baptism of Jesus, 1:11, and at the Transfiguration, 9:7. Jesus is God's *final* messenger, the heir of the vineyard, but like the earlier servants (i.e. the prophets of old) he too is killed by the 'tenants' (i.e. the leaders of Israel) on whom God's judgement will be meted out. The original parable has been extended and enriched by being placed in its present context as part of Mark's story.

Many of the additions made by the evangelists can be categorized as 'explanations' of an earlier tradition. However, there is an important exception: sayings in the Gospels which presuppose a setting *after* the lifetime of Jesus and which are attached only loosely to the adjacent traditions. In Matthew 10:18 Jesus warns the disciples whom he is sending out on their mission that they will be persecuted both by Jewish and by Gentile authorities. There is no evidence that such persecution took place in the lifetime of Jesus, though it certainly did in later decades. In Matthew 18:20 we read: 'Where two or three are gathered in my name, there am I in the midst of them.' This saying can hardly come from the historical Jesus, but it does make sense in a post-Easter setting in which disciples gather in the name of Jesus and, as the

Risen Jesus promises in Matthew 28:20, experience his continuing presence with them.

To sum up the first step in reconstructing the actions and
teaching of Jesus: the modifications and additions which stem
from the evangelists must be set aside, along with verses which
presuppose a setting in the evangelists' own day. In particular,
traditions both of the teaching and of the actions of Jesus must
be detached, again at least provisionally, from the contexts in
which they have been placed by the evangelists. The word 'provisionally' is chosen deliberately, since at least some of the
changes, additions and contexts provided by the evangelists may
turn out after further investigation to reflect accurately the
original teaching and intention of Jesus.

❧

After taking that crucial initial step, one or more of three criteria may be used to establish that a tradition may well be authentic. Close attention should be given to some traditions which
were an embarrassment to followers of Jesus in the post-Easter
period. If the post-Easter church has retained traditions which
run 'against the grain', they are probably authentic. For example:
Mark 1:41 refers to the anger of Jesus; Matthew and Luke omit
the reference, and in many copies of Mark scribes quickly
changed 'moved with anger' into 'moved with compassion'.
Similarly, the claim of the opponents of Jesus that he was mad
(Mark 3:21) was omitted by both Matthew and Luke. The reference on the lips of Jesus to his ignorance of the time when the
end would come (Mark 13:32) is not included by Luke. In
Chapters XIV and *XV* I shall lay considerable emphasis on the
value of traditions about Jesus which have survived even though
they were an embarrassment to later followers of Jesus. As we
shall see, some of them were such an embarrassment that it is
most unlikely that they were made up.

The 'criterion of dissimilarity' is also often helpful. If a Gospel
tradition is *dissimilar* to the teaching and practices of early
Judaism, then it can hardly have been taken over by the disciples
or later followers of Jesus and attributed to him. And if a tradition runs counter to Christian teaching in the post-Easter period, it can hardly have been created then. So if traditions of either

the sayings or the actions of Jesus are dissimilar *both* from early Jewish *and* from early Christian teaching or practice, then we may accept them with confidence as solid historical evidence.

The attitude of Jesus to fasting is a good example. In Mark 2:18 we read that while John's disciples and the Pharisees did fast (as was the general custom), the fact that the disciples of Jesus did not fast caused offence. We know that many very early Christian circles continued to fast. This is simply assumed to be a normal Christian religious observance in Matthew 6:16-18 and in the Didache chapter 8 which may date from about AD 100. In both cases Christians are told not to fast 'like the hypocrites', but the practice is not called in question. Since the failure of Jesus to fast cannot have been 'taken over' either from contemporary Jewish teaching or 'created' by Christians in the immediate post-Easter period, this must be an authentic tradition.

The criterion of dissimilarity does effectively isolate authentic sayings of Jesus. But if it is used as the sole criterion, serious distortion results. Since our knowledge both of Judaism and of early Christianity is limited, we can never be absolutely certain that a saying of Jesus is 'dissimilar' to both. This criterion undermines the Jewishness of Jesus, since everything which Jesus *shared* with his fellow-Jews is rejected as suspect. It also assumes that there was no continuity between Jesus and the early church: the early church never understood Jesus! If we are seeking to understand an individual, we do not normally concentrate *solely* on those views and attitudes which are not shared by his contemporaries and which are not accepted by his successors. If we were to do so, we would gain a very odd impression. Although in the past scholars have attached a lot of weight to this criterion, many recent writers have rightly been more sceptical of its value.

The 'criterion of multiple attestation' is often more useful than 'dissimilarity'. If we find a saying of Jesus in several strands of the traditions (Mark; Q; traditions found only in Matthew, Luke or John; and extra-canonical traditions with good claims to authenticity) then its widespread attestation is noteworthy. The same saying or character trait is unlikely to have been 'invented' within several independent Christian communities which were preserving parts of the Jesus traditions. As an example, we may note that three independent passages record that Jesus' acceptance of tax collectors drew critical questioning: Mark 2:13-17; Matthew 11:19 = Luke 7:34 (Q); and the partly pre-Lucan tradition at Luke 15:1-2. The authenticity of these and the related traditions can be established with reasonable confidence by appealing to the criterion of multiple attestation.[6]

✿

The initial step and the three proposed criteria provide a firm foundation for reconstruction of the actions and teaching of Jesus. To some this approach will seem to be much too cautious. Some attach far more weight to the criterion of dissimilarity than I do. They insist that unless Jesus traditions can be *shown* to stem from Jesus rather than from the early church, they should not be considered to be authentic. Scholars who have tried to reconstruct the intention of Jesus on this basis have not been particularly successful. Their use of an apparently rigorous method turns out to be illusory. Evidence which is accepted as authentic often turns out to fit all too neatly a particular theory which is being advanced; inconvenient evidence is set aside as inauthentic.

If sound historical methods are available, why are there so many different reconstructions of the career and intention of Jesus? Different methods and presuppositions are part of the answer. Equally important are the gaps in our knowledge of the religious, political and social world at the time of Jesus. Disciplined imagination has to be used to fill the gaps: naturally different historians will assess the probabilities rather differently. The Jesus story is set against the backdrop of two worlds which have both similarities and differences: the village world of Galilee and the world of the political and religious establishment in Jerusalem. Progress continues to be made in the reconstruction of those two worlds, but we shall never know enough to answer all our questions satisfactorily.

CHAPTER XII

JESUS: THE AFTERMATH

Tell me the personal background of someone who is studying seriously the life and teaching of Jesus, and I shall tell you what kind of Jesus will emerge. Is that comment a little cynical? Perhaps, but there is more than a grain of truth in it. The history of scholarly quests for the historical Jesus confirms just how easy it is to reconstruct Jesus in one's own image.

Steps can be taken to minimize the risk. Careful assessment and use of *all* the relevant evidence, as sketched in several of the preceding chapters, is imperative. Acquaintance with earlier attempts to set out a historical portrait of Jesus makes one alert to the pitfalls. One of the main pitfalls today is giving undue weight to one strand of the evidence at the expense of other strands. Jesus of Nazareth does not fit readily into either ancient or modern categories.

In this chapter I shall approach the question, 'Who was Jesus?' from an unusual angle. The impact of a religious or political leader can be judged in part by the eventual outcome of that person's distinctive aims. Only with hindsight some years after the death of a prominent person can his or her achievement be assessed adequately. So too with Jesus of Nazareth.

It is greatly to the credit of E. P. Sanders to have emphasized this point, for it has been regularly overlooked. In the opening pages of his impressive book, *Jesus and Judaism* (1985), Sanders refers to the question posed in 1925 by the distinguished Jewish scholar Joseph Klausner. 'How was it that Jesus lived totally within Judaism, and yet was the origin of a movement that separated from Judaism, since *ex nihilo nihil fit*, nothing comes from nothing, or more idiomatically, where there is smoke there is fire.'[1] In this chapter I shall pick up this question and look at several aspects of the *aftermath* of the Jesus movement. The swirling smoke is easy to find, but what about the fire?

E.P. Sanders lists eight 'almost indisputable facts' about Jesus' career *and its aftermath* :

1. Jesus was baptized by John the Baptist.
2. Jesus was a Galilean who preached and healed.
3. Jesus called disciples and spoke of there being twelve.
4. Jesus confined his activity to Israel.
5. Jesus engaged in a controversy about the temple.
6. Jesus was crucified outside Jerusalem by the Roman authorities.
7. After his death Jesus' followers continued as an identifiable movement.
8. At least some Jews persecuted at least parts of the new movement (Galatians 1:13,22; Philippians 3:6), and it appears that this persecution endured at least to a time near the end of Paul's career (II Corinthians 11:24; Galatians 5:11; 6:12; cf. Matthew 23:34; 10:17).

A few scholars would want to abbreviate even this minimal list. My own list would be rather longer, but never mind for the moment. This list forces us to consider how the various 'indisputable facts' are related to one another. For example, what is the connection between items 2 and 7? Why did the Romans crucify a Galilean who preached and healed? I shall return to this key point in *Chapter XV*. In this chapter I shall focus on items 7 and 8 in Sanders' list, though my discussion will be along rather different lines. It is, of course, these two items in the list that point us to the importance of the *aftermath* of the ministry of Jesus.

What was the relationship between the intention of Jesus during his lifetime and the aftermath following his death? As Sanders notes, there may have been no link at all: the resurrection appearances alone may account for the existence of the Christian movement. He accepts (and so do I) that the resurrection experiences of the disciples provided the motivating force behind the proclamation of Jesus as the Christ and as Lord, and much of its content. But we must then ask whether the resurrection is the *sole* explanation of the Christian movement, or whether there is more than an accidental connection between Jesus' own work and the emergence of the Christian church.

I shall concentrate on two points. First: shortly after the crucifixion some of the followers of Jesus accepted Gentiles into their movement, without insisting on circumcision as an entry rite. This proved to be the single most radical theological and social step they took,   and a primary reason why followers of Jesus were hounded by some of their fellow Jews after his death. What led them to do this? Had the actions and words of Jesus paved the way?

I shall then turn to an issue which is not on Sanders' list, though it is an indisputable aspect of the aftermath of the Jesus movement. Shortly after the crucifixion, followers of Jesus began to *worship* him as Lord and proclaim him as God's Son. Is there any fire behind this smoke? Or do we need to look no further than the resurrection experiences of the disciples and/or their experiences of the Spirit?

Gentiles and law

Paul's letter to the Galatians (c. AD 53) reveals that there were deep and painful divisions among the followers of Jesus over acceptance of non-Jews into their circles. Paul's own view was clear: circumcision was not required of Gentiles as an entry rite into the people of God; Jews and Gentiles should share table fellowship with one another openly and freely; the 'works of the law' were the very antithesis of 'faith in Christ'. In his face to face confrontation with Peter at Antioch (Galatians 2:1-14), Paul may have lost the battle; in the long run his views won the day.

Why did Paul take such a firm stand? One possible answer might be that as a Jew proud of his heritage he was doing no more than some other Jews of his day had been doing for some time, i.e., welcoming Gentiles freely without insisting on circumcision as commanded by the law of Moses. Plenty of evidence indicates that Judaism with its monotheism and high ethical standards was an attractive religion to many non-Jews. Although first-century Judaism was not a missionary religion, Gentiles who wished to associate themselves with local Jewish communities were welcome. However, circumcision, keeping the sabbath, and observing purity regulations were always the mark of full conversion.[4]

Paul's own explanation of the origin of his Gentile 'law free' mission is clear: he was called by God to proclaim Jesus as the Son of God among the Gentiles (Galatians 1:15-16). This insight may well have come to Paul as a bolt from the blue, but none the less the historian will want to ask about its earlier roots.

At this point there is a surprise. Jesus himself said nothing at all about circumcision. From time to time he accepted the faith of individual Gentiles, perhaps most notably the Roman centurion at Capernaum (Matthew 8:5-13 = Luke 7:1-10 [Q]). But Jesus did not call non-Jews into discipleship. Several traditions confirm that he confined himself very largely to Israel (e.g. Matthew 10:5; 15:24; Mark 7:24-30). So Jesus did not *directly* pave the way for later developments.

It is worth noting at this point that in the post-Easter period the convictions of followers of Jesus concerning table fellowship with Gentiles and circumcision were not anachronistically placed on the lips of Jesus. There was no command of the Lord to which appeal could be made, and that was that. So we should be wary of the assumption that sayings of Jesus were invented freely in the gap between the death of Jesus and the writing of the Gospels.

Is there no connection at all between the actions and words of Jesus and the later full acceptance of Gentiles? A mission to Gentiles is deeply embedded in resurrection traditions (Matthew 28:19; Luke 24:47; Acts 1:8; John 20:21), but this link seems to have been made later, for the disciples did not embark on mission to Gentiles immediately after Easter Day.

We still have a puzzle. It is not hard to find the smoke, but where is the fire? I believe that in deliberately turning repeatedly to those on the margins of society Jesus made a profound impact on his followers. The list is long: tax collectors, who were collecting taxes for an occupying power; 'sinners', who were apathetic about the law; those with physical disabilities of all kinds, who were all too often treated as second-class citizens. There are many such traditions in the various sources behind the Gospels. These traditions were transmitted orally by followers of Jesus over a long period, and eventually their deeper significance was discerned.

In commenting on his confrontation with Peter, Paul notes that he and Peter are both Jews by birth, and not Gentile 'sinners'. He then insists that a person's standing before God is established not by 'works of the law' (including circumcision), but by faith in Jesus Christ (Galatians 2:15-16). The immediate issue was table fellowship: Gentile 'sinners' were to be accepted freely. Surely Jesus' own action in sharing table fellowship with sinners (Mark 2:16-17; Matthew 11:19 = Luke 7:34 [Q]) lies in the background, even though we cannot trace a direct link.

The issue of table fellowship was closely related to the question of pure and impure food. In Romans 14:14 Paul seems to echo a saying of Jesus: 'I know and am persuaded on the authority of the Lord Jesus that nothing is unclean in itself.' Mark 7:15 records that Jesus said, 'There is nothing outside a person that by going in (i.e., by being eaten) can defile a person (i.e. render him or her impure ritually).' Mark himself believes that in taking this stand, Jesus 'declared all foods clean' (7:19b); he makes this declaration in an aside directly to his readers to make sure they appreciate the significance of what Mark thinks Jesus did.

However, Jesus is unlikely to have launched a wholesale attack on Jewish purity regulations, one of the pillars of the law. If he did, then it is difficult to explain why his followers came to this conclusion so slowly and painfully in the post-Easter period. It is much more likely that Jesus provoked reflection on priorities by saying, 'A person is *not so much* defiled by that which enters from outside as by that which comes from within . . .' (i.e. by impure thoughts and desires: Mark 7:20-3).

Both by his actions and his words Jesus seems to have paved the way, albeit indirectly, for the radical step taken by his followers in the post-Easter period. By looking carefully for the fire behind the smoke, we are taken to one of the most striking and distinctive features of the ministry of Jesus.

Jesus is Lord

Soon after the debacle of the crucifixion, followers of Jesus began to worship Jesus as Lord and proclaim him as God's Son. As the terms 'Lord' and 'Son of God' raise rather different issues, we shall consider them one by one.

'Jesus is Lord' quickly became a central Christian confession (Romans 10:9; I Corinthians 12:3; Philippians 2:11). In this confession Jesus is referred to as one who was 'more than merely human'. Christians in Paul's churches would have been aware that it was becoming customary to refer to the Roman emperor as 'Lord'. For them any such reference was impossible; their sole confession was 'Jesus is Lord'. But this confession of Jesus did not arise solely in the Graeco-Roman world: there is now evidence which shows that 'Lord' was used in some Jewish circles to refer to God.

Among the very earliest Aramaic-speaking Christians it became customary to refer to Jesus as 'Lord'. This is confirmed by Paul's prayer in I Corinthians 16:22, where he uses an Aramaic phrase *marana tha*, 'Come, (our) Lord Jesus' in a letter written to the Greek-speaking Corinthians. Presumably this Aramaic invocation was so well known that Paul did not need to translate it. Since Paul spoke and wrote Greek, the phrase must have a pre-Pauline origin, even though we cannot trace its roots with any precision.

We can affirm that within a few years of the crucifixion, Jesus was worshipped and confessed as Lord. Billowing smoke, but where is the fire? In this case we cannot trace a line of continuity to the lifetime of Jesus. Although conservative scholars sometimes talk about 'earlier hints', special pleading has to be invoked.

From time to time in the Gospels Jesus is referred to in the Greek text as 'Kyrios' (Lord). In a number of these passages, the term is simply a polite form of address, 'Sir'. In other cases, the post-Resurrection sense is used anachronistically – just as one might say, 'When the President was a College student . . .' Mark 11:3 is an instructive example. As Jesus and the disciples approach Jerusalem, the disciples are told to go and fetch a colt. If anyone asks why they are doing this, they are to say, 'the Kyrios (Lord) needs it'. Is this an anachronistic post-Resurrection usage? Or is it a polite form of address? The translators are divided. NRSV has, 'the Lord needs it', while REB has 'the Master needs it'.

If the confession 'Jesus is Lord' cannot be traced to the lifetime of Jesus, how did it come to be used so quickly and prominently in the post-Easter period? In this case we need look no further than the Easter experiences of the followers of Jesus (e.g. John 20:18, Mary Magdalene's confession, 'I have seen the Lord'), and their experiences of the Spirit (e.g. I Corinthians 12:3, 'No one can say "Jesus is Lord" except by the Holy Spirit').

Jesus is the Son of God

The conviction that Jesus is God's Son is found on page after page of the New Testament. At first sight, Paul's letters (the earliest New Testament writings) seem to be out of line. Whereas Paul refers to Jesus as 'Lord' 184 times, 'Son of God' is used only 15 times. But as is so often the case, statistics are misleading. Paul uses 'Son of God' in several key passages in which he is discussing the heart of the Christian message, 'Gospel truth'.

In the opening verses of the letter to the church in Rome, Paul's most sustained theological discussion, he uses the title three times. 'The Gospel concerns God's Son' (Romans 1:3); 'Jesus was declared to be Son of God with power . . . by resurrection from the dead' (1:4); 'I serve God by announcing the Gospel of his Son' (1:9). Since some of the vocabulary and turns of phrase in the first two of these passages are not Paul's own, he is drawing on an earlier credal summary from the early 40s. The first two statements bring together 'Son of God' and 'Lord': 'the Gospel concerns God's Son . . . Jesus Christ our Lord' (1:4c).

In Galatians 1:15 Paul links 'Son of God' closely with his radical change of direction from persecuting the church of God to proclaiming its faith in Jesus as God's Son. A little later in the same letter Paul makes a 'programmatic statement':

> When the fulness of time had come, God sent his Son, born of a woman, born under the law, in order to redeem those who were under the law, so that we might receive adoption as children (4:4-5).

The central ideas here, 'God's sending of his Son into the world for redemption', are also found in Romans 8:3, and also in John 3:17 and I John 4:9-10, 14. Since a similar theological expression is prominent in two quite unrelated strands of early Christianity, Paul's letters and the Johannine writings, it is likely that both have drawn independently on an early confessional statement about the significance of Jesus.

So it is clear that just like 'Jesus is Lord', 'Jesus is the Son of God' is a very early credal summary. Once again a striking claim about the significance of Jesus is an important part of the immediate 'aftermath' of his life and death. What led followers of Jesus to make these affirmations so soon after his violent death on a Roman cross?

Was it the resurrection appearances and their experiences of the Spirit? The first of the passages quoted above, Romans 1:3-4, does link 'Son of God' with the raising of Jesus from the dead. There has been a long-standing debate over the precise nuance of this pre-Pauline credal summary. Does it affirm that Jesus *became* Son of God at his resurrection, or does it state that through the resurrection God *declared* Jesus to be what he had been during his earthly ministry?

Fortunately we do not need to settle the debate, for there is evidence which confirms that in this case it is possible to trace a line of continuity from the 'aftermath' back to Jesus himself. Before we go further, it is important to note that the phrases 'God's Son' or 'Son of God' do not necessarily refer to 'divinity', to sharing God's *nature*, as in later Christian thought which refers to Jesus as being 'of one substance with the Father'. In the Old Testament, and in Jewish circles at the time of Jesus, 'son of God' referred to a special *relationship* to God. In the Old Testament 'son of God' is used of angels or heavenly beings (e.g. Genesis 6:2,4; Deuteronomy 32:8; Job 1:6-12), Israel or Israelites (e.g. Exodus 4:22; Hosea 11:1), and also of the king of Israel (notably in II Samuel 7:14 and Psalm 2:7).

There are several passages with good claims to authenticity in which Jesus refers to himself as God's Son. In Mark 14:36 Jesus addresses God: '*Abba*, Father, all things are possible to you. Take this cup (of suffering) from me.' Although Jesus immediately accepts God's will ('not my will but yours'), the fact that Jesus even asked to be allowed to avoid the 'cup of suffering' was an intense embarrassment to his followers – a prayer they are unlikely to have invented. In this verse the Aramaic word *Abba* is used, and then for the benefit of Greek speakers translated immediately as 'Father'. The same way of addressing God lies behind the opening line of the Lord's prayer in the shorter, more original Lucan version (11:2), 'Father, may your name be hallowed.'

The claim that in contrast to Jewish prayers which stressed the 'otherness' of God, *Abba* means 'Daddy' has been repeated in countless sermons. *Abba* is said to express a totally new, intimate way of referring to God. But this claim must be abandoned, for it rests on a faulty linguistic basis: *'abi* is the normal way a child addressed a parent in Aramaic at the time of Jesus. None the less, Jesus' usage *is* distinctive: *'Abba*, Father' is rarely if ever used by an individual in pre-Christian Jewish writings as a personal address for God. Two decades after the time of Jesus, Paul was still using *Abba* when writing to Greek-speaking Christians who did not know a word of Aramaic! In Galatians 4:6 and Romans 8:15 Paul insists that the gift of God's Spirit enables Christians to pray, 'Abba, Father.'

In a much-discussed Q passage (Matthew 11:27 = Luke 10:22) Jesus says: 'No one knows the Son except the Father, and no one knows the Father except the Son and anyone to whom the Son chooses to reveal him.' It is difficult to rule out the possibility that words of Jesus have been adapted in the light of post-Easter faith to speak more explicitly of Jesus as 'the Son' in an absolute sense. Perhaps Jesus originally drew on a proverb which spoke about the ways a son and a father know one another intimately.

Mark 13:32 must have been an embarrassing saying to many of the followers of Jesus, for it concedes that Jesus was ignorant about the precise date of 'the end': 'But about that day or hour no one knows, neither the angels in heaven, nor the Son, but only the Father.' Here we do have Jesus speaking about his special relationship to Jesus as 'God's Son'.

There is one further important passage in Mark. In Mark's version of the parable of the vineyard (12:1-7), the owner of the vineyard sends a series of servants to collect his share of the profits from the tenants of the vineyard. One by one they are rejected, some even killed. 'Finally he sent a beloved son to them saying, "They will respect my son".'

As this parable stands in Mark, it is an allegory: every part corresponds to deeper truth, starting with the depiction of Israel as a vineyard, and the prophets as servants sent by God to Israel. If we decide that Jesus never used allegory in his parables, then this parable cannot go back to Jesus. In recent years, however, many scholars have become more open to the possibility that Jesus did

use some allegory. Since Isaiah 5 already speaks of Israel as a vineyard, there is no reason why Jesus should not have done so.

I think that most of this parable does go back to Jesus. It
includes a slightly embarrassing admission: Jesus was sent to Israel
just as the prophets were, so a critic might ask, 'What was the difference between Jesus and the prophets?' The parable does not
bring out the difference as sharply as a later Christian parable-
teller would have done. Nor does the parable refer to Jesus as *the*
Son of God as a later Christian would have done: Jesus is *a son* of
the owner of the vineyard (God). Perhaps Mark the evangelist
has added the word 'beloved' to 'son', in order to draw attention
to the fact that at two points earlier in his story a voice from
heaven declares that Jesus is God's Beloved Son: at the baptism of
Jesus (1:11) and again at the Transfiguration (9:6). But in this
parable Jesus may well have spoken of his special relationship to
God as 'God's son'.

There is, then, a line of continuity between the post-Easter
confession that 'Jesus is the Son of God', back to several sayings
of Jesus himself. This observation can be extended a little. In the
post-Easter period both Paul and the Fourth Gospel stressed that
Christian believers shared the special relationship Jesus had with
the Father as his Son. Independently both took pains to stress
that while Jesus was *the* Son of God, believers were 'sons' in a different sense. Paul used the analogy of adoption (e.g. Galatians
4:5), while John chose a different word: Jesus is *huios* (Son),
believers are *tekna* 'sons' (e.g. John 1:12). There is even continuity here, for Jesus taught his disciples to pray, 'Father' (Luke
11:2), and thus share his relationship with God as 'sons'. From
this verse, and from numerous passages which speak of God as
Father, the following conclusion may be drawn: Jesus saw himself as 'the first of many to stand in a new and special relationship
to God as Father; that priority implies that his sonship was in
some sense superior to the sonship of all who would follow
him.'[5]

What is the relationship of God's Son to God's Messiah? If
Jesus spoke of himself, at least occasionally, as God's Son, was he
thereby also implying that he was the Messiah? Until recently,
this possibility would not even have been considered. However,
a recently published Qumran fragment from Cave 4, 4Q246, has

placed it firmly on the agenda. The fragment, which had been available unofficially and discussed since 1972, was finally published in 1992. On 1 September of that year a story about the fragment in the London newspaper, *The Independent*, carried the headline, 'Scroll fragment challenges basic tenet of Christianity'.

Part of 4Q246, column II, reads as follows:

1. He will be called son of God, and they will call him son of the Most High . . .
2. His kingdom will be an eternal kingdom, and all his paths in truth and uprigh[tness].[6]

Who is being spoken about? Several scholars have concluded that the fragment refers either to the expected Messiah as God's Son, or is 'messianic' in a broader sense, though other interpretations have been proposed.[7] Even if this fragment does refer to 'the Messiah' as 'the Son of God', the truth of the Christian Gospel is not threatened. We would have fresh evidence for a close link before the time of Jesus of two terms which have often been assumed to be unrelated to one another in Jewish thought. Christians picked up and developed radically these overlapping ideas. Perhaps we might even say cautiously that if Jesus saw himself as God's Son in a special sense, he may thereby have been hinting at his Messiahship. But the debate over the interpretation of 4Q246 is by no means settled.

❈

By looking at several aspects of the aftermath of the life of Jesus and trying to seek causes, we find that some light is shed on our central question, 'Who was Jesus?' As we have seen, it is not always possible to move back from the post-Easter period to the lifetime of Jesus, and in some cases the links are tenuous. But there are undoubtedly lines of continuity. The method of starting with the 'aftermath' has been vindicated: we have located several of the most distinctive features of the actions and teaching of Jesus.

CHAPTER XIII

JESUS: A MAGICIAN
AND A FALSE PROPHET

HOW WAS JESUS perceived by Jews who did not accept Christian claims about him? This is an important question, even if it is not often asked. If one wants to form an assessment of a religious or political leader, one should consider not only the accolades of followers, but also the barbed criticisms of opponents. The latter may turn out to be more revealing than the former. Opponents often see more clearly than followers what is at stake. So it is entirely reasonable to search for the polemical accusations made against Jesus. They form part of the 'aftermath' we considered in the preceding chapter.

How deep are the roots of the later anti-Jesus polemic? Do the criticisms levelled at Jesus both during his lifetime and later tell us anything about his intentions?

Once again it will be helpful to start by looking at the later smoke before searching for the fire. My starting point is Justin Martyr's extended debate with his Jewish adversary Trypho, written about AD 160.[1] Justin claims that the healing miracles of Jesus were the fulfilment of the messianic prophecies of Isaiah 35: 1-7. The miracles of Jesus were intended to elicit recognition of him as Messiah, but many who saw them drew the opposite conclusion: 'they said it was a display of magic art, for they even dared to say that *Jesus was a magician and a deceiver of the people* (*Dialogue* 69:7).' From the context there is no doubt that the term 'deceiver' is being used against the background of Deuteronomy 13: 5, with the special sense of a false prophet who leads God's people astray.

Justin believes that this conclusion was drawn already in the lifetime of Jesus. Was this an anachronistic judgement? Do Justin's comments simply reflect Jewish-Christian controversies in the middle decades of the second century? I hope to show that this polemic has deep roots: it puts us in touch with two of the earliest negative assessments of Jesus.

To label someone a 'magician' and/or a 'deceiver' ('false prophet') in antiquity was an attempt to marginalize a person who was perceived to be a threat to the dominant social order. If we can show that these terms were used by opponents of Jesus either during the lifetime of Jesus or soon after, an important corollary would follow: *at a very early point, the actions and teaching of Jesus must have been considered to be deeply offensive.*

'Magician' and 'deceiver' ('false prophet') are used in Deuteronomy 13 and 18 to refer to the treatment to be meted out to 'heretics' and apostates among the Israelites. Opponents who used these categories in their polemic against Jesus were drawing on Scripture. These polemical descriptions of Jesus became stock terms of abuse which were repeated from generation to generation, but these slogans packed a powerful punch because their roots were in Scripture.

Trypho's double accusation, 'Jesus was a magician and deceiver of God's people' is also found in two rabbinic passages which we referred to in *Chapter X*, pp.127-9. In *b.Sanh* 43a Jesus is referred to as one 'who has practised sorcery and enticed and led Israel astray'; in *b. Sanh*. 107b we read, 'Jesus the Nazarene practised magic and led Israel astray.' These two rabbinic traditions are very difficult to interpret in detail, and even more difficult to date with any confidence. Were it not for the close correspondence with Justin's *Dialogue* 69:7, it would be tempting to dismiss them as third-century (or even later) Jewish anti-Christian polemic. However, the semi-technical terminology used in Justin Martyr's Greek is almost as close as one could reasonably expect to the Hebrew of the rabbinic traditions, so we are in touch with stock items of abuse which had deep roots.

The comments about Jesus made by Josephus in AD 93 or 94 include a very similar polemical tradition. As we noted in *Chapter X*, later Christian additions to the text can be removed readily, leaving an authentic neutral or mildly hostile portrait of Jesus drawn by the Jewish historian himself. Josephus refers to Jesus as 'one who did surprising (or unexpected) deeds'. Depending on one's perspective, this could refer negatively to a magician, or positively to a miracle worker. Josephus then adds that Jesus 'brought trouble to' or 'led astray' many Jews.

Josephus states that Jesus was a miracle worker/magician who impressed rather gullible people, and led many Jews (and many Greeks) astray. Although the terminology in the terse assessment of Jesus differs from that used in the anti-Christian Jewish polemic quoted by Justin, and in the rabbinic traditions discussed above, there is notable agreement.

So far we have considered examples of the *double* polemical accusation that Jesus was a magician and a false prophet/deceiver. Both accusations are also found singly in a wide range of writings. Since these charges are closely related to one another, use of one or other polemical term often carries with it the implications of the other.

There is a third related line of polemic which is relevant. In ancient polemic, opponents often allege that both the 'magician' and the 'false prophet' are able to act as they do as the result of their close relationship to the devil or to demons. The claim that an opponent was possessed by demons or in some other way was closely related to the demonic world was easy to make and difficult to refute.

These three labels which are so prominent in ancient polemic have a specific social setting. They are used to marginalize and undermine the influence of individuals whose claims and behaviour are perceived to pose a threat to the stability of the dominant social order. In short, the polemic is a form of social control. With these considerations in mind, we turn now to the Gospels.

※

Matthew's Gospel reflects the double allegation that Jesus was a magician and a false prophet who deceived God's people. The threefold accusation that the exorcisms of Jesus have been carried out 'by the prince of demons' (9:34; 10: 25; 12:24, 27) is a way of alleging that Jesus is a magician, for exorcism is the best attested form of magic among Jews at this period. Matthew clearly has a special interest in this allegation: he is anxious to acknowledge it and to refute it.

At the climax of Matthew 12 the tables are turned on the scribes and the Pharisees: they are part of a generation which is possessed by seven evil spirits (12:43-5). They are demon-possessed, not Jesus. Here we are overhearing a bitter debate: Christians and Jews are involved in a bitter dispute and are trading the same taunt. The threefold accusation that the exorcisms of Jesus have been carried out by dint of collusion with Beelzebul, the prince of demons, is carefully balanced by a threefold insistence that Jesus acts 'by the Spirit of God' (12:18, 28, 31-2).

The final words attributed to the Jewish leaders in Matthew refer to the second half of the double allegation with which we are concerned. In 27:63-4 Jesus is referred to as 'that deceiver' and his life is summed up as 'deception'. This time Matthew does not reply directly to the polemic. He takes pains to convince the reader that the resurrection of Jesus from the tomb in which he was buried was not the 'final deception', but he simply lets the Jewish leaders' critical comments stand. Presumably he is convinced that readers of his Gospel will readily agree that the claim of the Jewish leaders that Jesus is a 'deceiver' is monstrous; perhaps the closing verses of the Gospel (28:18-20) were intended to prove the point.

In Luke 23:2,5 and 14 there are three references to Jesus leading the people astray. From Luke's perspective, such charges were mischievous, if not unexpected; they were all of a piece with the false allegations brought against Stephen and Paul. I think it probable that Luke was aware of what became the standard polemical claim that Jesus was a false prophet who led the people astray.

This accusation is certainly prominent in John's Gospel. In the central chapters we are able to eavesdrop on the disputes between the Johannine community and the local synagogue in the evangelist's own day. In chapter 7 there are three references to division among the people on account of Jesus (7:12, 25-7, 40). In 7:12 some who are antagonistic to Jesus claim that he is leading the people astray, i.e a false prophet. At the climax of the chapter the officers who were sent by the chief priests and Pharisees to arrest Jesus returned empty-handed, only to be asked why they had failed to bring Jesus with them (v. 45). The officers

answered, 'No man ever spoke like this man!' (v. 46) Their positive response to Jesus is immediately undermined by the taunt,
'Are you led astray, you also?' (v. 47).

In both verses reference to 'leading astray' is a formal allegation with roots in Deuteronomy 13. In John 4:19 and 9:17
acknowledgement of Jesus as a prophet is shown to be an acceptable if partial response to Jesus. So it is no surprise to find reference to Jesus as a *false* prophet in John 7:12 and 7:47, and, by
implication, in 7:52. There is little doubt that it is related to the
polemic Justin refers to in *Dialogue* 69.7 and 108.2, and to the
allegations found in the rabbinic traditions quoted above. In both
John 7:12 and 7:47 the claim that Jesus leads the people astray is
used to ridicule sympathetic responses to Jesus. This may well
have been the context in which this jibe was used in the evangelist's day. The evangelist refers to this and other allegations
against Jesus because he is confident that his Gospel as a whole is
an adequate response.

The claim that Jesus is a magician is not referred to explicitly
in John's Gospel. Perhaps this is not surprising, given the absence
of references to exorcism in this Gospel and the fact that exorcism is unquestionably the best attested form of magic among the
Jews before Bar Kokhba.[2]

In view of the role accusations of demonic possession (and
similar charges) play in ancient polemic, we half expect that both
parties to the ferocious disputes which lie behind the central
chapters of John's Gospel use this taunt. And this is exactly what
we find in the text. In John 8:44 'the Jews' are said to be 'of their
father the devil', while in 8:48, 52 and 10:20 Jesus is alleged to
have a demon. The evangelist is confident that his readers will
know where the truth lies.

The allegations that Jesus was a magician and that he was a
false prophet were known at the time the evangelists wrote.
Matthew knew the double form of the accusation. John (cer-
tainly) and Luke (probably) were aware that Jewish opponents of
Christian claims allege that Jesus was a false prophet who led
God's people astray.

The passages from the Gospels discussed so far put us in touch
with the viewpoints of the evangelists and confirm that they
were aware of polemical allegations against Jesus and sought to

counter them. Matthew, Luke and John all wrote in the 80s, at a time of mutual incomprehension, keen rivalry and sour disputes between Christians and Jews. The Gospels put us in touch with charges and counter-charges concerning the actions and teaching of Jesus towards the end of the first century.

◆

Does this polemic have roots in the lifetime of Jesus, some fifty years earlier? There are sound reasons for concluding that even in his own lifetime Jesus was labelled 'magician' by his opponents.

In Mark 3:22 and independently in Q (Matt 12:24 = Luke 11:15),[3] the exorcisms of Jesus are said to be carried out as a result of Jesus' association with Beelzebul, the prince of demons. We noted above that exorcism was the best attested form of magic among Jews in the first century and that magicians were regularly said to be demon-possessed. Hence there is little doubt that both the Marcan and the Q traditions are tantamount to a charge that Jesus was a magician. In his healing miracles and exorcisms Jesus undoubtedly used techniques which would have been perceived by contemporaries to be magical. Since few scholars have any reservations about the authenticity of these two traditions, it is highly likely that Jesus was written off by his opponents as a magician, and thus as a social deviant.

Already within Q and in pre-Marcan traditions (as well as in the completed Gospels), there is a response to this charge. Followers of Jesus would not have transmitted such a hostile assessment of Jesus unless a firm refutation of the allegation was juxtaposed.

The Q pericope contrasts sharply two ways of assessing the exorcising activity of Jesus: is Jesus in league with the prince of demons, or are his actions the result of his relationship to God? Jesus himself claims that his exorcisms were carried out 'by the finger of God', as signs of the breaking in of God's kingly rule (Matthew 12:28 = Luke 11:20).

Mark himself has shaped considerably the traditions he links together in 3: 20-35. In an editorial comment in v. 30 he points out that the saying of Jesus concerning blasphemy against the Holy Spirit (3:28-9) applies to those who claimed that Jesus was possessed by Beelzebul, and that he casts out demons by the prince of demons (3:22). R.A. Guelich has perceptively summed up the key point Mark is making: 'To attribute the work of the Spirit through Jesus to demonic forces is the ultimate calumny for which there is no forgiveness.'[4] Once again, as in the Q Beelzebul traditions, there are two opposing assessments of the actions of Jesus: are they to be ascribed to demonic possession, or to divine agency?

In Mark 3:22 the opponents are identified as 'the scribes who came down from Jerusalem'. They represent the dominant social order which Jesus is threatening.[5] Although the reference to Jerusalem is a note from the evangelist Mark himself, the scribes were probably identified as the opponents of Jesus in the earlier tradition Mark used.   There is no reason to doubt that both the actions and the teaching of Jesus brought him into conflict from time to time with the religious authorities of the day. In that social setting allegations of false prophecy and sorcery thrive; they are used to marginalize and undermine the influence of individuals whose claims and behaviour are perceived to pose a threat to the stability of the dominant social order.

❦

It is more difficult to establish that in his own lifetime Jesus was considered by some to be a false prophet who led Israel astray. However, cumulative evidence makes this a strong probability.

(i) As we have seen above, Matthew and John, and probably Luke, were aware of this polemical charge. There is no reason to suppose that it first arose at the time they wrote. Tension between Jews who accepted Christian claims about Jesus and those who did not did not arise overnight in the 80s. Given that in his lifetime Jesus was alleged by some to be a magician, and given the close links between the two allegations to which we drew attention above, it is highly likely that Jesus was said by some to be a false prophet.

(ii) John the Baptist was said to have a demon (Q: Matthew 11:18 = Luke 7:33). Since neither the synoptic evangelists nor Josephus (*Antiquities* 18:116-19) attribute miracle-working powers to John,[6] the polemical jibe recorded in Q labels him as a *demon-possessed false prophet*. Since John and Jesus were associated closely (*see Chapter XIV*), Jesus was almost certainly also margin-alized by some with the same accusation.

(iii) Although the evangelists do not emphasize that Jesus was a prophet, in two sayings, Mark 6:4 and Luke 13:33, Jesus refers to himself as a prophet. A number of other sayings and several of his actions confirm that he saw himself as a prophet.[7] Thus it would be surprising if some opponents did not dub him as a false prophet, perhaps even with Deuteronomy 13 in mind.

⚜

I have argued that the double allegation found in Justin's *Dialogue* 69. 7 and in the rabbinic traditions quoted above has deep roots. In his own lifetime Jesus was said by some to be a demon-pos-sessed magician. It is probable, but not certain, that he was also said to be a demon-possessed false prophet.

The allegations of the contemporary opponents of Jesus con-firm that he was seen by many to be a disruptive threat to social and religious order. His claims to act and speak on the basis of a special relationship to God were rightly perceived to be radical. For some they were so radical that they had to be undermined by an alternative explanation of their source: Jesus was a demon-possessed magician and a false prophet.

CHAPTER XIV

JESUS: DISCIPLE OF JOHN

IN THE PREVIOUS chapter I approached the question, 'Who was Jesus of Nazareth?' from an unusual angle. In this chapter I shall do likewise. Jesus was more similar to John the Baptist than to any other prominent Jewish leader of the time. So we will do well to compare and contrast Jesus and John.

In the first part of this chapter traditions about John which were an embarrassment to later followers of Jesus will be considered, for they linked Jesus and John closely together. I shall then turn to Josephus's portrait of John the Baptist which differs somewhat from Mark's.

John the Baptist: an Embarrassment

In the post-Easter period, Jesus, not John, was proclaimed as Messiah-Christ and Son of God, and worshipped as Lord. If Jesus and John were very similar, why should John not be accepted as the Messiah? There is some evidence that towards the end of the second century a few 'sectarian' groups did claim that John, not Jesus, was the Messiah. So followers of Jesus had good reason to play down traditions which drew attention to the similarities between Jesus and John. Embarrassing traditions are likely to be authentic. Would Christians invent very positive traditions about John which drew attention to his similarities to Jesus?

The Gospels all state or imply that Jesus was baptized by John. Mark's account is terse and straightforward: 'in those days Jesus came from Nazareth in Galilee and was baptized by John in the Jordan' (1:9). On reflection, however, the reader of Mark might well ask why Jesus needed to be baptized by John. John preached 'a baptism of repentance for the forgiveness of sins'(Mark 1:4), so was Jesus the Son of God sinful?

In one of a handful of fragments which has survived from the apocryphal Gospel of the Nazoreans (perhaps written early in the second century) this question becomes explicit. The mother of the Lord and his brothers say to Jesus, 'John the Baptist is baptizing for the remission of sins. Let us go and be baptized by him.' Jesus replies, 'In what way have I sinned that I should need to go and be baptized by him? Unless perhaps something which I said in ignorance'(§2).

This issue seems to lie behind the comment in Matthew's Gospel that when Jesus came to the Jordan to be baptized by him, John would have prevented him, saying, 'I need to be baptized by you, and do you come to me?' (3:14). Jesus does not need to be baptized by John – indeed the reverse is the case. In Matthew John agrees to baptize Jesus only after Jesus has indicated to him that he should proceed in order 'to fulfil all righteousness' (i.e. to carry out God's will) (3:14-15).

A similar hesitation over the baptism of Jesus by John can be discerned in Luke's rehandling of Mark's account of the baptism of Jesus. Luke does not include Mark's account of the beheading of John by Herod Antipas at the instigation of Herodias his wife (Mark 6:17-29; Matthew 14:3-12). But immediately before his account of the baptism of Jesus, he does include a very brief account of John's entanglement with Herod (3:19-20): 'Herod the tetrach, who had been reproved by him for Herodias, his brother's wife, and for all the evil things that Herod had done, added this to them all, that he shut up John in prison.'

Luke's account of the baptism of Jesus is squeezed into one sentence. It is as if Luke wants to pass over this incident as quickly as possible. In fact there is no explicit reference at all to John's role in baptizing Jesus. Luke simply notes that when all the people had been baptized, and when Jesus also had been baptized and was praying, the heaven was opened, and the Holy Spirit descended upon him in bodily form, as a dove. . . (3:21-22).

In John's Gospel, a further step is taken. John bears witness that he saw the Spirit descend as a dove from heaven and remain on Jesus (1:32-4). A reader familiar with the accounts of the baptism of Jesus in the synoptic Gospels will naturally assume from this passage that John baptized Jesus. But John the evangelist does not state this explicitly! He does not wish to suggest that Jesus, the Lamb of God who takes away the sin of the world (1:29) and who himself baptizes with the Holy Spirit (1:33), needed to go to John for baptism.

In view of these later hesitations, we can be certain that Mark's clear reference to the baptism of Jesus by John is authentic. By going to John for baptism, Jesus was expresssing his agreement with John, and his intention to become a follower of his.

▩

A second set of traditions about John the Baptist must have greatly embarrassed later followers of Jesus. Matthew, Mark and Luke all state that the beginning of Jesus' ministry was quite distinct from John's: Jesus began to teach and to heal in Galilee 'after John was arrested' (Mark 1:14; Matthew 4:12; Luke 3:21-23). Matthew even reminds the reader that John was 'in prison' (a phrase he adds to his source at 11:2) during the first part of the ministry of Jesus (see also 14:3).

But a very different picture emerges in several passages in John's Gospel which state that Jesus and John were active at the same time (1:29; 1:35-42; 3:22-24; 4:1-3). Two of the disciples of Jesus (and perhaps Jesus himself) were originally disciples of John (1:35-37). In other words, Jesus' ministry overlapped with John's. John's Gospel copes with the embarrassment of overlapping ministries by portraying John as a witness to Jesus, a 'Christian evangelist', and by including several negative references to John (1:8; 1:20; 3:28; 1:21; 3:30).

An important passage in Q also suggests that the ministries of Jesus and John may have overlapped. In Matthew 11:2-6 = Luke 7:19-23 John sends disciples to Jesus to ask, 'Are you he who is to come, or shall we look for another?' Jesus says to them, 'Go and tell John what you hear and see.' Jesus then refers to his healing activity and 'preaching of the good news' as fulfilment of Scripture (especially Isaiah 35: 5-6 and 61:1). In the verses in Q which follow Jesus speaks about John positively and in some detail. This lengthy Q passage implies, just as John's Gospel does, that there was a very close relationship between Jesus and John.

The synoptic evangelists (Matthew, Mark and Luke) portray

John as the forerunner of Jesus whose baptizing and preaching ministry was over (or nearly over) before Jesus appeared on the scene. This portrait has strongly influenced later Christian tradition. But John's Gospel and Q both suggest that the ministries of Jesus and John overlapped. And John states unequivocally that disciples of Jesus originally belonged to John's circle. Since these 'alternative' traditions run counter to the tendency to 'separate' Jesus and John, and to stress John's inferior role, they are undoubtedly historical.

ʊ

Another set of 'embarrassing' traditions takes us further. Although the synoptic Gospels do not state that Jesus himself was a 'baptizer', John 3:22 records that Jesus and his disciples went into the Judean countryside and spent some time there with them and baptized. The next verse notes that John was baptizing in the same area and implies that Jesus and John were both baptizing at the same time. A few verses later there is even a hint of rivalry: the Pharisees hear that Jesus was making and baptizing more disciples than John (John 4:1; cf. also 3:26). At this point the evangelist adds an aside in order to avoid linking Jesus and John too closely: it was not Jesus himself but his disciples who baptized (4:2).

Once again embarrassing traditions, even though they are found only in John's Gospel, are likely to be authentic. Jesus aligned himself with John and also baptized in continuity with John's baptism. However, from the evangelist's point of view, Jesus was not just another baptizer like John: Jesus is the one who baptizes with the Holy Spirit (John 1:33).

ʊ

There is a saying of Jesus which speaks about John so positively that it must be authentic:

> Truly I tell you, among those born of women no one has arisen greater than John the Baptist; yet the least in the kingdom of heaven is greater than he (Matthew 11:11 = Luke 7:28 [Q]).

In this saying Jesus seems to praise John to the sky in the first part, and then bring him firmly down to earth in the second. Perhaps the second half of the saying was added later in order to modify the first half. But a moment's reflection soon reveals that this is an unlikely solution. Would a Christian put John in his place by first proclaiming his greatness? John could easily have been assigned an inferior role by omitting the first half of this baffling saying.

The first half of the saying, with its warm praise of John, must be authentic. What does the second half mean? There are two possibilities. (i) Jesus may be referring to the *coming* kingdom: in that grand era, anyone in the kingdom will be more privileged than John the greatest of men in the present era. If this is the correct interpretation, here is a positive portrait of John in both parts of the saying. (ii) On the second interpretation, the least in the *present* kingdom are contrasted with John who is not even in the kingdom. Since this interpretation offers a more negative portrait of John, it is less likely.

⚏

By looking out for 'embarrassing' traditions in the preceding paragraphs, we have seen that there are a number of authentic traditions which link Jesus and John. Jesus was undoubtedly baptized by John, and then carried out a baptizing ministry himself in the same area as John. For some time before John was arrested, Jesus seems to have been a disciple of John's. If so, *John may well have influenced Jesus*. There is an obvious corollary: by looking closely at the historical evidence concerning John, we may gain some insights into the intention of Jesus. The similarities as well as the differences between Jesus and John are well worth exploring.

Josephus

At this point we must consider evidence of a rather different kind: Josephus's comments on John the Baptist. For rather different reasons, some of these traditions are likely to be authentic. They follow Josephus's account of the defeat of the army of Herod Antipas by the Nabatean king Aretas IV. Herod Antipas governed Galilee in dependence on Rome from 4 BC to AD 39.

116. But to some of the Jews it seemed that the Herod's army was destroyed by God, indeed as a just act of vengeance for his treatment of John, surnamed the Baptist. 117. For Herod had put him to death, even though he was a good man and had encouraged the Jews to lead righteous lives, to practise justice towards one another and piety towards God, and so doing to join in baptism. For only thus would the baptism be acceptable to God: they must not use it to gain pardon for whatever sins they committed, but rather for the purification of their bodies, implying that their souls had already been thoroughly cleansed by right behaviour. 118. When others too joined the crowds about him, because they were roused to fever pitch by his words, Herod became alarmed. He feared that John's ability to sway people might lead to some form of sedition, for it looked as if they would act on John's advice in everything that they did. Herod therefore decided that it would be much better to strike first and be rid of him before his work led to an uprising. . . 119. And so John, because of Herod's suspicions, was brought in chains to Machaerus . . . and there put to death. But the verdict of the Jews was that the destruction of Herod's army was a punishment of Herod, since God saw fit to inflict harm on Herod. (*Antiquities* xviii. 116-9)

As we saw in *Chapter X*, the writings of Josephus were preserved solely by Christians. Since Josephus's comments about Jesus were 'Christianized', we must ask whether anything of the sort has happened here. There are several reasons why this extended passage is not a later Christian interpolation. First, a Christian would surely have mentioned Jesus in connection with John.

And secondly, the reason given for John's death differs from Mark's account in 6:17-29, which is abbreviated in Matthew 14:3-12. A later Christian interpolator would not have allowed that to happen. Whereas Mark insists that it was John's ethical rebuke of Herod which led to his downfall, Josephus stresses that John's death was the result of Herod Antipas's political fears.

Thirdly, Josephus's comments fit in well with his general approach in this section of the *Antiquities*. The vocabulary and style do not suggest an interpolation.

Both Mark and Josephus could be correct in the reasons they give for John's death: given the political threats he faced, Herod may well have understood John's ethical rebuke to have had very strong political overtones. Mark's claim (6:17) that Herod Antipas had married quite inappropriately his brother Philip's wife, Herodias, is mistaken: in fact Philip was married to Salome, not Herodias her mother.

Both Josephus and Mark have 'shaped' their accounts of John in the light of their wider concerns. Few of Josephus's largely pagan and Jewish readers would have been interested in John's fiery prophetic preaching recorded by the evangelists, so it is not included. Josephus portrays John as a popular moral philosopher with a lustration rite, a portrait which would not have seemed odd to his readers. Mark's concerns are different. For Mark, the rejection and death of the prophet John foreshadow the rejection and death of God's final 'prophetic' messenger, Jesus.

In spite of the evident 'bias' of both Josephus and Mark, with judicious assessment both accounts of John are invaluable for the historian. Josephus provides important evidence external to the Gospels that John appeared on the religious scene about AD 28. He was known as John 'the baptist' because of the lustration rite he administered. John attracted such a large following that Herod feared an uprising. Josephus's account underlines the highly charged political environment in which John (and Jesus) lived, taught and died. Because John was perceived to be a political threat, he was put to death at Machaerus, Herod's mountain fortress not far from the east coast of the Dead Sea.

Similarities and differences

Jesus acknowledged that John was a prophet – indeed, more than a prophet (Matthew 11:9); once again, this high praise is authentic. Jesus links himself closely with John: John and Jesus are both sent by God: 'God's wisdom is proved right by both her children' (the original Q wording of Matthew 11:19 = Luke 7: 35). Since Jesus and John were so similar, *Jesus himself was undoubtedly a prophet.* This may seem to be labouring the obvious. But it needs to be said in view of the recent attempt to claim that Jesus was a sage. The case depends on isolation of wisdom traditions (including general maxims, riddles and proverbs) as the foundation of both Q and the Gospel of Thomas.[1] It can be sustained only by ignoring the clear evidence of both Mark and Josephus that Jesus and John were prophets who called for the renewal of Israel in God's name.

Jesus and John were both written off by opponents who claimed that their prophetic words were spoken not on God's authority but as the result of their possession by a demon (see Matthew 11:18 for John, and the previous chapter for Jesus). Some even confused Jesus and John (Mark 8:28 and cf. 6:14).

Both Jesus and John were opposed to the Temple establishment. This is a conclusion which needs some explanation. We shall see in the next chapter that Jesus' actions in the Temple 'triggered' his downfall. What was John's attitude to the Temple? A hint is given in a feature of John's baptism which is referred to in passing in Mark 1:5 and 9, and also in Matthew 3:11 = Luke 3: 16 (Q): whereas all the various Jewish lustration rites were self-administered, John carried out baptism himself. This probably led to his nick-name, the 'baptizer'. The Gospels and Josephus emphasize that John called people to repentance. In his role as baptizer, *John himself mediated God's forgiveness.* As Robert Webb has recently stressed, his role was 'parallel to the mediatorial role of a priest performing a sacrifice to mediate forgiveness in the sacrificial system (e.g. Leviticus 5:5–10).'[2] Webb goes even further (I think correctly) and suggests that John's baptism functioned at least implicitly as a protest against the Temple establishment.

Both John and Jesus suffered a similar fate at the hands of the political authorities, Herod Antipas and Pontius Pilate. Josephus notes that John and his followers were seen as a threat to political stability. In the next chapter we shall see that Jesus and his followers were also seen as a threat to political stability. In first-century Palestine religion and politics cannot be separated: prophetic calls for religious renewal had sufficiently strong political overtones to account for the downfall of both John and Jesus.

◘

Jesus and John differed in important respects. Unlike John, Jesus was not an ascetic (Matthew 9:19; 11:18 = Luke 7: 33-34). Unlike John's disciples, the disciples of Jesus did not fast (Mark

2:18). Unlike John, Jesus stopped baptizing (John 3:22; 4:2).
Unlike John, who remained in the wilderness, Jesus travelled
from village to village. Unlike John 'who did no miracle' (John
10:41), Jesus performed numerous healings and exorcisms.
Unlike John, Jesus shared table fellowship with tax collectors and
sinners. Unlike John, whose prophetic preaching focused on the
future, Jesus announced that God's kingly rule was breaking into
the present *now*, through his own actions and words (e.g.
Matthew 11: 2-5 = Luke 7:18-23 [Q]; Matthew 12:28 = Luke
11:20 [Q]).

How are these differences to be accounted for? Paul
Hollenbach (1982) discerns a shift in Jesus' ministry from baptizer to healer, and accounts for the change by referring to Jesus'
experience of the kingdom of God in his power to heal and
exorcize.[3] Robert Webb (1994) accepts this explanation and adds
a further observation: as a prophet, Jesus experienced God's call
at the time of his baptism by John, and only gradually understood
the full significance of that call. 'Jesus' shift from baptizer to
healer and exorcist implies a shift to an increased experience and
intimacy with the divine realm.'[4]

Such appeals to the personal religious experience of Jesus are
not fashionable: they are said to involve 'psychologizing' for
which the sources do not provide evidence. But surely a profound awareness of God's call and commissioning is fundamental
to the experience of the Old Testament prophets. Like the
prophets of old, in God's name John and Jesus also called for the
renewal of Israel.

In this chapter I have focused on 'embarrassing' traditions
which are likely to be authentic, and I have drawn attention to
the value of the comments of Josephus. By comparing and con-
trasting Jesus and John, fresh light is shed on the differing ways
they understood their call to address Israel prophetically in God's
name.

CHAPTER XV

JESUS: KING OF THE JEWS

IN THE PRECEDING chapter we saw that some of the traditions concerning the opening of the ministry of Jesus embarrassed his later followers. So too did his ultimate fate. In antiquity crucifixion was the most savage and shameful form of capital punishment. It was so barbarous and inhumane that polite Romans did not talk about it. Crucifixion was carried out by the Romans especially on slaves, violent criminals and rebellious subject peoples.[1]

The crucifixion of Jesus was an acute embarrassment to his followers. At the time of Jesus there was no expectation that a Messiah would suffer or be crucified, so proclamation of a crucified Messiah made no sense at all to Jews who heard it. Markus Bockmuehl notes that 'in the public mind this kind of ignominious death would have meant the end of any Messianic claim. A righteous man he might be – after all, even the highly regarded Maccabean martyrs had suffered a violent death. But he could not be the Messiah.'[2]

To Greeks, proclamation of a recently crucified person was 'folly' (I Corinthians 1:23). The reaction of Celsus, the pagan critic of Christianity (see p.35) was surely typical. He poked fun at Christians who claimed that Jesus was God's Son, 'although he was most dishonourably arrested and punished to his utter disgrace.'[3]

The first followers of Jesus could not possibly have invented the crucifixion of Jesus, for it left them open to ridicule. So there can be no doubt at all that Jesus was crucified by the Roman prefect Pilate as a political rebel. The disciples did not and could not gloss over this embarrassing fact. Very soon after what must have been a traumatic event for the disciples, they attached positive theological significance to the crucifixion of Jesus. About AD 50 Paul cites as 'Gospel truth' a much earlier tradition he had received: 'Christ died for our sins in accordance with the Scriptures' (I Corinthians 15:3). Luke reports that on the day of Pentecost Peter claimed that the crucifixion of 'this Jesus' was part of God's definite plan: by raising Jesus from the dead, God reversed the actions of wicked men (Acts 2:23-4). But even the positive ways in which the earliest Christians spoke about the death of Jesus could not hide the shame of crucifixion.

There is equally little doubt about the historicity of the inscription on the cross. Similar wording is found in all four Gospels:

Mark 15:26: 'The King of the Jews'
Matthew 27:37: 'This is Jesus, the King of the Jews'
Luke 23:38: 'The King of the Jews, this one'
John 19:29: 'Jesus the Nazorean, the King of the Jews'

The differences are not significant, but they do remind us that the Gospels do not give us absolute accuracy.

The inscription was intended to provide information about the offence to passers-by, and to act as a deterrent. Mark's earliest and simplest wording is probably what was written. 'The King of the Jews' announced the charge made against Jesus: he was put to death for claiming to be king of the Jews and thus usurping Rome's authority. From the evangelists' point of view, the inscription was profoundly true: Jesus was indeed the Messiah-King. None the less, the inscription, like the crucifixion itself, was deeply embarrassing, for it announced to all and sundry that Jesus had been condemned as a political upstart.

Why was Jesus put to death on a Roman cross? As soon as the possible explanations of this 'brute fact' are explored, we are brought face to face with the political and religious turmoil of the times. The close association of Jesus with John the Baptist is a further reminder of this. John, like Jesus, called for the renewal of Israel. His confrontation with Herod Antipas was construed by Mark and Matthew in religious terms, and by Josephus in political terms (see pp. 168-70). These judgements are not incompatible. The evangelists and Josephus are concerned with two sides of the same coin: in first-century Palestine politics and religion were inseparable. A challenge to the religious *status quo* carried strong political overtones, and vice versa.

The historian is bound to ask first of all whether the Romans were in fact justified in putting Jesus to death for political subversion. Did Jesus advocate the use of violence against the despised Roman authorities? If this notion turns out to be impossible, we must search for a more plausible explanation for the crucifixion of Jesus.

Jesus: a political revolutionary?

A positive answer to this question was given in the very first modern attempt to discuss the intention of Jesus with rigorous historical methods. Towards the end of the eighteenth century Hermann Samuel Reimarus (*see p.* 7) wrote:

> (Jesus was well aware that) by such a plain announcement of the kingdom of heaven, he would only awaken the Jews to the hope of a worldly Messiah; consequently, this must have been his object in so awakening them. . . . It was then clearly not the intention or the object of Jesus to suffer and to die, but to build up a worldly kingdom, and to deliver the Israelites from (political) bondage.[4]

Although variations on this theme were proposed from time to time, it was only in 1967 that the claim that Jesus was sympathetic to the 'freedom fighters' of his day made an impact. In that year S. G. F. Brandon's book, *Jesus and the Zealots*[5] was immediately seized on with glee by Christian and non-Christian political activists in several parts of the world, some of whom were prepared to use violence in the struggle against injustice and political oppression.

First of all we must clarify just who the 'zealots' were. The 'zealots' are often mentioned in standard books on the New Testament as a fourth group in first-century Judaism alongside the Pharisees, the Essenes and the Sadducees. Unlike the other three groups, the 'zealots' are said to have advocated the use of violence in order to rid the land of the Romans, the hated occupying power.

This picture is, however, misleading. The so-called zealots were by no means the only Jews opposed to Roman rule. Many others (including some Pharisees) shared their objectives, if not their methods. In addition, the term 'zealots' is inappropriate, since there is no firm evidence before AD 66 (the outbreak of the Jewish uprising against the Romans) that there was a group or sect known as the 'zealots'. None the less there is clear evidence that in the previous sixty years there were several (often competing) groups dedicated to the overthrow of the Romans. Their aims were both political and religious. The various resistance movements called for overt opposition to the Romans in order to restore the purity of the land of Israel which had been defiled by some of the actions of the Romans. The so-called zealots were *zealous* for the law and for the purity of Israel.

What is to be made of the claim that Jesus was a 'zealot' sympathizer? Brandon insists that the evangelists have painted a portrait of a 'pacifist' Jesus to suit the period after AD 70 when Christians had to prove to the Romans that their movement was politically harmless. The 'real' Jesus is hidden by the evangelists' whitewash: he was in fact associated with the freedom fighters of his day. But, it is alleged, the whitewash is so thin that it reveals some tell-tale clues for the keen observer.

Brandon notes that one of the disciples of Jesus is referred to as 'Simon, the zealot' (Mark 3:18). The NEB translates misleadingly, 'a member of the Zealot party'; as we have just noted, there was no such 'party' before AD 66.[6] The Greek word transliterates an Aramaic word which may mean no more than 'enthusiast'. In any case there is no evidence that once he became a disciple of Jesus, Simon retained any former sympathies with a group of 'enthusiasts' who may or may not have been freedom fighters.

Brandon dismisses the 'love your enemies' saying (Matthew 5:44 = Luke 6:27,35) too readily as a creation of Matthew's. But this is a Q logion which antedates our written Gospels; it has good claims to be accepted as a radical saying of Jesus with little or no precedent in first-century Jewish teaching.

Jesus' acceptance of tax collectors is well attested in several strands of the Jesus traditions. Since they were collecting taxes for the detested occupying power, they were despised and spurned by groups advocating violence against the Romans. It follows that if Jesus took a special interest in the tax collectors, he cannot have had close links or sympathies with resistance fighters.

A good deal of emphasis is placed on what is taken to have been the original intention of Jesus in entering Jerusalem and 'cleansing' the Temple. However, insufficient account is taken of the fact that at Passover time each year the Romans reinforced their garrison in Jerusalem. There would have been an immediate and vigorous response to a mere rumour of a major disturbance either on a major route into Jerusalem, or in the Temple precincts. If Jesus had intended to spark off a political revolt in Jerusalem at Passover, he and all his followers would surely have been arrested. The fact that only Jesus was arrested tells strongly against Brandon's theory.

Careful sifting of all the evidence of the Jesus traditions does not support the claim by Brandon (and others) that the 'real' Jesus was a political revolutionary. Too much inconvenient evidence has to be ignored in order to make out the case.

If Jesus was not put to death because he was a freedom fighter, or a sympathizer with such groups, how are we to account for his crucifixion by the Romans? There are several possible explanations. I shall discuss three, but it is important to note at the outset that they are not mutually exclusive.

Was Jesus crucified because he (or his followers) claimed that he was the (non-violent) King-Messiah? Was Jesus crucified because his anti-Temple sayings and his action in the Temple were a frontal attack on the political and religious establishment of the day? Or did Jesus fall foul of the *Jewish* authorities because over a period of time many of his actions and words had kindled messianic expectations and had been considered to be deeply offensive?

What can be ruled out confidently is any suggestion that Jesus was merely a sage, a teacher of proverbs, maxims and general ethical principles. It is very difficult to envisage a sage offering such subversive teaching that he ended up on a Roman cross. The Romans were often ruthless, but they did not crucify such people.

Jesus: the King-Messiah?

The inscription over the cross of Jesus read: 'The King of the Jews.' Did the authorities judge correctly that Jesus had claimed to be a King-Messiah? At the time the term 'Messiah' carried many connotations, but central to most of them was the hope that an anointed King of David's line would set up a glorious kingdom by removing Israel's enemies. Messiah means 'the anointed one'; 'Christ' is the Greek translation of the Hebrew 'Messiah' (cf. John 1:41; 4:25). So for many 'Messiah' and 'King' were almost synonymous terms.

The followers of Jesus were convinced that Jesus was indeed the King-Messiah. How did they reach that conclusion? Did the Christian confession of the Messiahship of Jesus arise only in the post-Easter period?

Paul refers to Jesus as 'Christ' on every page of his letters – 271 times in all in his seven undisputed letters. However, with only one clear exception and a handful of marginal cases, 'Christ' has become simply a name for Jesus; it no longer refers to the *Messiahship* of Jesus.[7] Elsewhere when Paul speaks about the significance of Jesus for Christians, he prefers to use 'Lord', or 'Son'/'Son of God', because these terms made sense to Gentiles. Without explanation, Messiah meant nothing in non-Jewish settings.

Paul's letters come from the 50s and are the earliest New Testament writings. Why does Paul use the name 'Christ' so frequently to refer to Jesus, even though he does not have Messiahship in mind? The only possible explanation is that long before Paul's day, 'Jesus is Messiah' was central in the earliest Aramaic-speaking church's confessions and proclamation.

Is the origin of this conviction the disciples' resurrection experiences, as in the case of the confession, 'Jesus is Lord' (*see pp. 149-51)*? The disciples were convinced that on the third day God had raised Jesus from the dead, *but this conviction would not have led them to conclude that Jesus was the Messiah*. For none of the varied first-century beliefs about resurrection had anything to do with messianic hopes. This time we have to look elsewhere.

As the Norwegian scholar Nils Dahl notes, 'Rarely has it been made clear how strange it is that precisely the title "Messiah" was applied to Jesus and became his name.'[8] It is no help to suppose that in the early post-Easter period the Jewish idea of the Messiah was simply hijacked and applied to Jesus. For there is a huge gap between Jewish messianic expectations and what Christians began to say about the Messiahship of Jesus. It is no exaggeration to refer the early church's 'Christianization' of Jewish messianic hopes.

At the time of Jesus there were many different expressions of the hope that one day soon God would intervene on behalf of his people – and by no means all of them included reference to an individual through whom God would act. Where the term 'Messiah' was used, it nearly always included reference to the political Messiah, the king of David's line. However, the first followers of Jesus avoided the term 'king' and notions of a political Messiah: to have referred to Jesus in these ways would have been suicidal in the highly charged political climate of the day. Not surprisingly, the phrase 'King of the Jews' never became a Christian confession. So it was by no means as natural as we might suppose for the first followers of Jesus to apply the term 'Messiah' to Jesus.

Nor can we explain the early Christian insistence that Jesus was the Messiah by appealing to Jesus' own claims. If Jesus had repeatedly stated explicitly that he was the Messiah, then it would have been natural for his followers to continue this claim, and to develop it in the light of their Easter convictions. But in our earliest Gospel, Mark, Jesus rarely speaks of his Messiahship. When Peter does confess, 'You are the Christ' (Mark 8:29), this is not greeted by Jesus with enthusiasm. Jesus immediately speaks solemnly about his coming suffering and rejection, which were not part of the expectations concerning the Messiah.

Why was the confession 'Jesus is Messiah' so prominent in the earliest post-Easter period? Neither the disciples' resurrection experiences, nor current Jewish messianic expectations, nor the preaching of Jesus himself turns out to be an adequate answer. The only possible explanation for early Christian usage is that Jesus was crucified as a messianic pretender. His actions had aroused messianic hopes among his followers. Those hopes may have been enough to rattle the authorities and force them to charge Jesus as a messianic pretender.

It is very difficult to judge exactly what lies behind the accounts of the Sanhedrin hearing. In their present form they are somewhat idealized. Jesus may have been questioned by the high priest at a less formal hearing than Mark suggests. However, the essential point would seem to be historically accurate. When badgered about his intentions and claims, Jesus at first refused to respond. When pressed, Jesus reluctantly conceded that he was the Messiah.[9] At Mark 14:62 some manuscripts record that the reply of Jesus to the high priest's question was, 'You say that I am' – those are your words, not mine. From the perspective of a later Christian scribe, a more direct answer, 'I am (the Messiah)', would have been preferable. So the evasive answer may well be original. Enough was enough. Jesus was passed over to Pilate who knew all too well the implications of 'Messiahship'.

The inscription on the cross sums up the charge against Jesus. It presupposes that Jesus was accused before Pilate on the ground that he made a royal-messianic claim. This inscription left the followers of Jesus open to the suspicion that they were politically subversive themselves. When they began to 'Christianize' the Messiahship of Jesus, his crucifixion led to ridicule. So it is unlikely that the inscription is a Christian invention. We must conclude that Jesus was condemned by Pilate for claiming to be a Messiah-King.

Jesus and the Temple

According to Mark's account of the trial before the Sanhedrin, false witnesses stood up and said, 'We heard him say, "I will destroy this Temple that is made with hands, and in three days I will build another, not made with hands" ' (Mark 14:58). At the scene of the crucifixion passers-by derided Jesus, 'wagging their heads, and saying, "Aha! You who would destroy the Temple and build it in three days, save yourself, and come down from the cross!" ' (Mark 15:29-30).

Did Jesus speak along these lines? Mark places the sayings on the lips of Jesus' opponents and thus implies that there was no truth in them at all. In *Chapter XIII* we discovered the importance of attending to the critical comments of opponents of Jesus. So we must consider carefully the possibility that Jesus did threaten the destruction of the Temple.

Earlier, at 13:2, Mark himself records that Jesus did predict the destruction of the Temple. As Jesus comes out of the Temple he says to one of his disciples, 'There will not be left one stone upon another, that will not be thrown down.' These three Marcan sayings against the Temple (and their parallels in Matthew) are unlikely to have been invented in the early decades of the early church; during those years completion of the building of the Temple, not its destruction, went on apace.

Two other anti-Temple sayings are relevant. (i) Luke does not include Mark 14:58 and 15:29-30, but in Acts 6:14 he notes that false witnesses claimed that Stephen spoke against the Temple: 'We have heard him say that this Jesus of Nazareth will destroy this place.' Luke himself, like Mark, regards the accusations as mischievous: both writers are reluctant to admit that Jesus made any such claim, but this partial 'cover-up' makes us suspect that he may well have done so, at least indirectly! (ii) Immediately after John's account of the 'cleansing of the Temple' Jesus says to his Jewish critics, 'Destroy this Temple, and in three days I will raise it up again' (2:19). As is often the case in John's Gospel, the opponents of Jesus misunderstand his words – and this allows the evangelist to clarify their true meaning. John explains that Jesus was speaking about the Temple of his body. Since John could hardly have allowed Jesus to say 'I will destroy this Temple, my body', a saying very similar to the three we have noted seems to have been changed from 'I will destroy this Temple. . . .' to 'Destroy this temple' (my body).

The prediction of the destruction of the Temple in Mark 13:2 does not imply that Jesus himself will be involved and it does not mention a rebuilding of the Temple. But the other four 'temple' sayings we have noted (Mark 14:58; 15:29; Acts 6:14 and John 2:19) all mention rebuilding, and three of them (John 2:19 is only a partial exception) do indicate that Jesus himself would be involved in the destruction of the Temple.

Is Jesus likely to have claimed quite openly that he would destroy the Temple and somehow be involved in its rebuilding? This seems very unlikely. However, in the early decades of the first century some Jewish circles did expect that in the 'last days' *God* would provide a 'new Temple', and thus the purity of Israel would be restored. A new Temple clearly implies the destruction of the existing Temple.

Perhaps Jesus spoke against the Temple in the form of a riddle. The variations in the anti-Temple sayings suggest that an original riddle-like saying may have been developed in different ways. No doubt many ignored the rather strange indirect attack on the Temple Jesus seemed to be making. But some of the leaders of the religious 'establishment' would have recalled readily that Jesus had recently entered the Temple and 'driven out those who sold and those who bought in the Temple' (Mark 11:15). Any hint, even in the form of a riddle, that the present Temple might be destroyed and replaced by a new Temple of some kind would be seen as a threat to be taken seriously.

Mark (followed by Matthew and Luke) implies that there was a direct link between the actions of Jesus in the Temple and the hardening of opposition on the part of some of the Jerusalem authorities. This was almost certainly the case. The 'overturning of the tables of the money-changers and the seats of those who sold pigeons' (Mark 11:15) may have been an 'acted parable': a prophetic declaration of God's judgement on the Temple (and, by implication, on Israel as a whole) and an expression of hope that God would soon replace it with some form of 'purified' new Temple.

There are two alternative explanations of the actions of Jesus in the Temple (Mark 11:15-18 and parallels) which we must discuss briefly. On the traditional view, Jesus cleansed the Temple. He protested against the actions of the money changers: their trade should not have been taking place within the precincts of the Temple. Jesus was attempting to restore 'pure' worship of God by showing that much current worship was based on mere 'externals'. Mark seems to have understood the actions of Jesus as a protest against blatant abuses. He himself is probably responsible for the citations of Scripture (11:17) which portray the Temple as a 'den of robbers' (Jeremiah 7:11), in sharp contrast to God's intention that the Temple should be a 'house of prayer for all the nations' (Isaiah 56:7).

While there was certainly an element of protest in the actions of Jesus, the traditional view ignores the fact that buying and selling in the Temple precincts was necessary in order to sustain Temple worship. Overturning a few money tables would not have brought buying and selling to a halt: to do that one would have needed an army! Hence the actions of Jesus are better understood as more than a protest against the money changers; they were a prophetic gesture against the Temple itself.[10] Open denunciation would have led to instant dismissal as a mere madman. But by his riddle-like sayings about the destruction and rebuilding of the Temple, and by his 'parabolic' actions in the Temple precincts, Jesus expressed his fundamental opposition to the Temple. As E.P. Sanders notes, 'Symbolic actions were part of a prophet's vocabulary.'[11] At the time there were several Jewish groups which, for diverse reasons, opposed the Jerusalem Temple, so we need not be surprised that Jesus adopted such a radical stance.

The Temple dominated the religious and political life of Jerusalem. The sheer size of the Temple itself and its precincts are difficult to appreciate unless one visits Jerusalem. Much of the Temple wall and foundations are still visible. The stones are massive: the stones at the southwestern corner of the Temple mount weigh 50 tons; one is almost 400 tons. No wonder that the disciples said to Jesus as he came out of the Temple, 'Look, Master, what large stones and what large buildings' (Mark 13:2) (see Plate 16).

Markus Bockmuehl has recently argued that the legitimate and necessary operation of the Temple was supported by a maze of intrigue, nepotism and corruption which is amply reflected in Josephus and early rabbinic sources.[12] In Chapter IX (p. 116) I suggested that the lifestyle of the wealthy priestly owners of the recently excavated houses near the Temple may well have caused outrage to Jesus.

So the prophetic words and actions of Jesus are hardly surprising. Nor need we doubt that they triggered his downfall.

A Messianic Prophet

In this chapter I have suggested that Jesus was condemned by Pilate as a messianic pretender. I have also suggested that the prophetic words of Jesus about the Temple, and his actions in the Temple, triggered his downfall. These are not alternative ways of understanding why the prophet from Galilee ended up on a Roman cross.

Were there deeper roots? Did Jesus give offence at earlier

stages of his ministry? Or should we draw a sharp contrast between a relatively trouble-free ministry in Galilee and the turmoil of the final visit of Jesus to Jerusalem?

Mark has a clear answer to these questions. Mark concludes a cycle of stories in which Jesus is in conflict with scribes and Pharisees in Galilee with these words: 'The Pharisees went out and immediately conspired with the Herodians against Jesus, how to destroy him' (3:6). The Pharisees and Herodians appear only once more: following the 'cleansing of the Temple' they are sent by the chief priests, scribes and the elders (11:27) to trap Jesus with a trick question about paying the Temple tax (12:13). For Mark, the Herodians represent the political powers of Herod Antipas (cf. 8:15) and Rome (12:13-17).

In this way Mark links Galilee and Jerusalem together: in both places the religious authorities (Pharisees) and the political authorities (Herodians) work together to try to secure the downfall of Jesus. For Mark, matters are brought to a head by what Jesus says and does in the Temple, but there are deeper roots which go right back to near the beginning of his Galilean ministry (2:1–3:6).

At this point we come across a baffling issue. The Pharisees, who have been prominent as opponents of Jesus in the early chapters of Mark, disappear from the stage at 12:13. They are not mentioned anywhere in Mark's passion narratives. Equally baffling is the fact that the issues which caused such offence to the scribes and Pharisees in the early chapters do not reappear when Jesus is questioned and accused by the high priest and by Pilate.

Mark implies that while the events in Jerusalem led directly to the condemnation of Jesus, he had caused offence to religious and political authorities long before he went up to Jerusalem. The careful reader notes that in 12:13 Mark does supply a link between the Pharisees and the Jerusalem authorities: the chief priests, elders and scribes sent some Pharisees and some Herodians to trap Jesus *in the Temple precincts*. Is this simply Mark's way of telling the story of Jesus? Or is it, at least in general terms, what happened?

In his recent influential historical reconstruction E. P. Sanders places a great deal of weight on the prophetic words and actions of Jesus in the Temple. Although I am hesitant about some points, I think he has correctly drawn attention to the Temple as decisive as far as the downfall of Jesus was concerned.[13] But in my opinion he has dismissed the conflicts between Jesus and the Pharisees.

Here I can make only two points briefly. First, Sanders believes that the conflicts between Jesus and the Pharisees have been heavily influenced by post-Easter disputes between Christians and Jews. However, some of the issues most prominent in post-Easter disputes are *not* mentioned in the Gospels, and vice versa (*see pp. 147-9*).[14] I do not think the conflict traditions can be brushed aside so readily. Although Jesus normally kept the Jewish law, he does seem to have caused offence by breaking conventions (e.g. fasting, Mark 2:18) and by calling for a re-ordering of priorities on a number of issues.

And secondly, as I argued in *Chapter XIII,* the later polemic is relevant: in his own lifetime Jesus was accused of being a magician (certainly) and of being a false prophet who led Israel astray (probably). The 'magician' charge relates to the exorcisms and healing miracles performed in Galilee: opponents refused to see them as signs of the breaking-in of God's kingly rule. The 'false prophet' accusation would certainly include calling in question well-established conventions concerning behaviour, i.e. issues which Jesus and the Pharisees argued about. I doubt whether the anti-Temple sayings and the 'cleansing of the Temple' alone would have led to the polemic to which I have drawn attention.

❦

Jesus was a prophet. Was he a *messianic* prophet? He did not make repeated explicit claims to be the Messiah. But as I have suggested above, Jesus conceded reluctantly to Pilate that he was the Messiah-King. Were some of his earlier words and actions an implicit claim to Messiahship? This is much disputed; the issues are complex and not easy to resolve.

However, a recently published Qumran fragment does suggest that some of the actions and words of Jesus were implicitly messianic. When John the Baptist sent disciples to make inquiries about Jesus, he answered as follows:

Go and tell John what you see and hear: the blind receive

their sight, the lame walk, the lepers are cleansed, the deaf hear, *the dead are raised, and the poor have the good news (Gospel) brought to them.* (Matthew 11:4-6 = Luke 7:22-3 [Q])

With these words Jesus is alluding to Isaiah 29:18f; 35:5; and 61:1f. The first two passages provide the general theme of an eschatological time when the deaf will hear, the blind see, and the lame walk. The climax comes with the allusion to Isaiah 61:1, 'the poor have the good news (Gospel) preached to them'. Was Jesus hinting that he was an expected end-time prophet, or even that he was the Messiah?

In a discussion of this passage in 1973, I drew attention to a recently published Qumran fragment (11Q Melchizedek, line 18) in which the herald of good tidings of Isaiah 52:7 is closely linked with Isaiah 61:1 and is identified as '*the* anointed one'. I then wrote as follows: 'Although it has frequently been assumed that the reply of Jesus to John would be understood as an indirect claim to be Messiah, there are some grounds for caution, even in spite of 11Q Melch. For it is difficult to find clear-cut evidence that Isaiah 61:1 was referred to the Messiah in late Judaism.'[15]

The missing evidence has now turned up in another Qumran document, 4Q521, published in 1992. One of the 17 fragments of 4Q521 opens in line 1 as follows: ' . . . heaven and earth will obey *his Messiah*' (fragment 2 ii). The lines which follow speak of care for the pious, righteous, the poor, the captives, the blind. And then in the very important line 12 we read, 'for he will heal the wounded, *give life to the dead and preach good news to the poor.*'

The correspondence with phrases in Matthew 11:4-6 (quoted in italics above), with Isaiah 52:7 and 61:1f., and with 11Q Melchizedek is striking. Although the fragment of 4Q521 quoted above opens with a reference to the Messiah, in the lines which follow it is not clear whether the one caring for the various needy groups is God or his agent, the Messiah. But in line 12 there is no doubt. God does not usually 'preach good news'; this is the task of his herald or messenger. So in line 12 at least, it is the Messiah who has the task of 'healing the wounded, giving life to the dead, and preaching good news to the poor'.[16]

In 4Q521 the Messiah 'preaches good news to the poor'. We now have evidence that before the time of Jesus Isaiah 61:1f., with its reference to the anointed prophet being sent to preach good news to the poor, was understood to be a *messianic prophecy*. It is highly likely that when Jesus referred to his own actions and words in terms of this passage (and the related ones), he was making an indirect messianic claim.[17] Jesus refers to himself as the fulfilment of Isaiah 61:1f. in another strand of the Gospel traditions, Luke 4:18-21, so on the basis of the criterion of multiple attestation we need not doubt that these are authentic words of Jesus.

Why was Jesus crucified? The inscription over the cross provides the answer: Jesus was condemned as a Messiah-King. The anti-Temple words of Jesus and his 'cleansing' of the Temple triggered his downfall. The events in Jerusalem immediately before the arrest of Jesus were not the beginning of the end, but the end of the beginnings in Galilee.

CHAPTER XVI

GOSPEL TRUTH
ABOUT JESUS

FRESH LIGHT ON Jesus and the Gospels? I hope that the promise of the sub-title of this book has been fulfilled. I have shown that we have plenty of evidence both inside and outside the New Testament Gospels for the life of Jesus – far more than for any other first-century Jewish prophet-teacher. Indeed we know as much about Jesus of Nazareth as we know about almost any person from antiquity. As we have seen, sifting, sorting and assessing the varied literary and archaeological evidence is by no means a simple task.

My predecessor at King's College London, Professor Christopher Evans, used to tell our students that rigorous study of the Gospels was as demanding and as rewarding as any scholarly work undertaken in our multi-Faculty College – not even our high-powered physicists were an exception. I hope that readers of this book will now agree that this was no exaggeration.

I have drawn attention to some important discoveries made in recent years. We began by looking at widely publicized claims concerning fragments of papyrus. The Magdalen College Oxford fragments of Matthew are very important indeed, but not because of their alleged first-century date. They come from a codex (book) which probably dates from the latter decades of the second century. This handsome codex is the oldest surviving codex which contained Matthew, Mark, Luke and John. It provides fresh evidence for my conviction that the early church settled on *four* Gospels, no more, no less, rather earlier than some scholars have maintained. In *Chapter VIII* I explained why the second-century church's decision to accept *four* Gospels was one of the most momentous steps taken in the history of early Christianity.

The discovery and eventual publication of the Dead Sea Scrolls has been the single most important step forward in the twentieth century for students of all parts of the Bible. In the case of many books of the Old Testament, we now have Hebrew manuscripts which are older by a millennium than the manuscripts known before eleven caves near Qumran began to reveal their secrets.

The claim that a fragment of Mark's Gospel has been found in Cave 7 has naturally attracted a great deal of excited interest. I have considered the theory carefully with an open mind. If correct, many of my views about the origin and date of Mark's Gospel would have to be revised, as would many of my conclusions about earliest Christianity. I am not at all unwilling to follow the evidence. Although I consider that it is very unlikely that a copy of Mark's Gospel found its way to Qumran in the first century, I do not rule out that possibility. The theory that 7Q5 is a fragment of Mark collapses, not for reasons of this kind, but because at a crucial point there is a damaged letter in the tiny fragment which cannot be the letter *nu*. If any other letter existed at this point, 7Q5 cannot be part of Mark's Gospel.

The Dead Sea Scrolls are important for students of the Gospels for other reasons. The 800 or so manuscripts do not include part of any early Christian writing. Since they were nearly all written *before* the time of Jesus, it is not surprising that they do not contain even a single indirect reference to Jesus or to any of his followers. However, the Dead Sea Scrolls do greatly enrich our knowledge of the world in which Jesus lived and taught. This was confirmed by discussion of three recently published fragments from Cave 4:4Q246 (*see pp. 154-5*); 4Q394-9 (=4QMMT, *see pp.31, 59*), 4Q521 (*see pp. 186-7*).

❧

In the second half of this book I assessed the historical evidence for the actions and teaching of Jesus of Nazareth. By reading the Gospels 'against the grain', it proved possible to reconstruct a clear picture of the actions, words and intentions of Jesus. Three unconventional methods were used.

I insisted that it is essential to consider the 'aftermath' of Jesus. It is quite in accord with sound historical method to look closely at the post-Easter period. In the very conservative religious and social climate of the first century, followers of Jesus took radical steps in his name, and made profound claims about him. In spite of the monotheistic heritage they refused to abandon, at a very early point they began to *worship* Jesus. How could all this have happened if Jesus of Nazareth was merely a sage or a conventional teacher? As we saw, at some points there is no pre-Easter precedent for later developments; at other points, there are clear and important lines of continuity. The latter direct us to some of the most distinctive features of the life of Jesus.

I attach rather more weight than most recent writers to traditions strongly *critical* of Jesus (*see Chapter XIII*). I am convinced that the later polemical comments made about Jesus have deep roots. In his own lifetime Jesus was considered by some to be deeply offensive. Were his exorcisms and healing miracles signs of the partial presence of *God's kingly rule,* or were they the result of collusion with the prince of demons? Was Jesus a prophet sent *by God*, or was he a false prophet who was deceiving Israel? The polemical traditions confirm that in his own lifetime the relationship of Jesus *to God* was a central issue.

I also argued that traditions within the four Gospels which were an embarrassment to the later followers of Jesus are authentic. With careful scrutiny, they tell us a good deal about Jesus. The similarities between Jesus and John the Baptist confirm that Jesus, like John, was a radical prophet. As we saw, the significant differences point to further distinctive features of the ministry of Jesus. The inscription over the Cross, 'The King of the Jews', announced to passers-by the charge brought against Jesus, but it points us to the reason why Jesus was put to death: he was a messianic pretender.

Jesus was a charismatic prophet with unusual healing gifts. His actions and words flouted deeply-held religious and social conventions: they were perceived by the religious and political 'establishment' to be a threat to law and order. Although Jesus avoided making explicit claims about himself, there is little doubt that some of his actions and words were in effect an implicit claim to Messiahship. They were certainly perceived to be so by many who followed Jesus in Galilee, and by many in the crowds which followed him to Jerusalem. Although his riddle-like anti-Temple comments and the so-called cleansing of the Temple triggered his downfall, earlier confrontations with scribes and Pharisees were a contributory factor.

♉

Do the Gospels contain 'Gospel truth'?   In the opening chapter we saw that this phrase is used today in two ways: to refer *either* to the absolute reliability of every single word of the Gospels, *or* to the truth of the Gospel message about Jesus Christ which the evangelists sought to proclaim. Along with Origen (third century) and Martin Luther (sixteenth century) I do not believe it is possible to establish the accuracy of every word of the Gospels (*see pp.8-10*). Nor do I think that 'the truth of the Gospel' is thereby placed in jeopardy.

There are two main reasons why we cannot claim that the Gospels preserve 'Gospel truth', if we understand this phrase to refer to their historical accuracy in every detail.

First, Jesus spoke Aramaic; at some point Aramaic traditions were translated into Greek. Translation from one language into another always involves an element of interpretation. When two languages are unrelated, as is the case with Aramaic and Greek, there is an unavoidable loss of precision. So we do not have direct access to the very words of Jesus.

And secondly, as we saw in Chapter IV, the gap between the lifetime of Jesus and the writing of the four Gospels is considerable. Although it can be bridged, care is needed. There are good grounds for concluding that on the whole Jesus traditions were transmitted faithfully from one generation to another. None the less, as soon as we set the Gospels side by side in columns, we become aware of the variations in wording. For example, there are variations in the words of the Lord's Prayer, the words of Jesus at the Last Supper, and the wording of the inscription over the Cross. And in addition, the evangelists shaped and developed the traditions in order to make them relevant to their reader. They felt free to do this because their primary concern was to proclaim the significance of Jesus Christ; they did not intend to summarize what Jesus had said and did in the manner of a modern secretary taking minutes as records of important board meetings.

In short, if we take 'Gospel truth' to refer to the absolute accuracy of every word and phrase, then the evangelists fall short: that was not their primary intention. They give us four *portraits* of Jesus, and four portraits are infinitely more revealing than four photographs.

❦

How do matters stand if we take 'Gospel truth' to refer to the evangelists' theological convictions about Jesus of Nazareth as Messiah-Christ, Son of God, and Lord? As a Christian, I affirm the 'Gospel truth' proclaimed by Matthew, Mark, Luke and John. But that is not a commitment I make solely on the basis of historical evidence: I cannot *prove* to myself or to anyone else that in the life, death and resurrection of Jesus, God disclosed his purposes for his creation. All I can say is that my theological affirmation is *not inconsistent* with the historical evidence as I understand it.

This is such an important point that it must be taken further. No amount of historical evidence for the life and teaching of Jesus ever *proves* 'Gospel truth'. After all, some who saw and heard Jesus for themselves drew the conclusion that he was a magician and a false prophet. *Proof* cannot reside either in any new papyrus fragment (however early its date), or in any artefact uncovered by archaeologists.

The historian can even conclude that the tomb in which Jesus was buried was empty *without* affirming the 'Gospel truth' that God raised Jesus on the third day. Some historians have in fact done this: they simply leave open what happened to the body of Jesus. The resurrection is not an historical event which can be investigated with historical methods. The historian can comment on what happened in the light of the disciples' experiences of the 'aliveness' of Jesus, but the nature and reality of those experiences cannot be established by historical methods. Can a historian *prove* that a young couple have fallen in love, rather than into a delusion?

On the other hand, in theory at least, 'Gospel truth' is open to *falsification* by historical evidence. If historians were to conclude that Jesus did not exist, then Christianity as it has been understood by most Christians down through the centuries would be holed beneath its waterline. In the light of the evidence discussed in this book, the existence of Jesus is firmly established: so this is a purely hypothetical example.

Let me give further examples to illustrate the relationship between 'Gospel truth' and historical evidence. If Jesus really was a political insurgent, in key respects the evangelists' portraits would be totally unreliable. If Jesus was condemned *justly* as a political rebel, it would have been impossible for followers of Jesus to claim that God had reversed the 'wicked deed' of crucifixion by 'lawless men' (cf. Acts 2:22). The disciples' post-Easter proclamation of 'Gospel truth' about Jesus would be undermined.

Or if Jesus did in fact utter blasphemies against God (cf. Mark 14:64), how could his followers possibly have claimed that in raising him from the dead, God had *vindicated* Jesus? God's vindication of Jesus lies at the heart of the varied traditions about the resurrection of Jesus in the New Testament. In raising Jesus from the dead, how could God accept openly that Jesus had *acted correctly* in repudiating him in the most profound way possible?

Down through the centuries Christianity has taken many forms – and it still does so today. None the less, Christians of all persuasions have always insisted that God has disclosed his purposes for humanity in the life, death and resurrection of Jesus; for Christians, this is 'Gospel truth'. So if historical reconstruction of the actions and teaching of Jesus is at odds with this central theological conviction, then 'Gospel truth' is called in question.

Gospel truth cannot be confirmed by historical evidence, but it does depend on the *general reliability* of the evangelists' portraits of Jesus. For this reason the historical evidence discussed in this book must be of perennial interest to Christians. I have chosen the term 'general reliability' deliberately. We do not have precise historical *records* in the Gospels: we have *four* different portraits of Jesus written by evangelists who were concerned to set out the story of Jesus in order to proclaim his significance.

Notes

Chapter I (pp. 1-10)

1. Carsten Peter Thiede, *The Earliest Gospel Manuscript?* Exeter, Paternoster, 1992.
2. Bernhard Mayer, ed., *Christen und Christliches in Qumran?* Regensburg, Friedrich Pustet, 1992.
3. For this paragraph and the quotation I am indebted to Roland Bainton, 'The Bible in the Reformation', in ed. S. L. Greenslade, *The Cambridge History of the Bible* Vol. II, Cambridge, CUP, 1963, pp. 1-37, especially pp. 12-13.
4. I have quoted Henry Chadwick's admirable translation, *Origen: Contra Celsum*, Cambridge, CUP, 1953.

Chapter II (pp. 11-19)

1. There is one possible rival: papyrus fragments of parts of Matthew 23:30-9, POxy 2683 (known to New Testament scholars as P77). I owe this point to Professor Peter Parsons (Oxford) who has kindly helped me to clarify a number of other points made in this chapter.
2. At this point Roberts is quoting W. Schubart, *Griechische Paläographie*, p.136. See 'An Early Papyrus of the First Gospel', *Harvard Theological Review* 46 (1953) pp. 233-7.
3. C. H. Roberts appended a note to a second edition of P. Roca-Puig's monograph, *Un papiro griego del Evangelio de San Mateo* (Barcelona, 1962).
4. For a fuller discussion, see E. G. Turner, *Greek Manuscripts of the Ancient World*, 2nd ed. revised and enlarged by P. J. Parsons, Oxford, OUP, 1987, pp. 21-2.
5. 'Papyrus Magdalen Greek 17 (Gregory-Aland P64) A Reappraisal', *Zeitschrift für Papyrologie und Epigraphik* 105 (1995) pp. 13-20. This article has been reprinted with minor corrections

in *Tyndale Bulletin* 46 (1995) pp. 29–42.

6. Both terms are used in the specialist literature.

7. *Greek Literary Hands*, Oxford, OUP, 1956.

8. G. Cavallo, *Richerche sulla maiuscola biblica*, Studi e testi di papirologia 2, Florence, Le Monnier, 1967; G. Cavallo and H. Maehler, *Greek Bookhands of the Early Byzantine Period, A.D. 300–800*, London, University of London, 1987.

9. See *Greek Bookhands*, pp. 5 and 34.

10. In *The Church Times* on 6 January 1995 Professor Neville Birdsall wrote as follows: 'On the publication of *The Times*'s report on 24 December, I compared the facsimiles of the Magdalen and Barcelona parts of this manuscript with the materials in my library, especially the study of the Italian expert Professor G. Cavallo devoted to the evolution of that style (1967). There can be no doubt of the congruence of the style of the papyrus with many examples quoted by Cavallo.' Dr S. R. Pickering (Macquarie University, Sydney) and Dr David Parker (Birmingham) have both kindly sent me drafts of articles they are preparing on P64; independently, they make similar points. See also note 26 below.

11. Mr T. C. Skeat has pointed out to me that the papyri are probably from the library of Philodemus of Gadara, who died c. 40 BC. If this is so, there can be no comparison with any Christian fragments.

12. In their list of the characteristics of the 'Biblical Majuscule' script, G. Cavallo and H. Maehler draw attention to both the formation and the shape of letters. See their *Greek Bookhands*, p. 34, and also Cavallo's *Richerche sulla maiuscola biblica*, pp. 4–12.

13. I owe this point to Dr David Parker of Birmingham.

14. Parsons continues, 'It is, for example, arguable that styles which contrast wide and narrow letters appear at Herculaneum in i B.C., but in Egypt not until ii A.D.' See his extended discussion of the problems of dating manuscripts in *The Greek Minor Prophets Scroll from Nahal Hever (8HevXIIgr)* (DJD VIII) ed. E. Tov, Oxford, OUP, 1990, pp. 19–26, here pp. 22–3. See also Parsons' contribution on palaeography in eds. P. Skehan, E. Ulrich, Judith E. Sanderson, *Qumran Cave 4. IV: Palaeo-Hebrew and Greek Biblical Manuscripts,* (DJD IX) Oxford, OUP, 1992, pp. 7–13.

15. After I had completed this chapter, Dr Klaus Wachtel of the Institut für neutestamentliche Textforschung at Münster kindly sent me proofs of his forthcoming article to be published in *Zeitschrift für Papyrologie und Epigraphik,* 'P64/P67: Fragmente des

Matthäusevangeliums aus dem 1. Jahrhundert?' Wachtel provides a fine very detailed critical appraisal of Thiede's theory and reaches broadly similar conclusions to those set out above.

In a letter to me at the beginning of May 1995 Professor Parsons mentioned that he had consulted a meeting of papyrologists about the dating of the Magdalen fragments: most opted for the third century, one doubtfully for the fourth.

16. See for example, C. H. Roberts, *Manuscript, Society and Belief in Early Christian Egypt*, London, OUP for the British Academy, 1979, p. 13; C. H. Roberts and T. C. Skeat, *The Birth of the Codex*, Oxford, OUP, 1983, pp. 65f.

17. See J. Merell, 'Nouveaux Fragments de Papyrus 4', *Revue Biblique* 47 (1938) pp. 5–22. Merell's discussion takes up only four pages; the rest of the article consists of his transcription of the text, plus photographs.

18. Colin Roberts, *Buried Books in Antiquity*, London, The Library Association, 1963, pp. 11–13. See also his *Manuscript* (as in note 16) p.8.

19. I owe this paragraph to a letter dated 20 June 1995 from Mr T. C. Skeat. He also pointed out to me that A. S. Hunt was very reluctant to date any Christian papyri, or any codices in general, earlier than the fourth century.

20. Philip W. Comfort, 'Exploring the Common Identification of Three New Testament Manuscripts: P4, P64 and P67', *Tyndale Bulletin* 46 (1995) pp. 43–54. This article is followed by Carsten Peter Thiede's reply, 'Notes on P4 = Bibliothèque Nationale Paris, Supplementum Graece 1120/5', pp. 55–8. On the question of dating Comfort wrote: 'If P4 can be dated to the end of the first century or early second century, it should readily follow that p4 is not far behind.'

In his reply Carsten Thiede also accepts that the manuscripts were written by the same scribe. He gives two reasons why they did not belong to the same codex: whereas the Paris fragments are dark brown, the Oxford/Barcelona scraps have a much lighter hue; there is a difference in the way the start of a new section of the text is indicated. However, the different colouring of the papyri is not significant; it can be accounted for by the appalling state in which the fragments were found. The latter point will be discussed in full in a forthcoming article to T. C. Skeat.

21. *Manuscript* (as in n.16) p. 13.

22. 'The Origin of the Christian Codex', *Zeitschrift für Papyrologie und Epigraphik* 102, (1994) pp. 263–8. See also C. H. Roberts and T.

C. Skeat, *The Birth of the Codex*, London, OUP for the British Academy, 1983.

23. 'Origin', p. 264.

Chapter III (pp. 20–32)

1. Small numbers of scrolls were also found in other places near the Dead Sea. Strictly speaking the term 'Dead Sea Scrolls' refers to *all* the writings discovered. However, this term is often used to refer to the largest and most important of the Dead Sea Scrolls, the writings found in the eleven caves near Qumran. The Scrolls are referred to by the number of the cave in which they were found, followed by 'Q' for Qumran, and then the scroll or fragment number. So 7Q5, the alleged fragment of Mark, is fragment 5 from Cave 7 at Qumran.

2. See Otto Betz and Rainer Riesner, *Jesus, Qumran and the Vatican*, New York, Crossroad, English translation 1994 (2nd German edition, 1993).

3. For a full discussion of the theories of Baigent and Leigh, Robert Eisenman and Barbara Thiering, see the excellent book by Otto Betz and Rainer Riesner (note 2). In my opinion Betz and Riesner are justifiably extremely critical of these recent publications.

4. See Volume III of *Discoveries in the Judaean Desert*, eds. M. Baillet, J. T. Milik and R. de Vaux, Oxford, OUP, 1962.

5. The fragments are probably too small for the new carbon 14 analysis.

6. The discussion which followed is documented fully by Thiede in his *The Earliest Gospel Manuscript?*

7. *The Earliest Gospel Manuscript?* p.55.

8. See *Qumran Cave 4. IV: Palaeo-Hebrew and Greek Biblical Manuscripts*, eds. P. Skehan, E. Ulrich, Judith E. Sanderson, (DJD IX) Oxford, OUP, 1992.

9. *The Dead Sea Scrolls. Major Publications and Tools for Study*, Atlanta, Scholars Press, 1990. See also, P. Kyle McCarter, 'The Mystery of the Copper Scroll' in ed. Herschel Shanks, *Understanding the Dead Sea Scrolls*, London, SPCK, 1993, pp.227–41.

10. In chapter 4 of *The Earliest Gospel Manuscript?* pp. 42–4, Thiede appeals to a fragment of Menander and a fragment of Virgil as comparable examples. While his point is well made, it is worth noting that both examples contain more certain letters than 7Q5.

11. For fuller information on this point, see S.R. Pickering and R.R.E. Cook, *Has a Fragment of Mark been Found at Qumran?*

Sydney, The Ancient History Documentary Research Centre,
Macquarie University, 1989, pp. 12-13.

12. *Has a Fragment of Mark been Found at Qumran?* p.6.

13. See *The Earliest Gospel Manuscript?* p. 69

14. As Thiede readily concedes, O'Callaghan himself was more cautious: he admitted that this *nu* was 'the most difficult point in
the papyrus.' *The Earliest Gospel Manuscript?* pp.34-5.

15. Bernhard Mayer (ed.), *Christen und Christliches in Qumran?*
Eichstütter Studien, Neue Folge Bd 32, Regensburg, Pustet,
1992.

16. This was the verdict of the original editor, M. Baillet, in *Biblica*
53 (1972) pp. 510-11. See especially S.R. Pickering and R. R. E.
Cook, *Has a Fragment of Mark been Found at Qumran?* pp.11-12. I
have been in correspondence with J. A. Fitzmyer concerning the
new photograph. In a letter of 15 June 1995 he mentions that he
has been impressed by it, and now considers the O'Callaghan/
Thiede identification to be unlikely but not impossible. He is
awaiting further study of the photograph, and the reactions of
others to it.

17. W. Slaby, 'Computerunterstützte Fragment-Identifizierung' in the
Eichstätt symposium volume (see note 13) pp. 83-8, notes that a
computer search based on the *ten sure letters* of 7Q5 resulted in its
only possible identification being Luke 3:19-21!

18. An unidentified Greek fragment from Cave 4 at Qumran has
recently been published. It is approximately the same size as 7Q5
– and it also contains only one certain word, *kai* (and). See
Qumran Cave 4 (as in note 8), p. 78.

19. I have quoted (with minor changes) M.A. Knibb's translation,
The Qumran Community, Cambridge, CUP, 1987.

20. See John J. Collins, *The Scepter and the Star: the Messiahs of the
Dead Sea Scrolls and other Ancient Literature*, New York, Doubleday,
1995, p.58 and the further references given there.

Chapter IV (pp. 33-48)

1. I owe this reference to L. Vaganay and Christian-Bernard
Amphoux, *An Introduction to New Testament Textual Criticism*,
Cambridge, CUP, 1991, p. 96.

2. See Tjitze Baarda, 'ΔΙΑΦΩΝΙΑ – ΣΥΜΦΩΝΙΑ: Factors in the
Harmonization of the Gospels. Especially in the Diatessaron of
Tatian', in ed. W. L. Petersen, *Gospel Traditions in the Second
Century*, Notre Dame and London, Notre Dame Press, 1989, p.
134.

3. On the textual tradition of Virgil's writings, see chapter 5 of R. D. Williams and T. S. Pattie, *Virgil, his Poetry through the Ages*, London, The British Library, 1982, pp. 73-83.

4. One Greek manuscript, Codex Washingtonianus, includes the following passage (usually known as the Freer logion) after verse 14 in the longer ending of Mark's Gospel:

> And they excused themselves, saying, 'This age of lawlessness and unbelief is under Satan, who does not allow the truth and power of God to prevail over the unclean things of the spirits. Therefore reveal your righteousness now' – thus they spoke to Christ. And Christ replied to them, 'The term of years of Satan's power has been fulfilled, but other terrible things draw near. And for those who have sinned I was delivered over to death, that they may return to the truth and sin no more, in order that they may inherit the spiritual and imperishable glory of righteousness that is in heaven.

With the exception of the NRSV, these verses are not quoted in the notes of modern translations. In Codex Washingtonianus they follow immediately after the reference in 16:14 to the failure of the disciples to believe those who saw the Risen Jesus. They are clearly intended to account for the disciples' lack of faith and to rehabilitate the disciples following their desertion of Jesus at the time of his arrest (Mark 14:50).

Chapter V (pp. 49-62)

1. Vincent Taylor, *The Formation of the Gospel Tradition*, London, 1933, pp. 41-3; also p. 107. I owe these references to D.E. Nineham, 'Eye-witness Testimony and the Gospel Tradition I', *Journal of Theological Studies* 9 (1958) p. 14.

2. *The Preface to Luke's Gospel: Literary Convention and Social Context in Luke 1. 1-4 and Acts 1.1*, Cambridge, CUP, 1993, pp. 116-25.

3. *The Death of the Messiah*, New York, Doubleday, 1994, Vol. II, p.1184.

4. I owe the main points in the preceding two paragraphs to an unpublished paper by Professor Alan Millard of Liverpool University, 'Writing and the Gospels'. Professor Millard is undertaking important fresh research in this area.

Chapter VI (pp. 63-76)

1. J. Kloppenborg, *The Formation of Q*, Philadelphia, Fortress, 1987, p.80.

2. F. Gerald Downing, 'A Paradigm Perplex: Luke, Matthew and Mark', *New Testament Studies,* 38 (1992) pp. 15-36.

3. M.D. Goulder, *Luke. A New Paradigm,* Sheffield, JSOT, 1989, Vol. I, p.44.

4. A. Harnack, *The Sayings of Jesus,* London, Williams and Norgate, 1908.

5. G.N. Stanton, 'On the Christology of Q', *Christ and Spirit in the New Testament* (FS C.F.D. Moule), eds. B. Lindars and S.S. Smalley, Cambridge, CUP, 1973, pp. 27-42.

6. M. Sato, *Q und Prophetie,* Tübingen, Mohr, 1988; D.R. Catchpole, *The Quest for Q,* Edinburgh, T. & T. Clark, 1992; C.M. Tuckett, *Studies in Q,* Edinburgh, T. & T. Clark, 1995.

7. J. Kloppenborg, *The Formation of Q,* Philadelphia, Fortress, 1987; Burton Mack, *The Lost Gospel,* Shaftesbury et al., Element, 1993.

8. Burton Mack, *The Lost Gospel,* p. 115.

9. 'The Sayings of Gospel Q', in ed. F. van Segbroeck et al., *The Four Gospels 1992* (FS F. Neirynck), Leuven, University Press, 1992, Vol. I, pp. 361-88.

10. See note 4.

11. For a fuller discussion see G.N.Stanton, *A Gospel for a New People: Studies in Matthew,* Edinburgh, T. & T. Clark, 1992, pp. 12-18.

Chapter VII (pp. 77-95)

1. *The Death of the Messiah,* New York et al., Doubleday, 1993, Vol. II, p. 1347.

2. On POxy 2949, see R.A. Coles in ed. G.M. Browne et al., *The Oxyrhynchus Papyri,* Vol. 41, London, Egypt Exploration Society, 1972, pp. 15-16; D. Lührmann, 'POx 2949: EvPt 35 in einer Handschrift des 2./3. Jahrhunderts', *Zeitschrift für die neutestamentliche Wissenschaft* 72 (1981) pp. 216-22. On POxy4009, see D. Lührmann and P. Parsons in ed. P. Parsons et al., *The Oxyrhynchus Papyri,* Vol. 60, London, Egypt Exploration Society, 1993, pp. 1-5.

3. Eusebius, *Historia Ecclesiastica,* VI.12. I have quoted the translation by H.J. Lawlor and J.E. L. Oulton, Vol. I, London, SPCK, 1927.

4. *The Historical Jesus,* San Francisco, Harper, 1991.

5. See especially R. Brown, *The Death of the Messiah,* Vol. II, Appendix I, pp. 1317-49; J.H. Charlesworth and Craig A. Evans in eds., B. Chilton and Craig A. Evans, *Studying the Historical Jesus,* Leiden, Brill, 1994, pp. 503-14; J.P. Meier, *A Marginal Jew: Rethinking the Historical Jesus,* New York, Doubleday, 1991, pp. 116-18.

6. These points (and others) are rightly pressed by Raymond Brown, *The Death of the Messiah*, II, pp. 1332-3.

7. *Fragments of an Unknown Gospel and other Early Christian Papyri*, eds. H. I. Bell and T. C. Skeat, London, The British Museum, 1935, p. 1. Between 1935 and 1938 over fifty publications were devoted to the Egerton Gospel, which is on permanent display in the British Library in London.

8. The square brackets are only an approximate indication of the gaps in the text. The translations are my own. I have used the Greek text of the edition by Bell and Skeat, and the Greek text printed in Aland's *Synopsis*. For PKöln 255, I have used the reconstructed Greek text by D. Lührmann, 'Das neue Fragment des P Egerton 2 (Köln 255)', in eds. F. van Segbroeck et al., *The Four Gospels 1992: FS F. Neirynck*, Leuven, University Press, 1992, Vol. III, pp. 2243-4.

9. J. D. Crossan, *The Historical Jesus*, Edinburgh, T. & T. Clark, 1991, p. 428.

10. See, for example, J.H. Charlesworth and Craig A. Evans (note 5) pp. 514-25; F. Neirynck, 'The Apocryphal Gospels and the Gospel of Mark' in ed. J.-M. Sevrin, *The New Testament in Early Christianity*, Leuven, University Press, 1989, pp. 123-77, esp. pp. 161-7; J. P. Meier, *A Marginal Jew* (note 5), pp. 118-20.

11. Macmillan, New York, 1993.

12. *The Historical Jesus*, p. 428.

13. B. Layton, *The Gnostic Scriptures*, Garden City, Doubleday, 1987, p. 376.

14. 'Thomas and the Synoptics', *Novum Testamentum* 30 (1988) pp. 132-57, here pp. 139-40. Tuckett also notes that in POxy 1, the saying about 'splitting the wood' is part of logion 30, whereas in the Coptic version it is part of logion 77. Since the compiler of the Coptic version has altered the order of the earlier Greek version, why should the order of sayings of Jesus in the Gospels not have been altered?

15. See C. M. Tuckett's detailed discussion (note 14).

16. C.M. Tuckett, (note 14) pp.145-6.

17. This point is pressed by J. P. Meier, *A Marginal Jew* (note 5) I, pp. 134-7.

18. See T. Baarda in ed. W. L. Petersen, *Gospel Traditions in the Second Century*, Notre Dame Press, 1989, pp. 133-54.

19. See Jacob Neusner, 'Who Needs "The Historical Jesus"? An Essay-Review', *Bulletin for Biblical Research* 4, 1994, p.115.

20. I have cited Morton Smith's own translation, *Clement of*

Alexandria and a Secret Gospel of Mark, Cambridge, Harvard University, 1973, p. 447.

21. *Four Other Gospels: Shadows on the Contours of the Canon*, Minneapolis, Winston Press, 1985, p.118.

22. For the recent literature, see J. H. Charlesworth and Craig A. Evans (note 5) pp. 526-33.

Chapter VIII (pp. 96-110)

1. Irenaeus uses the phrases 'old covenant' (or 'old testament') and 'new covenant', though the latter phrase is not used to refer to the authoritative writings produced in the 'new' Christian era. Only a decade or so later, however, Tertullian and Clement of Alexandria used these terms to refer to what we now know as the Old and New Testaments.

2. A. F. J. Klijn, *Jewish-Christian Gospel Tradition*, Leiden, Brill, 1992.

3. These quotations are taken from Origen's commentary on John. See Tjitze Baarda, 'ΔΙΑΦΩΝΙΑ – ΣΥΜΦΩΝΙΑ Factors in the Harmonization of the Gospels, Especially in the Diatessaron of Tatian', in ed. W. L. Petersen, *Gospel Traditions in the Second Century*, Notre Dame, Notre Dame Press, 1989, pp. 137-8.

4. In the preceding two paragraphs I have summarized Tjitze Baarda's article referred to in the preceding note.

5. See T. C. Skeat, 'The Origin of the Christian Codex', *Zeitschrift für Papyrologie und Epigraphik* 102 (1994) pp. 263-8.

6. See T. C. Skeat, 'Irenaeus and the Four-Gospel Canon', *Novum Testamentum* 34 (1992) pp. 194-9.

7. For a recent challenge to the consensus, see G. M. Hahneman, *The Muratorian Fragment and the Development of the Canon*, Oxford, Clarendon Press, 1992. Hahneman argues for a fourth-century provenance. In a thorough review in the *Journal of Theological Studies* 44 (1993) pp. 691-7, E. Ferguson concludes that Hahneman has not made out his case. In order to move to proof, 'there must be something only possible in the fourth century or something impossible in the second century. Despite Hahneman's effort, neither has been shown to be the case.' The evidence for the four-gospel codex in the second century which I have noted is an important consideration which tells against Hahneman's theory.

8. The Muratorian Canon also comments on a number of other early Christian writings, some of which are 'in', some 'out'.

9. In one passage Justin states explicitly that 'the memoirs of the apostles' are 'Gospels' *(I Apology* 1:66). Justin makes little or no

use of John, so he is not necessarily referring to the four canonical Gospels.

10. For an excellent full discussion, see Martin Hengel, 'The Titles of the Gospels', in his *Studies in the Gospel of Mark,* London, SCM, 1985, pp. 64–84.

Chapter IX (pp. 111-121)

1. J. Murphy-O'Connor, *The Holy Land,* Oxford University Press, 1992, p.413. For detailed discussion, see R.A. Batey, 'Jesus and the Theatre', *New Testament Studies* 30 (1984) pp. 563-74.
2. See especially, E. M. Meyers, 'Roman Sepphoris in Light of New Archaeological Evidence', in ed. Lee I. Levine, *The Galilee in Late Antiquity,* New York, Jewish Theological Seminary, 1992, p.325.
3. J. C. H. Laughlin, 'Capernaum: from Jesus' Time and After', *Biblical Archaeological Review* (56) 1993, pp. 55-61.
4. 'The "Caiaphas" Ossuaries and Joseph Caiaphas', *Palestine Exploration Quarterly* 126 (1994) pp.32-48.
5. See J. Zias and James H. Charlesworth, 'CRUCIFIXION: Archaeology, Jesus and the Dead Sea Scrolls' in ed. J. H. Charlesworth, *Jesus and the Dead Sea Scrolls,* New York, Doubleday, 1992, pp. 273-89. See also J. Zias and E. Sekeles, 'The Crucified Man from Giv'at ha-Mivtar – a Reappraisal', *Biblical Archaeologist* (48) 1985, pp. 190-1.

Chapter X (pp. 122-134)

1. His *Histories* start with an account of events in AD 69. He provides his readers with information about the Jewish people (some of which is inaccurate), but in the books which have survived little is said about the Jewish revolt against Rome.
2. *The Unknown Sayings of Jesus,* London, SPCK, 2nd edition, 1964.
3. Otfried Hofius, 'Unbekannte Jesusworte', in ed. P. Stuhlmacher, *Das Evangelium and die Evangelien,* Tübingen, Mohr, 1983, pp. 355-82.
4. For a fuller discussion of this saying, see p.44-5.

Chapter XI (pp. 135-144)

1. *I Apology* 66.3; 67.3; *Dialogue with Trypho* thirteen times; note especially *Dialogue* 103.8 and 106.3.
2. See D. E. Aune, *The New Testament in its Literary Environment,* Philadelphia, Westminster, 1987, pp. 66-7.
3. The genre of the Gospels has recently been discussed most

impressively by R. A. Burridge, *What are the Gospels?*,
Cambridge, CUP, 1992. See also G. N. Stanton, *A Gospel for a
New People: Studies in Matthew*, Edinburgh, T. & T. Clark, 1992,
pp. 59–71; 'Matthew: ΒΙΒΛΟΣ, ΕΥΑΓΓΕΛΙΟΝ, or ΒΙΟΣ?', in F.
Van Segbroeck et al., *The Four Gospels 1992*, Leuven University
Press, 1992, Vol. II, pp. 1187–202.

4. See D. E. Aune (note 2) p. 35.
5. This is in fact the first time the noun 'Gospel ' is used in the
plural to refer to more than one Gospel writing.
6. In this case it is worth noting that rigorous use of the criterion of
dissimilarity does not allow us to be certain! From Luke 3:12 and
7:29 we learn that John the Baptist also associated with tax collectors. So even though it is unlikely, it is at least possible that
something which was characteristic of the teacher-prophet John
was transferred to Jesus.

Chapter XII (pp. 145-155)

1. *Jesus and Judaism*, London, SCM, 1985, p. 3 and pp. 18-19.
Sanders refers to J. Klausner, *Jesus of Nazareth. His Times, His Life
and His Teaching*, E.tr. London and New York, 1925 p. 369.
2. *Jesus and Judaism*, p.19.
3. I have chosen the term 'social step' carefully. The theological
steps taken were of course crucial for the development of the
new movement: proclamation of Jesus as the Messiah-Christ and
as Lord, and *worship* of him.
4. In his fine book, *Jew and Gentile in the Ancient World*, Princeton,
University Press, 1993, Louis Feldman shows convincingly that
Judaism was attractive to many Gentiles. However he exaggerates
the extent to which Judaism actively sought converts. See Scot Mc
Knight, *A Light among the Gentiles: Jewish Missionary Activity in the
Second Temple Period*, Minneapolis, Fortress, 1991, who shows
convincingly that first-century Judaism was not a missionary religion; Jews were a 'light among the nations' because they were
'thoroughly woven into the fabric of the Roman world' (p.117).
5. Raymond Brown, *An Introduction to New Testament Christology*,
London, Geoffrey Chapman, 1994, p.87.
6. I have quoted *The Dead Sea Scrolls Translated*, by Florentino
García Martínez, Leiden, Brill, 1994, p. 138.
7. See the fine discussion of the main possibilities in J. J. Collins,
*The Scepter and the Star: The Messiahs of the Dead Sea Scrolls and
Other Ancient Literature*, New York et al, Doubleday, 1995, pp.
154-72.

Chapter XIII (pp. 156-163)

1. For a fuller discussion of most of the points made in this chapter, and for full bibliographical references, see my essay, 'Jesus of Nazareth: A Magician and a False Prophet who Deceived God's People?' in eds. Joel B. Green and Max Turner, *Jesus of Nazareth: Lord and Christ,* Carlisle, Paternoster, 1994, pp. 164-80.

2. See P. S. Alexander, 'Incantations and Books of Magic', in E. Schürer, *The History of the Jewish People in the Age of Jesus Christ* III.1, eds. G. Vermes, F. Millar and M. Goodman, Edinburgh, T. & T. Clark, 1986, §32.VII, pp. 342-79, here p. 342·

3. In most recent reconstructions of Q, this tradition is accepted as Q material. See the brief discussion in J. Kloppenborg, *Q Parallels: Synopsis, Critical Notes and Concordance,* Sonoma, Calif.: Polebridge, 1988, pp. 90-2.

4. R. A. Guelich, *Mark 1 – 8:26,* Word Biblical Commentary 34A, Dallas: Word, 1989, p. 180.

5. A. F. Segal's comments are instructive: 'The logic from the scribes' perspective is that if Jesus were from God, he could not oppose the ideas of the legitimate authorities of Judea. Since he does oppose them, his power must have other sources.' *Rebecca's Children: Judaism and Christianity in the Roman World,* Cambridge, Harvard UP, 1986, pp. 144-5·

6. Cf. John 10: 41. Mark 6: 14 is an apparent exception, but on any view this is a puzzling verse·

7. I have summarized and discussed the evidence briefly in *The Gospels and Jesus,* Oxford, OUP, 1989, pp. 177-83. See especially D.E. Aune, *Prophecy in Early Christianity and the Ancient Mediterranean World,* Grand Rapids, Eerdmans, 1983, pp. 153-89.

Chapter XIV (pp. 164-172)

1. See Burton Mack, *The Lost Gospel,* Shaftesbury et al., Element, 1993. J.D. Crossan sees Jesus as a Jewish Cynic-sage: *The Historical Jesus,* Edinburgh, T&T Clark, 1992·

2. Robert Webb, 'John the Baptist and his Relationship to Jesus', in eds. B. Chilton and C. A. Evans, *Studying the Historical Jesus,* Leiden, Brill, 1994, p.192.

3. See Paul Hollenbach, 'The Conversion of Jesus: From Jesus the Baptizer to Jesus the Healer', *Aufsteig und Niedergang der römischen Welt,* Berlin, de Gruyter, 1982, II.25.1, pp. 196-219.

4. Robert Webb (as in note 1), pp. 225-6.

Chapter XV (pp. 173-187)

1. See especially Martin Hengel, *Crucifixion*, London, SCM, 1977. There is no evidence that at the time of Jesus crucifixion was ever carried out by Jews.

2. Markus Bockmuehl, *This Jesus, Martyr, Lord, Messiah*, Edinburgh, T. & T. Clark, 1994, p. 55.

3. *Contra Celsum* 6:10. I have cited H. Chadwick's translation, *Origen: Contra Celsum*, Cambridge, CUP, 1953.

4. *Reimarus: Fragments,* ed. C. H. Talbert, Fortress, 1970, pp. 137, 150.

5. S. G. F. Brandon, *Jesus and the Zealots*, Manchester, Manchester University Press, 1967.

6. NRSV has 'Simon the Cananaean', a rather odd translation of the Greek word which comes from an Aramaic word meaning 'zealot' or 'enthusiast'. REB has 'Simon the Zealot'. 'Zealot' with a capital letter does imply (incorrectly) that Simon was a member of a well-known group.

7. The exception is Romans 9:5. Paul has been listing the privileges his fellow Jews have enjoyed at God's hand. At the end he writes: 'The patriarchs are theirs, and from them by natural descent came the Messiah' (REB). Here 'Christos' is not merely a proper name, as is usual in Paul's letters, but a reference to Jesus as the Messiah.

8. *Jesus the Christ*, p. 39.

9. It is possible that the reading, 'You say that I am' is a harmonization with Matthew 27:64, where the context is a little different.

10. This is E. P. Sanders' view. See his *Jesus and Judaism*, London, SCM, 1985, and his *The Historical Jesus*, London, Allen Lane, 1993. See also Markus Bockmuehl, *This Jesus* (note 2), pp. 60–76.

11. *The Historical Jesus*, p. 253.

12. *This Jesus,* (note 2), pp. 69–70.

13. See his *Jesus and Judaism* (note 10).

14. See also Martin Hengel and Roland Deines, 'E. P. Sanders' "Common Judaism", Jesus, and the Pharisees', *Journal of Theological Studies,* 46 (1995), pp. 1–70, especially p. 7.

15. G. N. Stanton, 'On the Christology of Q', in eds. B. Lindars and S. S. Smalley, *Christ and Spirit in the New Testament,* Cambridge, CUP, 1973, pp. 30–1.

16. For the text, see F. García Martínez, *The Dead Sea Scrolls Translated,* Leiden, Brill, 1994, p. 394. For an excellent discussion, see J. J. Collins, *The Scepter and the Star,* New York, Doubleday, 1995, pp. 116–23.

17. Matthew sees the point and states explicitly in 11:2 that 'these are the deeds of the Messiah'.

For Further Reading

General

Bockmuehl, Markus, *This Jesus*, Edinburgh, T. & T. Clark, 1994. An excellent clear introduction.

Borg, M., *Conflict, Holiness and Politics in the Teachings of Jesus*, New York and Toronto, Edwin Mullen, 1984. Stimulating and influential.

Borg, M., *Jesus: a New Vision*, San Francisco, Harper & Row, 1987. A lively presentation of a distinctive point of view.

Borg, M., *Jesus in Contemporary Scholarship*, Valley Forge, Trinity Press International, 1994. Excellent survey; concentrates on North American writers.

Burridge, Richard A., *Four Gospels, One Jesus?* London, SPCK, 1994. Probably the best introduction available.

Crossan, J. D., *The Historical Jesus*, Edinburgh, T. & T. Clark, 1991. A major, rather idiosyncratic study.

Harvey, A. E., *Jesus and the Constraints of History*, London, Duckworth, 1982. A valuable fresh approach.

Meier, John P., *Jesus a Marginal Jew*, New York, Doubleday, Vol. I, 1991; Vol. II, 1994. When complete, this trilogy will be unsurpassed: magisterial, but accessible.

Riches, J., *Jesus and the Transformation of Judaism*, London, Darton, Longman and Todd, 1980. Argues that in several respects Jesus adopted a critical stance towards Judaism.

Sanders, E. P., *Jesus and Judaism*, London, SCM, 1985. Impressive and learned, but not daunting to the non-specialist.

Sanders, E. P., *The Historical Figure of Jesus*, London, Allen Lane, 1993. An abbreviated and more wide-ranging version of his 1985 book.

Stanton, G. N., *The Gospels and Jesus*, Oxford, OUP, 1989. Complements the present book.

Theissen, Gerd, *The Shadow of the Galilean: the Quest of the Historical in Narrative Form*. London, SCM, 1987. Unusual approach which is very informative.

Vermes, G., *Jesus the Jew*, London, SCM 2nd ed., 1985; *The Religion of Jesus the Jew*, London, SCM, 1993. Two sympathetic studies by a Jewish scholar.

Wright, N.T., *Who was Jesus?* London, SPCK, 1992. A lively critical appraisal of books by Barbara Thiering, J.S. Spong, A.N. Wilson and others.

Chapter II. First-Century Fragments of Matthew's Gospel?

There is an introduction to the New Testament papyri and the textual evidence for the Gospels in *Chapter IV* of this book.

More specialized literature is referred to in the notes to this chapter.

Chapter III. Mark's Gospel among the Dead Sea Scrolls?

Betz, Otto, and Riesner, Rainer, *Jesus, Qumran and the Vatican: Clarifications*, New York, Crossroad, 1994. Assesses critically several recent books which have tried to forge direct links between the Dead Sea Scrolls and earliest Christianity. Highly commended.

Charlesworth, James H. (ed.), *Jesus and the Dead Sea Scrolls*, New York, Doubleday, 1992. A set of excellent essays by leading specialists. A good bibliography is included.

Fitzmyer, J.A., *Responses to 101 Questions on the Dead Sea Scrolls*, London, Chapman, 1992. A very useful introduction by a leading specialist.

García Martínez, Florentino, *The Dead Sea Scrolls Translated*, Leiden, Brill, 1994. This is the most complete translation available. Also included is an excellent introduction and bibliographical references for more advanced study.

Shanks, Herschel, (ed.) *Understanding the Dead Sea Scrolls*, London, SPCK, 1993. This book includes excellent introductory essays by a number of specialists.

VanderKam, James C., *The Dead Sea Scrolls Today*, Grand Rapids, Eerdmans, 1994. Up to date, with balanced judgements.

Chapter IV. How Reliable are the Manuscripts of the Gospels?

There are three helpful guides to the textual criticism of the New Testament:

Aland, Kurt and Aland, Barbara, *The Text of the New Testament*, Grand Rapids, Eerdmans, revised edition 1989.

Metzger, Bruce, *The Text of the New Testament,* Oxford, OUP, 1964; revised edition, 1992.

Vaganay, L., and Amphoux, Christian-Bernard, *An Introduction to New Testament Textual Criticism*, Cambridge, CUP, 1991.

Chapter v. Between Jesus and the Gospels

Hengel, Martin, *Studies in the Gospel of Mark*, London, SCM, 1985. This is an immensely learned discussion of the traditional approach to Mark.

Stanton, G. N., *Jesus of Nazareth in New Testament Preaching*, Cambridge, CUP, 1974, and *The Gospels and Jesus*, Oxford, OUP, 1989. These books include discussion of form criticism.

Chapter vi. Q: a Lost 'Gospel'?

Kloppenborg, J., *Q Parallels: Synopsis, Critical Notes and Concordance*, Sonoma, Calif., Polebridge, 1988. This a very useful reference tool. The notes to this chapter refer to the most important recent books, but they are not for beginners.

Chapter vii. Other Gospels: Peter, Egerton, Thomas and 'Secret Mark'

Charlesworth, James H., and Evans, Craig A., 'Jesus in the Agrapha and Apocryphal Gospels' in eds. Bruce Chilton and Craig A. Evans, *Studying the Historical Jesus*, Leiden, Brill, 1994, pp. 479-534.

Crossan, John Dominic, *Four Other Gospels. Shadows on the Contours of Canon*, Minneapolis et al., Winston, 1985. The four writings featured in this chapter are all discussed, but with rather different results.

Patterson, Stephen J., *The Gospel of Thomas and Jesus*, Sonoma, Polebridge, 1993. A thorough discussion, though rather one-sided, on Thomas's dependence on the canonical Gospels.

Chapter viii. One Gospel and Four Gospellers

Bruce, F.F., *The Canon of Scripture*, Glasgow, Chapter House, 1988. Clear and reliable.

Campenhausen, H. von, *The Formation of the Christian Bible*, 1968; E.Tr. Philadelphia, 1972. Dated, but still valuable.

Metzger, B.M., *The Canon of the New Testament. Its Origin, Development, and Significance*, Oxford, OUP, 1987. Magisterial.

Roberts, C.H., and Skeat, T.C., *The Birth of the Codex*, London, OUP (for the British Academy), 1983. A classic.

Chapter ix. Jesus the Archaeological Evidence

Batey, Richard A., *Jesus and the Forgotten City*, Grand Rapids, Baker, 1991. An imaginative reconstruction of life in Sepphoris at the time of Jesus. Excellent sketches and photographs.

Freyne, Sean, *Galilee, Jesus and the Gospels: Literary Approaches and Historical Investigations*, Philadelphia, Fortress, 1988. A more advanced book by a leading specialist on Galilee.

McRay, J.,*Archaeology and the New Testament*, Grand Rapids, Baker, 1991. Wide-ranging text book for students: good reference tool.

Millard, A.R., *Discoveries from the Times of Jesus*, Oxford, Lion, 1990. Lavishly illustrated, with judicious comments. A fine introduction.

Myers, E.M., Netzer, Ehud, Meyers, Carol L., *Sepphoris*, Winona Lake, Eisenbrauns, 1992. Written by archaeologists with plenty of experience at Sepphoris. The standard study.

Chapter X. Jesus Traditions Outside the Gospels

Elliott J. K., *The Apocryphal New Testament, A Collection of Apocryphal Christian Literature in an English Translation based on M. R. James* Oxford, Clarendon, 1993. This is now the standard translation of the texts, with good introductions and bibliographies.

Jeremias, J., *Unknown Sayings of Jesus*, London, SPCK, 1964. Still a classic.

Layton, B., (ed.), *The Gnostic Scriptures: A New Translation with Annotations and Introductions*, Doubleday, Garden City, NY, 1987. Reliable translations.

Maier, John P. *A Marginal Jew: Rethinking the Historical Jesus* , New York et al., Doubleday, Vol. I, 1991. Chapter 3 includes a fine discussion of the relevant passages in Josephus. Chapter 4 surveys other pagan and Jewish writings.

Robinson, J. M. (ed.), *The Nag Hammadi Library in English*, (E. J. Brill, Leiden 1977)

Tuckett, C. M., *Nag Hammadi and the Gospel Tradition*, London, T. & T. Clark, 1986. Through and reliable.

David Wenham, ed., *The Jesus Tradition outside the Gospels. Gospel Perspectives:* Vol. 5, Sheffield, JSOT 1984. A set of interesting essays.

Whittaker, M., *Jews and Christians: Graeco-Roman Views,* Cambridge, CUP, 1984. Includes good translations and comments on all the relevant texts.

Chapter XI. Jesus Traditions Inside the Gospels

Several of the books listed under **General** above include discussion of methods to be used in reconstructing the historical Jesus.

Chapter XII. Jesus: the Aftermath

Dunn, J. D. G. *The Parting of the Ways between Christianity and Judaism and their Significance for the Character of Christianity*, London, SCM, 1991. Excellent introduction to the issues at stake between Jews and Christians in antiquity.

Brown, Raymond, *An Introduction to New Testament Christology*, London, Geoffrey Chapman, 1994. A good place to start reading on this central topic.

Collins, John J., *The Scepter and the Star. The Messiahs of the Dead Sea Scrolls and Other Ancient Literature*, New York, Doubleday, 1995. Up-to-date impressive fresh study.

Chapter XIII. Jesus: a Magician and a False Prophet

Twelftree, Graham H., *Jesus the Exorcist*, Tübingen, Mohr, 1993. Will be the standard discussion for a long time to come.

Wilken, Robert L., *The Christians as the Romans Saw Them*, New Haven and London, Yale, 1984. A wide-ranging sensitive discussion.

Chapter XIV. Jesus: Disciple of John

Webb, Robert, 'John the Baptist and his Relationship to Jesus', in eds. B. Chilton and C.A. Evans, *Studying the Historical Jesus*, Leiden, Brill, 1994, pp. 179-230.

Webb, Robert, *John the Baptizer and Prophet: a Socio-Historical Study*, Sheffield, JSOT, 1991. The finest study available.

Scobie, C.H., *John the Baptist*, London, SCM, 1964. Dated, but still a good introduction.

Wink, W., *John the Baptist in the Gospel Tradition*, Cambridge, CUP, 1968. Clear exposition of the evangelists' portraits of John.

Chapter XV. Jesus: King of the Jews

Hengel, Martin, *The Cross of the Son of God*, London, SCM, 1986.

Hurtado, Larry, *One God, One Lord: Early Christian Devotion and Ancient Jewish Monotheism*, Philadelphia, Fortress, 1988. How did followers of Jesus come to worship him?

Rivkin, Elias, *What Crucified Jesus?* London, SCM, 1984. An evocative study by a Jewish scholar.

Several of the books listed under **General** are relevant.

General Index

Abba (Father) 152-3
Alexander, Loveday 54-5
Antipas, Herod (*see* Herod Antipas)
Aramaic 193

Baigent, Michael 21
Baillet, M. 23
Barth, Karl 72
Biblical Uncial
    (style of handwriting) 11
biographies, Gospels as 137-9
Bockmuehl, Markus 173, 183
Brandon, S.G.F. 175-7
Brown, Raymond 78
Bultmann, Rudolf 72, 137

Caiaphas 117-18
Canon, four-Gospel 108-10
Capernaum 54, 114-15, 148
Catchpole, D.R. 73
Cavallo, G. 14
Cave 4 (*see* Qumran)
Cave 7 (*see* Qumran)
Celsus 8-9, 35, 173
Celsus, Library of 136-8
circumcision 61, 147-9
Clement of Alexandria 93-5, 133
Clement of Rome 98
Codex Bezae 39, 44-5, 133
Codex Sinaiticus 14, 39, 46
Codex Vaticanus 14, 39, 46
Codex Washingtonianus 199
codex 17-19, 59, 103-4, 136, 186
computer searches 29
Cook, R.R.E. 27-9

criterion of dissimilarity 142-3
criterion of multiple attestation 143-4
cross, inscription on the 174-5, 180,
    190
Crossan, J.D. 80-1, 83, 87, 95
crucifixion 118-19, 127, 173-4
    (*see also* cross, inscription on the)
Cynics 74

Dahl, Nils 178-9
Dead Sea Scrolls (*see also* Qumran)
    1, 20-30, 84, 112, 135, 189
deceiver (*see* prophet, Jesus as a false)
Diatessaron, Tatians's 101-2, 109
Didache 131, 143
Downing, F.G. 69

Ebionites, Gospel according to 100-1
Egerton Gospel 81-4
Eisenman, Robert 22, 32
Ephesus 136-8
Erasmus 37
Essenes 20, 30
Eusebius 50, 58, 79
Evans, C.F. 186
eyewitnesses 1, 52-62

false prophet (*see* prophet, Jesus
    as a false)
Fitzmyer, J.A. 24, 25
form criticism 56-62
Fourth Gospel (*see* John's Gospel)

Galilee 184
genre 136-9

Gentiles, mission to 147-9
Gnostics 84, 87-90, 92-3, 99, 102-3,
    106-8
Gospel truth 4, 7-10, 92-3, 151,
    191-3
Goulder, M.D. 70
Griesbach, J. J. 69
Guelich, R.A. 162

Harnack, A. 72
Hebrews, Gospel according to the
    101
Herculaneum 15
Hermas, *Shepherd* of 108
Herod Antipas 113, 115, 165,
    168-70, 171
Hofius, Otfried 132-3
Hollenbach, Paul 172
Holtzmann, H.J. 63
Horbury, William 118
Hort, F.J.A. 41

Ignatius of Antioch 98, 131-2
inscription on the cross (*see* cross,
    inscription on the)
Irenaeus 49, 96, 104-5, 109

Jenkins, R.G. 28
Jerusalem 115-18
'Jesus boat' 115
Jesus seminar 86, 92
Jesus traditions, Paul's use of 96-7,
    129-31
John the Baptist 162-3, 164-72, 185-
    6, 190
John's Gospel 52, 55-6, 61, 82, 95,
    102-3, 105-6, 110, 118, 120,
    128, 159-60, 165, 167
Josephus 124-7, 134, 157-8, 168-70
Justin Martyr 102, 108-9, 137-8,
    156-7

Kähler, Martin 60
Klausner, J. 146
Klijn, A.F.J. 100
Kloppenborg, J. 67, 73-4

law, Jesus and the 147-9
Layton, Bentley 87
Leigh, Richard 21
Lord (Kyrios) 149-51
Lord's Prayer 45-6, 62, 71, 191
Lucian of Samosata 124, 134
Lührmann, D. 73
Luke's Gospel 55, 61, 105-6, 118,
    140, 159, 165
Luther, Martin 8

Mack, Burton 74
Maehler, H. 14
Magdalen College, Oxford (*see under*
    papyri, P64)
magician, Jesus as 156-63, 185
Marcion 89, 99-101, 102
Mark's Gospel 95, 105, 116-17, 129,
    137, 140-1, 161, 184
    dating 23-6, 49-52
    'longer ending' 43-4, 47
    origin 24-6, 49-52
    'shorter ending' 43-4
Mark, 'Secret Gospel' of 93-5
Matthew's Gospel 52, 80-1, 97, 140,
    158-9, 165
    Luke's use of 69-71
Melchizedek, 11Q (*see under*
    Qumran, Cave 11)
Messiah, Jesus as 31-2, 154-5, 177,
    178-80, 185-7
miniscules 39-40
miqva'ot (ritual baths) 114, 116
Montanus 103
Muratorian Fragment (or Canon)
    105-7, 109
Murphy-O'Connor, Jerome 113

Nag Hammadi Library 84-5, 87
Nahal Hever 15
Nazoreans, Gospel according to the
    101, 165
Neusner, Jacob 93

O'Callaghan, José 3, 23, 24
oral traditions 49-62
Origen 8-10, 35, 101

Osiander, Andreas 8
ossuary 117-19

palaeography 12-16
Palatial Mansion 115–16
Papias 50-2, 58, 64, 99
papyri 37-8
  P4 (Luke, Paris) 16-19, 48
  P45, P46, P47 (Chester Beatty
    papyri) 38
  P52 (John, Manchester) 4, 38, 81
  P64 (Matthew, Magdalen College,
    Oxford) 1-2, 11-19, 48, 103,
    138, 188
  P67 (Matthew, Barcelona) 15
  P66, P75 (Bodmer papyri) 38, 46
papyrology 12-16
Papyrus Egerton 2 (see Egerton Gospel)
Parsons, Peter J. 15-16
Peter 49-52, 105, 115, 149
Peter, Gospel of 78-81, 95, 102
Pharisees 175-6, 184-5
Pickering, S.R. 27-9
Pilate 123, 126-7, 171, 173, 180
Pliny the Younger 123
prophet, Jesus as a 163, 182-3, 185,
  190
prophet, Jesus as a false 156-63, 185

Q 54, 63-76, 141, 161, 166, 167-8,
  186
  Q as a 'Gospel' 71-76
Qumran (see also Dead Sea Scrolls) 3,
  20-32, 121
  Cave 4 20
    4Q171 31
    4Q246 154-5
    4Q285 32
    4Q521 186-7
    4QMMT = 4Q394-9 31, 59
  Cave 7 22-29
    7Q5 3, 23-9, 189
  Cave 11
    11QMelchizedek 186
Qumran, Community Rule (IQS)
  30-1

rabbinic writings 127-9, 134, 157,
  160
Reimarus, H.S., 7
Resurrection (of Jesus) 192
ritual baths (miqva'ot) 114, 116
Roberts, C.H. 11-17, 24
Robinson, J.A.T. 2
Robinson, James A. 74-5

sage, Jesus as a 66, 74, 124, 177
Sanders, E.P. 145-6, 183-5
Sato, M 73
Sepphoris 112-14
Shanks, Herschel 21
Simpson, O.J. 53
Skeat, T.C. 12, 17-18, 28, 104
Smith, Morton 93-4
Son, Son of God 151-5
Suetonius 123-4

Tacitus 122, 134
Tatian 101-2, 109
Taylor, V. 52
Teacher of Righteousness 31-2
Temple (Jerusalem) 171, 177, 180-3
Thiede, C.P. 1, 2, 3, 12-16
Thiering, Barbara 21, 22
Thomas, Gospel of 68, 84-93, 95,
  132, 133
Thomas, Infancy Gospel of 83
Tiberias 114
Tödt, H.E. 72
Tuckett, C.M. 73, 90-1
Turin Shroud 119-20
Turner, E.G. 12

uncials 38-9
Unknown Gospel (see Egerton
  Gospel)

Webb, Robert 172
Weiss, J. 63

'zealots' 175-7